TEAMING UP

TEAMING UP

Shared Leadership in Youth Ministry

Ginny Ward Holderness

WITH

Robert S. Hay

Westminster John Knox Press

Louisville, Kentucky

Book design by Jennifer K. Cox
Cover design by Pam Poll
Cover art: Teens together. F. Cruz. Courtesy of SuperStock.
Other images © 1996 PhotoDisc, Inc.

First edition
Published by Westminster John Knox Press
Louisville, Kentucky

This book is printed on acid-free paper that meets the ∞
American National Standards Institute Z39.48 standard.

PRINTED IN THE UNITED STATES OF AMERICA
97 98 99 00 01 02 03 04 05 06 — 10 9 8 7 6 5 4 3 2 1

Library of Congress Cataloging-in-Publication Data

Holderness, Ginny Ward, date.
    Teaming up : shared leadership in youth ministry / Ginny Ward
Holderness with Robert S. Hay. — 1st ed.
        p.   cm.
    Includes bibliographical references and index.
    ISBN 0-664-25624-4 (alk. paper)
    1. Church work with teenagers. 2. Church group work with teenagers.
3. Group ministry. 4. Christian leadership. I. Hay, Robert S., date. II. Title.
BV4447.H63 1997
259'.23—dc21   97-1730

To Jim, J. B., and Lorinda
Janice, Robert, and Kevin

Contents

Foreword

We have been through periods of too much structure and of too little structure these last several decades of youth ministry—periods of too much visibility of adult leaders and of too little "hands-on" adult leadership, times of too much shallow recreation and those of too much study, both of which miss the deep seriousness with which youth seek meaning and integrity. In a way that is stimulating to think about and concretely helpful in carrying out a ministry, *Teaming Up: Shared Leadership in Youth Ministry* makes one want to rejoice in the kind of balance that is achieved here.

Not many people risk providing actual accounts illustrating what they mean by general principles and advice, even though it is always the case that we do not really understand or *know* what is meant by an idea until we see it embodied, the general in the particular, the vision in the action. Ginny, however, provides the reader with actual accounts of her ideas on developing an effective youth-led youth ministry. She instructs the reader on how to enlist effective leaders, both youth and adult, create "lock-ins," and develop a variety of youth retreats that meet the different needs of youth by including a myriad of activities. She also gives actual illustrations of establishing rituals that grow out of youth experience. We all know how important these rituals are in theory, but we are not always sure about what they look like in practice.

Ginny *is* an advocate of the team approach to youth ministry. Throughout the book she stresses that youth should not only be receivers of tantalizing activities; they should be involved in planning and leading. The genius of this approach is having theory and rationale stated as well as interpreted into action. There are no foundational statements from which one moves deductively to "practical applications" here, but rather there is an interactive process where theory and practice inform each other. It is a way in which all youth workers should continue to learn as long as they live. This is a key document for anyone who cares about doing a *good* job in youth ministry.

Robert Hay, a youth minister of experience, also contributes to the insights and practices throughout the book. Robert's methods of developing youth ministry are quite valuable and admirable. A few years ago he participated in a consultation on youth ministry at Columbia Seminary and those present gained much from his knowledge. Robert and Ginny, two experienced professionals in youth ministry, broaden our vision as we see how they complement, correct, and enrich each other's ideas—a kind of demonstration, if you will, of the partnership they advocate.

Recently I invited Ginny to write her reflections on the present state of youth ministry, information I needed for a presentation I was to give on the history of youth ministry. I wish that her entire letter could be included here, because it beautifully states the *feeling* about youth and youth ministry that permeates this whole book—a genuine love for the youth and the joy in working with them, excitement about the new Presbyterian Youth Connection, and an expectation that, if you take youth seriously, the future will be a better one for them, as well as for the church, and indeed, for the world. There is hope here.

When I "presented" Ginny to the public at the time of the publication of her book *The Exuberant Years,* I made the following statement: "Her writing has within it the kind of intrinsic authority that arises out of experience, reflection, and commitment—and the sure knowledge that hard work is required, but is infinitely rewarding." That statement is still true.

Moreover, two of the young people with whom she is now working, John and Turner Merritt (my great nephews!), share my delight in her ministry.

Sara Little
Professor of Christian Education Emerita
Union Theological Seminary in Virginia

Acknowledgments

It would be impossible to name all the people who have in some shape or form contributed to this book, because the list would include young people, adult leaders, parents, and mentors from the last thirty years, in my case, and the last twenty years, in Robert's case. It would include people from all the churches we've served in youth ministry: For me, Second Presbyterian Church and Pulaski Heights Presbyterian Church in Little Rock, Arkansas; Shelby Presbyterian Church in Shelby, North Carolina; First Presbyterian Church in Concord, North Carolina; and First Presbyterian Church in Dalton, Georgia. For Robert, First Presbyterian Church in Selma, Alabama, and First Presbyterian Church in Marietta, Georgia.

It would include young people and adults who have participated in our many workshops and who have taught us more than we have taught them. We are especially grateful for the young people and the adult leaders at our respective churches in Dalton and Marietta, who helped shape this book and their youth min-istries by struggling in partnership to respond to God's call to be faithful. Since I promised the Dalton youth that they'd see their names in print, some of them will find that only their first names are mentioned, although the names used in various illustrations are not the actual individuals described in the situation.

Most of all we'd like to thank our own sons and daughter, who are the best teachers of how to love and relate to young people: Robert Hay, Jr., Kevin Hay, J. B. Holderness, and Lorinda Holderness. Our families and our ministries would not be complete without the love and support of our spouses, Jim and Janice. As many youth ministers and leaders would say, "Thanks for being a part of, and putting up with, the delightful craziness that goes with our calling."

A special word of thanks goes to our editor, Stephanie Egnotovich at Westminster John Knox Press, who helped us make sense of what we're trying to say.

Introduction

▼

The team approach to youth ministry has caught on. In fact "team" is the newest buzzword. Just check the titles of books in the business section of the local bookstore. Churches have found that recruiting a team of leaders, instead of the usual "couple" to "take the senior highs," greatly improves the youth ministry program of the local church.

Commitment is higher in the team approach; adult leaders discover that they don't have to go it alone. Someone is there (in fact, several someones) to share in the plans, the struggles, and the excitement. Just knowing you don't have to be responsible for coming up with a program every Sunday night . . . just knowing it's not a reflection on you if Sunday night bombs . . . just knowing you won't be burned out by January . . . these are all happy products of team ministry.

It's exciting to see so many adults involved in youth ministry and doing it well. I have been leading youth ministry workshops for almost twenty years. Every year the participants seem to be smarter, more skilled, and more in tune with the vision of youth ministry. They come to workshops with ideas and great stories about the young people in their churches. They don't seem as lost as they did years ago.

In 1981, I wrote a detailed description of how to develop a team of adult leaders, *Youth Ministry: The New Team Approach.* It described the team as having a clear goal: To involve as many young people as possible in the total life of the church, in its worship, explorations (or study), ministry within the congregation, service, and fellowship. Churches of all sizes responded by recruiting and training enthusiastic adults to form these leadership teams.

Supported by a team, a clear goal, and a planning process, adults who loved young people were motivated to make youth ministry happen. With all these enthusiastic adults running around, the young people began to see that indeed the church of Jesus Christ cares about them. The church was responding to some basic needs of youth—to be wanted, to be needed, and to be seen as responsible members of the Christian community.

It' a joy to hear that many churches have faithfully pursued the goal of involving youth in the total life of the church. Young people today are taking on all kinds of leadership roles in our churches. Youth ministries have been energized by this sharing of leadership between youth and adults.

In light of this development, my earlier book needed an update. The team has been expanding! The new team now includes adults and youth together—working, playing, learning, sharing, caring, and leading—in partnership.

Young people are taking ownership of their youth ministries. And as they do, the old problem of how to motivate youth to participate is fading away. In churches where young people plan and lead their own program, the young people are there. It's their program. They own it. And since they own it, they take care of it. Churches are seeing a new level of caring and commitment in their young people.

I saw a need for this level of commitment in my own church. The adult leaders had been doing a great job, but something was missing. The enthusiasm of the young people had reached a plateau. We needed a new vision. So we began playing with ideas for how to increase the level of youth participation. The young people were ready for leadership roles. For five years, we experimented with a variety of group formations—design teams, leadership teams, leadership/planning teams, care groups, leadership/care groups. Every new configuration taught us that there are many valid ways to structure a program.

We likened youth ministry to an amoeba, changing shape as we continued to explore and grow. New young people would emerge as leaders; different adult and youth teams would form. New issues and needs would cause us to push out in a different direction. The amoeba took its shape from the dedication and enthusiasm of young people and adults working together in partnership.

Youth ministry is not created by adults who tell youth how it's going to be. Young people and adults create it together. The key is to include the young people in the early stages of dreaming how it's going to be.

So how do you teach adults and young people to create youth ministry? What this book offers is a model for (1) team ministry that is a partnership between adults and young people; (2) youth ministry where young people can begin to take responsibilities and try on leadership roles in a supportive, caring environment; and (3) helping adults teach leadership skills to young people—how to teach, nurture, and support, and to know when to let go or to rescue.

Since I am a promoter of team ministry, I decided not to write this book alone. My good friend Robert Hay, an associate pastor for youth, has collaborated with me on this project. We have the same vision for team ministry, but we come from different backgrounds. For most of my ministry I have played the coordinator role, teaching adult leaders how to do youth ministry. Robert has spent most of his ministry with the young people, playing the role of a pastor.

Four years ago we discovered that youth ministry requires both roles—the coordinator and the pastor. The coordinator oversees the big picture, sees that all the parts of the program fit together to fulfill the goals, and sees that adult leaders develop the skills they need to relate to the young people. The pastor spends time with the young people, develops relationships, builds trust, and is the caring adult friend.

Knowing that both roles were essential for adult leadership, Robert and I began to teach each other how to play the "other" role. I began spending more time with the young people; Robert began spending more time with his adult leaders. What we discovered was that young people can take on the roles of coordinator and pastor, of planning and caring.

Young people can do the pastor role—that is, building relationships, and caring and being there for one another. This role can be challenging, however, for the youth. It's not always natural for young people to reach out in friendship to every person who walks through the door. If, however, young people are involved in developing a vision of a caring youth ministry, then they are much more likely to work on building relationships with others.

For some young people, the coordinating and planning role is the challenge. Again, if young people are in on the design of youth ministry, they will develop skills in planning and coordinating.

As you read this book, we hope you will discover ways to develop a team ministry of adults and young people in partnership. If you already have team ministry, consider ways to expand your present team ministry. Take from this book what is helpful to your situation. Learn to ask the right questions. Not just "How do we get youth to come?" but "How can we challenge young people to grow in commitment and be active as participants and leaders?" Not just "How can I get these kids to behave?" but "How can they take ownership of their own youth ministry?"

In chapter 1 we look at how the team approach has changed since the publication of my previous book in 1981. Chapter 2 contains suggestions for exploring the issues affecting today's teenagers, such as loneliness, stress, and brokenness. These issues should be of major concern for the church as it ministers to young people. We also look at the church's role in providing a sanctuary, a safe place for young people who are faced with so many pressures.

In chapter 3 we discuss eight essentials for youth ministry. And we look at what is necessary for faithful youth ministry to happen. Chapter 4 discusses several Bible passages and offers a theological foundation for youth ministry. Studying these passages with your young people, youth council, parents, and/or adult leaders is helpful for keeping youth ministry focused on God and God's Word. Bible study can help you stay on track or get back on track.

In chapter 5 we discuss how to move from adult-driven to youth-driven youth ministry. You'll be encouraged to look at your situation and assess the involvement of adult leaders and of young people. The expanded team approach suggests creating leadership/care groups, which are teams of young people and adult leaders.

Chapter 6 focuses on how to develop effective youth leaders. We offer a design for a leadership lock-in or retreat, an event that contains activities for helping young people discover their leadership gifts and skills. It includes practical guidelines, such as how to lead a game, a group discussion, or a meeting. Appendix 1 contains material to photocopy for creating leadership notebooks for participants to use at the leadership lock-in.

The next three chapters provide specific guidelines for developing an effective youth ministry program. In chapter 7, "Youth Ministry: Dreamed," we suggest ways to engage young people and adult leaders in dreaming and visioning the possibilities for youth ministry. A day retreat model for youth councils can be found in appendix 2. In chapter 8, "Youth Ministry: Developed," we suggest how to develop these dreams. It follows a youth council as it takes the ideas from the day retreat to the rest of the young people. This chapter focuses on planning and includes a description of leadership/care groups and a sample year's calendar. Chapter 9, "Youth Ministry: Delivered," describes key elements for "making it happen." We talk about how to start the year, plan and coordinate good programs, and effectively publicize these activities within the community. Appendixes 3–5 offer specific ways to involve youth in the life and ministry of the church, conduct youth-led retreats or workshops, and to develop activities that will facilitate group interaction.

Chapter 10 focuses on the roles and responsibilities of the adult leaders and includes a job description, a section on discipline, and tips on recruiting leaders. In chapter 11, we present a four-session leadership training program for adult leaders. In chapter 12 we focus on parents. Many churches are realizing that young people should not be treated as an isolated group. Churches are recognizing the need for healthy family relationships and are therefore ministering to the whole family. Appendix 6 contains a list of general youth ministry resources for additional information for youth leaders, parents, and churches. Throughout the book there is some duplication of material, especially games and exercises, because we have found that many activities are effective in several different settings.

We hope that in these pages you find what you need to help you take a long, hard look at your youth ministry. We hope you will talk over ideas with your leaders, your pastor, your young people, and your parents. We are confident that you will be able to take these ideas and adapt them to your own situation. Above all, seek God's guidance as you prayerfully consider the challenges of youth ministry.

ONE

The Team Approach Lives

The team approach to youth ministry is alive and well and living in a lot of churches all over the world. No longer are youth leaders struggling all alone. They are struggling together. And that's the way it should be. It is exciting to see the varieties of team leadership that are happening in churches of all sizes. Churches are examining their needs and designing the type of team ministry that fits those needs.

Adults involved with youth are realizing that going it alone is not fun, healthy, or even successful. Youth ministry is too much for one person. When a church recruits one person or a young couple to be the youth leaders, they are inviting leader burnout. Statistics show there's a sixteen-month average for turnover in youth ministry staff. That is, youth professionals just do not stay in a position much longer than sixteen months—and some move on in even less time. Churches shortchange their young people when they have one leader. There should be several adults with whom the young people can develop relationships. This is even more important when we realize that not all young people will relate to that one adult.

Youth programs suffer from the burden of being carried by too few leaders. The church needs a variety of adults involved in and committed to youth ministry. Look at your church's total program. Which areas are going especially well? Note the number of leaders involved. For example, the women's organization may be one of your more successful programs. Most likely this is because there are many women in leadership roles. A program that thrives is one that has a lot of people involved in responsible leadership. Volunteers are happier and work better when they are a part of a team. We find the greatest model for the team approach in the New Testament. At the beginning of his ministry, Jesus recruited a *team* of twelve.

So we recruit a *team* of leaders to work with youth. There can be many configurations of this team. The basic approach in my earlier book was to recruit a team of ten adults to work with a group of youth. That may sound unrealistic, but churches, both small and large, have been adapting it to their situations. Some small churches cut it down to five or six adults, but still pursued the recruitment of a team, because they believed that having a team of enthusiastic adults showed the young people that the church really does care about them.

The Team Approach Is for Both Small and Large Churches

It needs to be said clearly, right here at the start, that the team approach is for everybody. It has been used at small churches, large churches, and everything in between. The team approach was first introduced at a smaller church conference. The participants were from churches with fewer than 125 members. Those participants helped shape the concept. They were enthusiastic about ways to adapt the team approach to their situations. The key word is "adapt." Tap the creativity of your young people and adult leaders. For they are the ones to teach the church how to use the team approach.

Benefits for the Small Church

1. Small churches often feel limited in what they can do. The team approach gives small church youth ministry new life. It offers more than expanded leadership. It offers a variety of ways young people can be involved in the life of their churches.

2. Young people should have opportunities to get to know a variety of adults. Since small churches have fewer young people, the natural inclination is to recruit just one leader. But it doesn't matter how many young people a church has; they still need the opportunity to develop relationships with more than one adult. The more adults they know, the easier it will be for the young people to be involved in the life of the church.

3. Having fewer young people is an advantage in the relationship department. Relationships can develop more quickly in the smaller church. Each and every young person can have one-on-one time with the adult leaders.

4. Small churches usually do a good job of intergenerational ministry. They have to, since they are limited in the number of age-group ministries they can provide. Adult-youth partnership in team ministry gives small churches another opportunity for intergenerational ministry.

5. Since they have the support of a team, adult leaders can do youth ministry and take other leadership roles in the life of the church without fear of burnout. Sharing leadership means that time and energy are shared as well.

6. Young people see that they are important to their church. Any church that makes the effort to re-

cruit a team, no matter how big a team, is serious about its young people.

Benefits for the Large Church

1. Team leadership is essential for the personal-relationship aspect of youth ministry. It is impossible for one or two leaders to build relationships with every young person in a large church.

2. Team leadership is necessary in order to involve a large number of young people in a variety of activities. Large churches can benefit by developing teams of young people and adults for leadership. A youth minister from a large church once told me that he had too many young people to do the varieties of activities suggested by the team approach. His concept of youth ministry was a huge gathering of young people listening to the person with the microphone. He would lead, or he would have a guest speaker, a concert, or a huge game that everyone can play at the same time.

Somewhere we got the idea that all young people need to be doing the same thing at the same time. They don't. Dividing into smaller groups and teams offers the large church a wide range of possibilities. The church can offer specialized groups, such as Bible study, prayer, drama, music, puppetry, sports, dance, video teams, and service/mission teams. Diversified ministry is a necessity in larger churches. Adult ministries are diversified; youth ministries, too, should be diversified.

3. Large churches have more adults, and therefore, more possibilities for adult leaders to emerge. That doesn't mean that recruiting is necessarily any easier. But when you have lots of teenagers, there should be lots of adults and young people in partnership, seeking ways to do faithful ministry. Since more adults are needed, it is important that more efforts be made to pursue them.

The Original Team Approach

In the original team approach, ten was the operative number of adult leaders because the adult team members were recruited to work in pairs, two in each of five areas of ministry. The areas are listed here with a brief description of the kinds of activities that happen in the area.

Worship: includes experiences of worship as a group or with the entire congregation, prayer breakfasts, devotions.

Explorations: the study of topics and issues, mini-courses on various subjects, Bible study.

Ministry within the congregation: all that the young

people do with and for older and younger members of the congregation.

Service (to the community): young people being of service to those outside their own congregation.

Fellowship: everything else—recreation, socials, eating out, retreats, trips, group building.

Smaller churches could, if they recruited a smaller leadership team, combine areas such as ministry within the congregation and service, or ministry within the congregation and worship. Or a smaller church could recruit one leader per area and have a team of five instead of ten.

The adult leaders had the responsibility for planning and carrying out four or five activities in their respective areas. They concentrated on one particular area of ministry. They were free to attend activities when other leaders had the program responsibility. In this way they had a chance to build relationships with the young people without having to worry about "leading." Leaders liked having the support of a team. They enjoyed having a partner in their area. It was less frightening than going it alone.

For each activity the two area leaders had two or three "responsible persons" (youth volunteers) to help plan and carry out the activity. This little planning team provided a good setting for building relationships and for giving young people leadership opportunities.

In the fall, all the young people and all the adult leaders were encouraged to attend the planning retreat at which the entire year's calendar would be planned. The object was to get everyone on board early in the year. Seeing a calendar full of activities encouraged the young people to stay involved and to invite friends. It showed parents and other church members that their church had an active youth program.

This program offered a systematic approach to youth ministry that gave leaders and young people a balanced youth ministry program; the goal of involving all youth in the total life of the church; a structure for involving young people in the planning of their own program; a plan to achieve that program; a year's calendar; and a way to involve more adults in youth ministry.

As churches worked on incorporating the team approach, it became obvious that several aspects needed revision. In my own ministry, we revised it each year, always trying to find ways to heighten the involvement of young people. As a result, team ministry has expanded. It is now adults and young people together in partnership. Young people now are involved in the early stages of dreaming and designing their youth ministry. Leadership/care groups composed of young people and adult leaders are replacing "responsible persons." Youth councils have been given new roles and responsibilities. The focus of the fall retreat has shifted from planning to group building.

The Expanded Team Approach: Adults and Young People in Partnership

Even though, in the original team approach, young people were involved in planning and carrying out their own program, the structure of team ministry was rather adult-oriented. After all, what was exciting about team ministry was moving from the lone-ranger approach to a team of enthusiastic adults who love youth. Getting a team of adults involved was a major accomplishment.

As the team concept expands to involve young people and adults together in partnership, adult leaders are asked to share power and leadership with the young people. It's not always easy for adults to do this. As any adult will tell you, it's easier to do things yourself. Sharing power and leadership requires extra work. But the adults need to lead the way in turn-

ing youth programs around, from being adult-driven to becoming more youth-driven. One of the ways adult leaders can encourage youth ownership is, at every turn, to ask the question, Can a youth be doing this? (We will discuss this approach in subsequent chapters.)

We want to be clear about adult-youth partnership. It is a partnership. We are not advocating turning youth ministry over to the young people. It should not be totally youth-run with no adults involved in decision making and leadership. But we want to motivate young people to take ownership, which means we need to help adults encourage young people to "drive" their own youth ministries. Young people need to be involved at a deeper level.

Involving Young People in Dreaming and Designing Their Youth Ministry

It typically happens that the adult leaders meet and decide how to do youth group each year. They look at last year's program and decide what to keep and what to do differently. The tendency is either to do it the same way every year until it falls apart or to start over every year.

Even in churches where the young people choose their activities, it's usually the adults who set up the structure. One of the changes in the team approach is to get the young people in on the whole process earlier. Young people should be given the opportunity to struggle with the big questions: What are we trying to do? What do we want for the young people in our church? How can we develop a faithful youth ministry that responds to the needs of our particular young people?

Young people are capable of making needed changes in youth ministry. It was the youth at Dalton First Presbyterian who brought about the change in the focus of the fall retreat. They said the retreat was too work-oriented. They recognized that the group needed the retreat for growing together, bonding, and developing relationships. Teenagers are capable of making this kind of evaluation—if they are given a chance. If young people are accustomed to adults calling the shots, they may be slow getting to this point. But if adults hang in there and let the young people know that they will be heard and that the program needs their direction, then gradually the young people will come around.

You may be picturing your youth sitting there looking blankly at you while you ask for their help. That could happen. Do not be discouraged. This book offers some specific ideas for engaging young people in the dreaming, developing, and delivering of their youth ministry. This may be a radical change for you, your young people, and your church. You'll need to be patient, understanding, and persevering.

Building Leadership/Care Groups Composed of Young People and Adult Leaders

After spending time dreaming of what their youth ministry can be and deciding what they want to do with it, the young people and the adult leaders should figure out a system or structure that will carry out their dreams. They will need to design a way for all youth to become an important part of youth ministry. Young people and adult leaders together should ask: How can we engage young people in planning and carrying out their program? How can we encourage them to develop a caring relationship with each other? How can they have ownership in the program? How can they become responsible and accountable for the care of their youth ministry?

One way is to use the leadership/care group model. A leadership/care group can be as small as two people or as large as fifteen. If you have six young people, you can have two leadership/care groups. The groups plan and lead activities. But they do more than that—they care. They care about the youth program, and they care about one another.

Every youth on your membership roles becomes a part of a leadership/care group. Include those who are not church members but attend your activities. Include those who are members but are inactive. Since there are inactive youth listed in each group, you might have a group of fourteen with only five who show up for a planning session. We assign inactives to leadership/care groups intentionally, so we won't forget or neglect them. We need to keep pursuing ways to reach inactives. This should be as much a role of the leadership/care groups as planning programs.

Forming the Groups

It's quite a process configuring these groups. You need a good balance in each. Mix active youth with less active, outgoing with shy. Have a variety of ages. Separate those who tend to have troublesome behavior, for such youth do better when separated. Surely you've noticed that certain young people are less likely to create a problem when they don't have their buddies to "encourage" them. You can bring out the best in your rowdies by separating them and mixing them with other young people.

Adult leaders who know the youth fairly well and some young people who understand the purpose of leadership/care groups should cooperate to create these groups. I was nervous when I first did this, thinking that the young people I asked would try to compose groups on the basis of their own friendships. I was pleasantly surprised that they recognized the need to mix the groups.

These groups make possible a youth-driven youth ministry. It is still a partnership with the adult leadership, but we recommend emphasizing the youth-driven aspect, since so many youth ministries are adult-driven. Real partnership doesn't occur until the young people gain some ownership. When young people begin to get excited about their youth ministry, then you'll see a healthy youth-drivenness. It's exciting to see young people having an impact on their churches.

What Leadership/Care Groups Do

The young people in the leadership/care groups have the responsibility of seeing that activities happen. They plan and lead. They encourage and support one another. They invite friends and those who haven't been around lately. They handle problems and make decisions. They share leadership responsibilities with all those in the group. And they maintain control of the group when they are responsible for an activity.

How they carry out these functions depends on the group. Some groups may develop a level of caring, sharing, and praying that necessitates regular meetings. Others may meet only occasionally, when they have a particular activity to plan and lead, or to get personal updates and check on those who haven't been to activities in a while. Each situation is different. Your groups may meet regularly one year; the next year they may not. The key is having young people and adult leaders who are aware of

their purpose, who evaluate and decide where youth ministry is headed next.

Ways to Plan

One way these groups plan activities is to have five leadership/care groups, corresponding to five areas of ministry—worship, explorations (in the original team approach it was called "study," but this sounds too much like school), ministry within the congregation, service, and fellowship. If five is too many, then combine the areas. Each group plans three or four activities in its area. The young people in a group become quite knowledgeable about their particular area. Sometimes young people need assurance that just because they are not planning fellowship activities, they will not miss out on fellowship activities. Everybody gets to participate in everything. This model simply provides a way to divide up the responsibilities of planning.

Another option is to have each group choose activities from all five areas. In this way, one group can plan a service project, a worship experience, and a fellowship activity. The number of activities assigned to each group depends on the total number of activities and the number of groups. Work out whatever is feasible for your situation.

Each leadership/care group should have at least one adult and one youth designated as its leaders or conveners. They call the group together and set the agenda. This is a good opportunity for adult-youth partnership. Each set of adult-youth leaders has a designated group to get to know, to phone, to keep up with, to track. Thus, a system is in place for making sure every young person has a connection to the church. This system offers a structure for caring for all the young people. Everyone has a better chance of getting individual attention. Too often young people who are less active get "lost" if there isn't an intentional plan for keeping up with them.

The original team approach advocated "responsible persons" instead of leadership/care groups. Three or four responsible persons signed up for each activity. Adult leaders were to call these people together to plan an activity. Some adult leaders found it hard to keep up with their responsible persons. Time would get away from them, the activity would be coming up, and they wouldn't have time to get the responsible persons together. So the adult leaders ended up doing the planning and leading themselves.

There are many ways to plan with youth. The important thing is to devise some way to: (1) involve young people in the planning and leadership of their own activities; (2) encourage young people to care about one another; (3) enable young people to claim ownership of their own youth group; and (4) require young people to hold one another accountable for their youth ministry.

How do you find out what is best for your situation? Ask the youth! Listen to the youth!

New Life for Youth Councils

Those who have read my earlier book, *Youth Ministry: The New Team Approach,* know that I did not like youth councils. Well, I now have a youth ministry committee, which is much the same as a youth council.

I still believe there is a good argument for not having youth councils, and that is: All young people should be involved in planning and leading youth ministry, not just a select few. So often, those elected or appointed to youth council are the only ones motivated to be involved in youth ministry. The other young people in the group tend to hold back until they get a chance to be on the youth council.

There is also the problem of exclusivity, of having certain young people selected or elected and others left out. It puts church in the same category as school and other organizations that are selective and exclusive. It puts church in the business of having a popularity contest. The most popular get elected.

Yet, even in light of this argument, I have made an about-face on this issue. Robert has helped me to see the value of youth councils in providing a structure that holds young people and adults accountable for youth ministry. We still recommend that all youth be involved in planning and leading, but that involvement needs to be overseen by some responsible group. If you are in a small church, the entire youth group could serve the functions of a youth council.

Responsibilities of a Youth Council

The responsibilities of a council or committee could include some or all of the following:

- to dream and envision what youth ministry will be
- to set up a system or structure for making the dream happen
- to look at the needs of the young people
- to set goals, objectives, and themes for the year
- to evaluate the various programs or areas of youth ministry

- to advocate youth concerns
- to oversee the youth ministry activities
- to plan the program
- to develop young people in leadership

Having a youth ministry committee has kept me from taking charge and making plans. I'm not the one to set up the structure for youth ministry. If I'm not sure how we should do Sunday night activities this year, or how we should do the Bible discussion, I go to the youth council. What I do is set up the initial meeting for the council to do its dreaming and developing.

A youth council provides a logical place to start—with a group of young people and adults who have made a commitment to do youth ministry. The young people on the committee have ownership. They are accountable. They develop the adult-youth partnership that drives youth ministry. They work to create the vision. They promote youth ministry. They see their service on the committee as a calling from God. They have been called to lead others in youth ministry. They model leadership. They, in partnership with adult leaders, are the leaders of the leadership/care groups.

Forming the Youth Council

How is the youth council or committee formed? How do council members recognize that they are called to serve? There are two possibilities. For denominations that have representative governments, it would be in keeping with their tradition to elect youth council members. To keep it from being a popularity contest, young people need to know that the process is like electing elders. Elders are called out by their congregation to hear God's call to lead. Likewise, young people are called out by their people to lead their particular ministry. Many churches find that this is a tradition that works well for them.

Having young people and adults volunteer to

serve is also in keeping with church tradition. Therefore, young people and adults can be recruited for the council, much the same way as church members are recruited to serve on committees. Volunteers respond to God's call to serve in a particular way.

The volunteer method involves more than saying, Okay, who wants to be on the council? Prospective council members need to know that they are responding to God's call to serve. When it's time to recruit members for the youth council or youth ministry committee, consider having an application form, asking the young people and the adults to write why they want to serve on the committee. You'll find a description of the responsibilities of a youth council/youth ministry committee on page 9.

We tell our young people and adults that serving on the youth ministry committee is an important job, one that takes extra time and leadership. They shouldn't apply unless they are committed to the goals of youth ministry and to making our program great! We try to give lots of young people opportunities to serve, so if one is not recruited the first year, they should be able to serve the next. We also welcome any young person or adult who wishes to attend a meeting.

Let your youth ministry committee evolve; you may need to change its composition from year to year. My first committee was composed of eight adults and six young people. For the first year, all that group did was listen and advise. I presented the ideas and got the committee's feedback. I still made the decisions. The second year, we expanded the committee to include an equal number of adults and young people. I presented the issues. They made the decisions.

By the third year, we had eight adults and twelve young people (two per class of seventh- through twelfth-graders). This is our present configuration. The young people talk more than the adults on the committee. They make suggestions; they come up with new ideas. Both young people and adults have ownership of the youth ministry program. They are serving their church in an important and needed way. They are no longer rubber-stamping my ideas. They are shaping the program.

Every year we make changes, sometimes with the committee and sometimes with the entire youth ministry program. It is healthy for youth ministry to take a different shape each year. Youth ministry is not a static, staid animal. It changes shape as it evolves. Just because you structured your leadership/care groups according to the five areas one year does not mean you need to do it that way every year.

Youth groups constantly change. The age configuration changes. One year you'll have a younger senior high group, because of a huge freshman class; another year it's an older group. You could have a different group even by the middle of the year, with more young people getting involved.

Sometimes you'll find that the youth themselves are different each year. They vary in their commitment to the church. One year, you'll have a more serious group, with young people wanting to do a Thursday afternoon Bible study. But try the Bible study the next year, and they don't show. It's just not the same.

Youth councils or youth ministry committees can be a vital part of your youth ministry program. They keep adult leaders from making all the decisions. They push you toward being youth-oriented. They enable you to look to the young people for advice, direction, and leadership. They empower the young people to take ownership of their youth group. They encourage adult-youth partnership.

The Fall Retreat

When I am asked to name one activity that ensures a solid, exciting, faithful youth ministry, I say, group building. When I am asked the best way to do group building, I say, have a fall retreat. A group can only do so much group building on Sunday nights. You need a block of time where young people and adults can be together—preferably away from home—to build relationships, where they can get to know each other and get to know each other better.

I've heard it said that it takes fourteen contact hours to build a group. The young people and their adult leaders need fourteen hours together to get to know each other well enough to begin to "bond," to be comfortable, to develop trust, to feel safe. If your group came together only on Sunday nights, it would be around Christmas before they began to "become a group."

A one-night retreat can provide twelve hours or so of group-building time. A two-night retreat gives you up to twenty-five hours together. Sometimes, because of scheduling conflicts, churches can only manage to pull off a one-day retreat. Still, that's six to ten hours of time together, which puts you ahead of trying to get the contact hours once a week.

The fall retreat can provide leadership/care groups with a chance to do some team building in addition to group building. Team building differs in that you use exercises that help a group learn how to work together. The groups could spend the afternoon of the retreat doing a ropes course or other team-building activities.

When leadership/care groups are first formed, many young people look at the list of their group members and are disappointed that they will not be with their "friends." The fall retreat is a good team-building time for these groups. The young people are given a context for relating to people they might otherwise never get to know, and at the end of the retreat, they find they have made new friends.

In the original team approach, the fall retreat was the fall planning retreat. It was a highly structured work retreat that started out with group building. Then, part of the afternoon and the entire evening of the one-night retreat were spent planning the year's calendar (October to May), or, in some cases, a half-year.

The young people brainstormed ideas for activities in all five areas. They marked their three favorite activities in each area. The votes were tallied, and the result was a balanced program of activities for the year. Then they listed all the activities on large newsprint calendars. Responsible persons were recruited to work on each activity. This still is a viable planning retreat model. But it is very work-oriented.

The new fall retreat is more relaxed. There is more free time, which gives the adult leaders and the young people time for informal interaction. That kind of time is crucial for building relationships.

As you read this, you may be debating which kind of retreat to suggest. Having the whole year planned out, on a calendar, and planned by the youth, is an attractive idea. On the other hand, young people need group-building time. And they need downtime from stressful activities at school and elsewhere. What should you do? Ask the youth.

If you have a youth council or youth ministry committee, you have a ready-made group of young people and adults who can decide the kind of retreat to have. With the council planning the retreat, it is more likely that the fall retreat will serve the needs of the young people in your church. This retreat needs to have a focus, a purpose. It is too valuable to be haphazardly planned. The council should struggle with the issues: What do our young people need? What do we hope will happen on this retreat? What is our theme? What is our goal?

Expand and Adapt the Team Approach

There is no one right way to do the team approach. As you read on, keep the word "adapt" in mind. Twenty different people could read this book, use it, and come out with twenty completely different youth ministries. That would be wonderful! As you young people and you adult leaders use this book, you will discover ways to change your own team approach. You will come up with better ideas than the ones you find in this book. That's the way the creative process works.

It's exciting to think about the dynamic things that can happen when young people and adults, in partnership, in churches, stay on the move, evaluating, and evolving. No longer will we hear, "that's the way we've always done it." Keep growing.

Youth Council or Youth Ministry Committee[*]

There are many ways to form the membership of the council/committee. Here are three possibilities:

1. All the adult leaders and one or two representative youth from each class
2. An equal number of youth and adult leaders, and a representative from the session or church board
3. One or two representatives from each class, and eight adults, as follows: the coordinator of the senior highs; the coordinator of the junior highs; a junior high adult leader; a senior high adult leader; a junior high church school teacher; a senior high church school teacher; a junior high parent; and a senior high parent.

The council meets monthly or every six weeks and is responsible for:
- setting the direction for youth ministry
- implementing team ministry
- looking at needs of youth
- doing long-range planning
- evaluating youth ministry
- advocating youth concerns
- connecting youth ministry to other programs relating to youth—choir, church school, Scouts, church leagues

It might also be a good idea for you to create a "Think Sheet" for your youth ministry committee. This allows you to put on paper goals, objectives, and plans, and encourages continual evaluation. A sample form might look like this:

> The youth ministry committee sets the direction for youth ministry.
> - It identifies purpose and mission.
> - It gathers and analyzes data about youth.
> - It formulates policy and recommends such to the session.
> - It designs broad strategies.
> - It advocates youth concerns.
> - It develops leadership.
> - It oversees youth ministry activities.
>
> As part of the process of setting the direction, evaluate our church's "youth friendliness."
> - Is our congregation a "youth friendly" place?
> - Are youth present?
> - Do youth have power?
> - Are they valued?

Questions to Think About

Where is Jesus Christ present and at work in young people's lives?
What are we teaching youth about grace and stewardship?
What does faith have to do with growing up?
What do our understandings of gospel, church, and ministry teach us about youth ministry?

*This page may be reproduced as needed.

TWO

....

Youth Today

At a recent youth ministry committee meeting we were discussing our spring calendar. The young people started talking about having a relaxation retreat, a retreat with built-in downtime. The more we talked, the clearer it became that what they wanted was a spirituality/faith retreat, one in which they would have relaxed time to sit around and talk about faith.

Clearly the fast-paced retreats that we are all used to doing with young people are in need of revision for today's youth. The old philosophy of "keep them busy" is ridiculous. Young people today are so busy and so stressed out that they need downtime.

My teenage daughter once brought me a cartoon from the Sunday paper. It was a picture of a mom and dad looking out the window at their daughter sitting under a tree. The daughter looks peaceful and carefree. The parents' comment is something like: "Wouldn't it be nice to be young and carefree again?" Next to the daughter is a cartoon balloon that shows what she is thinking. In that balloon are depicted problems at school and with friends and fears about rejection, grades, career choice, and the future. It represents many of the issues facing teenagers today. And the point is clear: No, mom and dad, I am not young, and life is not carefree. I don't feel like a child anymore, not with these problems.

So here's the note to parents and youth leaders: Alert! There are some hurting, stressed-out young people out there. And they are ours! We need to find out all we can about youth today, about what occupies their minds and hearts.

The George H. Gallup International Institute produces resources, statistical studies, and survey results on teenage behavior, lifestyle, attitudes, concerns, and issues. In the introduction to *The Religious Life of Young Americans,* George Gallup writes:

Young Americans face unprecedented challenges—diminishing economic opportunities, changing gender roles, the lure of self-fulfillment as an ultimate personal goal, and a spiritual and ethical environment pervaded by cultural and religious relativism, to name a few.

At the same time, these young people find they have fewer personal and institutional resources upon which to draw. Family networks are weaker. Diminishing government resources are pulling the floor beneath the urban young who are the most disadvantaged.

What role are religious institutions playing in the lives of these young people?[1]

This is the question that faces us in youth ministry: What role is the church playing in the lives of young people? In order to discover what that role is, we need to know our youth. What's going on in their lives? What worries them? Statistical studies can give us, based on their surveys, a prioritized list of the concerns facing teenagers today. But you have a more accurate source: You can ask your own young people. The results will be more personalized than any study, for you can find out their concerns about their families, their school, their friends, their faith.

Though teenage concerns vary in different parts of the country and in different situations—rural, suburban, city, small town—three issues are common in the experiences of today's young people. These three critical issues are stress, brokenness, and loneliness. Other issues facing young people today face all of us—consumerism, the decline of the nuclear family, and environmental problems, among others. But since there are differences in each location and in each young person's life, we encourage you to use the questions in each section of this chapter. Ask your young people.

What better way to get to know them and to begin building relationships. These questions can be used in a one-on-one conversation or in a group discussion.

The following discussions are in no way a definitive study, but are intended to encourage readers to consider the issues.

Stress

Stress was once considered an adult condition but not anymore. If you've been picturing teenagers as bored, sitting in front of a TV or video game, you haven't looked lately. Young people will tell you they are stressed-out. This stress has many sources: (1) busyness—an ever-increasing number of activities; (2) pressure—from family, peers, school, and economic conditions, and from themselves; and (3) their consumer—gotta have it now—behavior.

Ask Your Young People:
1. What is your stress factor? Choosing a number from one (basically calm) to ten (very stressed-out), how would you rate your life in the stress department?
2. List the things that are stressful for you right now.
3. Why do you think these things that you listed in response to item #2 are causing stress in your life?

Busyness

One of the major problems with planning youth ministry in the local church today is scheduling. In youth ministry workshops, I hear over and over: "We can't have a retreat. Weekends just aren't available. Our kids have soccer, band competitions, cheerleading clinics, dance, play practice, the SAT exam, and jobs." Sunday isn't sacred anymore. Schools and recreation centers have all kinds of activities on Sundays. Even if they do have Sunday night free, many young people have to do homework then because they've spent the weekend involved in activities.

Our young people are pulled in so many directions. They want to do well in school. They have to do well in school if they hope to go to college. They want to participate in a lot of activities. They want to be popular. They want friends. They want to be with their friends. Parents want them to spend time with the family. It's rare to find a family that can manage to eat a dinner together.

And here we in the church are adding more busyness by wanting them to participate in youth activities. More than that, we want them to be involved in all aspects of the life of the church. And we're hoping it will be of their own free will and a priority. We don't want much, do we?

Yet isn't that what we're about? Isn't that what this book is about? Yes it is, and you will find lots of ways to involve young people as you read on. But your goal is not just to get them involved. They don't need one more activity to keep them busy. Faith is not about busyness. Faith is about a relationship with God that shapes the way young people make choices about their lives and lifestyles.

Ask Your Young People:
1. How many of you eat supper with your families at least once a week? How do you "do" dinner at your house—Who cooks? Is everyone there at the same time? Is there conversation?
2. What makes your life busy? What activities are you involved in—after school? in the evenings? on weekends?
3. Of all your activities other than school, which do you wish you could drop? Could you drop that activity? Why? Why not?
4. What would you like to make time for? What would you add to your life's schedule? Can you do it? Why? Why not?
5. How does the church play a role in your life?

Pressure

If you're busy and pulled in different directions, and trying to do it all, you know what pressure is. Young people experience that kind of pressure. You've heard a lot about peer pressure. It's real, but the good news is that it's not all bad. Young people can have a tremendously positive influence on each other. That's why parents are so concerned over choice of friends. They want their sons and daughters to spend time with young people who have good values and who aren't likely to get into trouble.

Since teenagers spend a lot of time with peers, they experience pressure as they have to decide daily whether or not to do what their friends want to do. They get a lot of practice in decision making, but it does add to the pressure of their lives.

Parents are another source of pressure, precisely because they want so much for their children. Of course, they want them to be happy and successful. But sometimes parents have an agenda for their children's future. They may want them to go into a particular occupation, or to go to a specific college, or to excel in a certain sport, or to live in their home town.

Studies show that grades and school performance are the number-one worry of adolescents. The competition for college admission has increased, and with it the pressure to get good grades. Young people experience tremendous anxiety the day the report card goes home. A lot of this has to do with trying to live up to parents' expectations. To teens parents never seem to be satisfied. The young person is proud to have a B; the parent asks why it isn't an A.

Grades impact a young person's self-esteem. A stigma goes with being a poor student. A teenager who gets poor grades may be penalized when it comes to sports and extracurricular activities. One who gets good grades is often treated better by teachers. A person's worth is directly connected to a grading system. It shouldn't be that way, but it is. And that creates pressure.

Parental expectations and restrictions are another source of pressure. Many parents don't know how to give their young people the space needed to develop independence and to practice decision making. Teenagers get lots of negative messages: "Why can't you be like your brother?" "You never do . . ." or "You always are . . ." "How can you be so stupid?" There are many situations in which young people don't want to go home because they will be yelled at, nagged, or abused. Physical, emotional, and sexual abuse is a reality, and something of which we in the church need to be aware.

There is also pressure to grow up quickly. Kids are not allowed to be kids. They take on responsibilities that would have been unheard of for young people twenty years ago. Today's young people take care of younger siblings. Many have to juggle a schedule split between divorced parents. Some prepare meals, because a parent is not around at dinnertime. Many hold down jobs, either to help with family income or to pay for their own activities and personal items. And they have to make adult decisions about their own behavior.

Young people today have to make critical choices at younger ages. If a young person wants to get into a certain college, he or she often needs to set the course in eighth grade. No eighth-grader wants to be thinking that far ahead, but many have to. Many young people are setting their sights on scholarships, and in order to compete, they have to plan and make choices in junior high school.

Finally, young people are the source of their own pressure problems. Youth today are driven. They pressure themselves to perform at higher levels. They push themselves. They choose to be overworked. They cram as much as possible into a day. Of course, you'll still find the "lazy" or unmotivated youth, but we are seeing fewer of them. How many young people twenty years ago carried personal calendars? They need them today.

Ask Your Young People:

1. What kind of pressures do you experience? What is the source of the pressure—parental expectations? peers? school? family situation? yourself? Describe an experience in which you felt pressure.

2. What kinds of positive peer pressure do you experience? What kinds do you see being experienced by other youth in your school?

3. What kinds of negative peer pressure do you experience? What kinds do you see being experienced by other youth in your school?

4. Would you say that the young people in your school are driven to do well at school? Why are they driven?

Consumerism

It is easy for adults and young people alike to become caught up in a consumer mentality. Whatever it is, we need it. And we need it now. Children are raised in a "buy" mode rather than a "wait" mode. Then, when we get it, we consume it. If it's packaged, we toss the package. And so we consume our environment. We seem to consume everything within our reach—food, drink, natural resources, time, energy, people. Young people today are learning to, as the saying goes, "love things and use people." They learn to use people to get ahead. And they need to get ahead in order to keep up in this expensive, consumer-dominated world.

Advertising is responsible in part for the consumerism problem, convincing us that we need what we didn't know we needed. Parents play a major role, when they model the need for bigger houses, better cars, better-paying jobs. We need more money to buy more things. Even a college education ends up being a means to an end, to buy a better position in life.

Buying and owning is seen as a way to soothe our battered souls, to solve problems of loneliness, rejection, and bruised self-esteem. Commercials tell us we'll feel better if we buy the product. So we keep on buying, whether we have the funds or not.

The commercializing process is started on young children. By the teenage years, young people are seasoned consumers. In their desire for popularity, young people believe they need certain jeans, athletic shoes, jackets, or whatever is "in" in order to even be considered a candidate for popularity. The "gotta have it" attitude is a part of the teenagers' lifestyle.

Since the church teaches a different set of values, young people and adult leaders have a lot to talk about: a lot of issues and challenges.

Ask Your Young People:

1. What's in? What shoes, shirts, jackets, and so on do you and other teenagers feel "you have to have?" Is being "in" a concern for you and your friends? Is it hard to be your own person, to be an individual who doesn't have to have certain "things?"

2. How important is money? Have the young people write down the list of items that appears below or copy the list and distribute it to your group. In the first space, have them place a number, from one to ten, as to how they personally would rank the importance of each item. One is least important; ten is most important. In the second blank, have them rank what they think the importance of each item is to people in general. Not all the items have to do with money. Ask them to think of additional values they'd like to include, and let the group discuss these as well.

3. Where do values come from? Discuss the role of parents, media, and faith.

Item	Important to me personally	Important to other people
A high-paying job	_____	_____
A big house	_____	_____
An expensive car	_____	_____
Travel	_____	_____
Expensive clothes	_____	_____
A wealthy spouse	_____	_____
Good health	_____	_____
Freedom	_____	_____
Respect	_____	_____
An exciting life	_____	_____
Being physically attractive	_____	_____
Faith in God	_____	_____
Family	_____	_____
_____	_____	_____
_____	_____	_____

Brokenness

We are a broken people living in a broken world. Young people are experiencing the effects of the brokenness of families, of the economy, of the world—peace, environment, politics. Evidence of all this hits us constantly through the news. Every community differs in the intensity of these problems. How is your community affected by these issues? Ask your young people.

Brokenness of Families

When parents separate and divorce, their children are hit hard. Teenagers often hide their feelings and withdraw during tense times. Others "act out" with destructive behavior. Many blame themselves.

Having an intact nuclear family doesn't guarantee a healthy family. Families experience brokenness at many levels. When communication is lacking between family members, there is brokenness. When parents are so consumed by their own problems that they cannot deal with their children, there is brokenness. And this kind of brokenness can end in abuse—physical and emotional.

Another common response is the determination to avoid a similar situation. It is not unusual for young people to say they don't want to have children. They don't want to raise children in a world that has so many problems.

Ask Your Young People:
(Be careful. The following sections contain some questions that may be too sensitive or personal for some young people. Young people should not be pushed to answer.)

1. In what ways are families "broken"? What are the problems facing families today? Which of these problems do you think is the most serious in our community?

2. What are the long-term effects of these problems? What happens when we can't "fix" the brokenness?

3. How can the church help families?

Brokenness of the Economy

Many teenagers' parents have lost jobs or been forced to change jobs. It's often hard for families to make ends meet. Financial problems consume both parents and young people. The future is uncertain and, therefore, frightening.

Young people used to dream of going into the helping professions—psychology and sociology, for instance. Today, if you ask teens about their future, making money is the first concern for most. This is not because they are greedy or uncaring kids. It's rooted in reality and experience. In the majority of families, a single income is not enough to support the standard of living people want.

A pressing question families fear is how to pay for college, especially when reality is often a bill of $100,000—for one child. And then there may be graduate school to consider. The high cost of education has changed lifestyles. Parents are going back to school while working, in order to obtain a higher-paying job. Students are working their way through school. Everyone is in need of a good job, and there are not enough good jobs to go around. Many of our nation's homeless are college graduates who cannot find jobs to support themselves and their families.

Ask Your Young People:
1. Spend some time talking about how families are handling the financial crises of "making it." Ask: Do you have family members who work at more than one job? What are the effects on your family of the high cost of living?

2. Is higher education a possibility for you? What are some of the ways your family is trying to make college a reality?

3. How stressed are you over financial issues? In what ways have you seen finances cause brokenness?

Brokenness of the World— Peace, Environment, Politics

Young people see that the world is broken. They are hopeful about peace, until violence in the Middle East erupts again, or in Bosnia, or in Rwanda, or in Oklahoma City. Many youth ask if peace can ever be a possibility. With the presence of guns and drugs on school grounds, they see violence winning out.

The environment is broken—rain forests are being destroyed, the ozone layer is being depleted, and pollution, toxic waste, chemicals, and garbage are clogging our water, air, and land.

Politics is broken. It once was a mark of honor to live in a country that has a two-party system and a democracy. But something has gone sorely wrong. Many have lost faith in our leaders. Faith in our judicial system is broken. Many feel that our system encourages people not to take responsibility for their actions: people are not to blame for their actions, for something in their past gave them just cause to commit the crime.

Ask Your Young People:

1. Where do you see possibilities for peace? What incidents and acts of peace are going on in the world? In your community?

2. Are any of your heroes or role models politicians? Why? Why not? How would you change the political system?

3. What is the role of the church in relation to brokenness?

Loneliness

What happens when stressed-out children live in a broken world? They experience loneliness. Do you wonder how young people can be lonely when they have so much to do? The loneliness young people are experiencing is an emptiness that comes from parent inattention, the lack of supportive friendships, and battered self-esteem.

Parental Inattention

Parents work longer hours these days. Many are workaholics. In addition to their jobs, many have outside commitments and interests. As a result, children and teenagers often come home to an empty house.

There seems to be a pattern in raising children that has left a void in parent-teen relationships. When the children are young, parents spend time with them, driving them to activities, playing with them after school, and attending school functions.

Then, when the children are old enough to go to the neighbor's house to play and don't need mom or dad to fulfill their every need, parents are able to do some of the things they've been putting off. They are relieved not to be quite so needed anymore. What these parents don't realize is that pre-teens and teenagers need their parents just as much as younger children do, but in a different way.

What teenagers need from parents is a listening ear. That's the key to developing close communication between parents and teenagers. In addition, young people need their parents to support them as they are developing independence, shaping values, and making decisions. Instead, some parents back off during the teen years, assuming that teenagers don't want them around. Parents are sure their teens won't listen to them anyway. But that's just the point. With teenagers, parents need to listen more than instruct, support more than correct, empathize more than criticize.

Ask Your Young People:

1. How many of you have experienced loneliness? Talk about a time when you experienced loneliness.

2. Describe parent-teen relationships. How much time do you spend with your parents? Is there communication between you?

3. How would you improve communication with your parents? What do you wish you could talk to your parents about?

Lack of Supportive Friendships

For young people, one of the precursors of depression and suicide is the lack of friends. Developing friendships is an important social skill that most young people learn during their childhood and teenage years. But not all young people have close, supportive friends. All teenagers need at least one close friend in whom they can confide.

The need for friends is so great that some young people will do anything to be accepted. This is when the negative aspects of peer pressure can take over. Acceptance is often the reason young people become involved in drinking, drugs, sexual activity, and gangs.

Ask Your Young People:
1. Do you have one really close friend? What are the qualities of a close friendship?

2. Do you know teenagers who will do just about anything to be accepted? What kinds of things do they do?

3. What is a gang? Are there gangs in your school? What kind of gangs? What goes on in these gangs? Why do you think teenagers are attracted to gangs?

Battered Self-Esteem

Too many young people suffer from poor self-image. Being put down is a way of life for many teenagers. Even their parents sometimes tell them that they are stupid, worthless, and can't do anything right. Statistics have shown that an average father-son relationship consists of thirty minutes a week spent together. Out of that thirty minutes, twenty-seven are instructional. Not one minute is affirmative.

It's amazing to me how often I meet a young person's parent for the first time and say, "I am crazy about your son," to be met with a parent's reaction of amazement. They say, "You are?" Then they say something like, "Well, he must be different around you." Is it any wonder young people feel unloved and unwanted? Those who are in families that are in conflict feel this pain even more.

Young people often perceive that their parents don't care. Then they wonder, if their parents don't care, why anyone else should. The situation is the same at school. When I asked a group of boys to name a teacher who really liked them, two of them could not think of a single teacher. And they sincerely believed that they had never been liked by any of their teachers. In a local news report about a teacher of the year, the comment most often repeated by students was, "He doesn't put you down." Obviously these young people were accustomed to having teachers who did put them down. Teachers and parents should not be shattering self-esteem.

How can young people become healthy adults if they grow up in homes and schools that constantly knock them down? How are they to have hope for the future? How are they to recognize that God loves them, when they see so little evidence of love and affirmation?

Ask Your Young People:
1. Have the young people list on one side of a sheet of paper what they don't like about themselves. Then, on the other side, have them list what they like about themselves. Which list is longer? Ask them why the list of negative traits is usually longer.

2. How many of you have teachers who are supportive and affirming? Tell about one. How many of you have teachers who put you down?

3. Can you name one person who really makes you feel good about yourself?

4. How can you help other teenagers see that they are loved by God?

Unhealthy Responses to Crisis

Stress, brokenness, and loneliness are taking their toll on our teenagers. How do these issues affect your young people? Again, ask them. Unfortunately, many young people deal with crisis in unhealthy ways. They make choices that result in serious problems that have long-range consequences. Teens believe the myth that they are indestructible. They believe "it's not going to happen to me." Your young people can tell you which are the most serious problems in their schools and among their peers.

Watch carefully for the following behavior.

Drug and Alcohol Use

Today, when we talk about problems with drugs and alcohol, we talk about them as substance abuse. Alcohol seems to be the drug of choice. Young people start drinking at a younger age than ever before.

Teenagers are consuming more and consuming it faster. Many young people use designated drivers, but death due to a drunk driver is still a leading cause of death among teenagers.

Drug use also continues. Many teenagers can tell you where to find drugs, especially marijuana, narcotics (including heroin), hallucinogens, barbiturates, and amphetamines (including cocaine). Huffing (sniffing household products) is a dangerous practice among young people today.

Ask Your Young People:
1. How would you describe the drinking and drug-use situation in your community? Is there a lot of drinking? Where and when? What do teenagers do about drinking and driving?

2. How available are drugs? Which kinds of drugs are teenagers using?

Sexual Activity

Since young people are looking for acceptance, love, and intimacy, it is no surprise that teenagers are sexually active. But they confuse sex with intimacy. Teens often back into sexual activity, going further on a date than they intend.

Young people do not communicate with each other about sex. Talking about sex with the opposite sex is essential for developing healthy male-female relationships. Both sexes need to develop refusal skills, the ability to say no, to be assertive without being aggressive or demeaning to the other person. Refusal skills are necessary at any age, from the child who needs to refuse to get into a car with a stranger to the adult who needs to refuse to be harassed on the job.

Refusal skills are essential for women today, as many are finding themselves in situations of date rape. This horrifying development in boy-girl relationships has prompted churches, schools, and families to talk more about sexuality, to provide sex education, to try to build self-esteem in young people, and to encourage communication in dating relationships.

Despite the AIDS epidemic, teenagers still engage in unprotected sex. Again, they believe it won't happen to them; they won't get AIDS.

Some of our teenagers asked us to say clearly in this book that alcohol can mess you up when it comes to making decisions about sex. The young person with the highest self-esteem and the strongest inten-

tion of not getting involved can "throw it all out the window" if he or she has been drinking.

Through the church and through relationships in youth ministry, young people should find a safe place where they can be themselves and be loved and supported. Many churches are providing retreats and other educational experiences that use good curricula and good leadership in the area of sexuality. One such curriculum is *God's Gift of Sexuality,* published by the Presbyterian and Reformed Educational Ministry of the Presbyterian Church (U.S.A.) and the Reformed Church in America. This curriculum is particularly good because of its emphasis on communication and its involvement of parents. It gives parents and youth a context in which to talk to each other in a nonthreatening setting.

Ask Your Young People:
1. Have any of you been a part of a sexuality course in the church? What did it involve? In what ways was it helpful?

2. How do you make decisions about sexual activity? What values play a role in your decision making?

3. Can you and your parents talk about sexuality?

Depression and Suicide

With all that young people have to cope with these days, it is not surprising that depression is a teenage problem. What is most tragic is teenage suicide. Nothing is more devastating than having one of your young people or one of their friends take his or her life. Suicide is on the rise in the teenage population.

It is of such concern that we want to share some of the warning signs of suicide. Be alert to the following conditions: withdrawal from friends; loss of weight or appetite; alcohol or drug use; death of a parent, sibling, or friend; divorce; breakup with girl- or boyfriend; a prolonged illness, depression; extreme happiness following depression; giving away of possessions; and talk about suicide.

If a young person talks about suicide, you must report it to a counselor or to a family member. If a young person comes to you, listening is important, but at some point in the conversation, you need to tell the young person that you can't keep this disclosure private. Someone needs to be told. You can help determine the seriousness of the young person's intent by asking if he or she has been planning to commit suicide, and if so, ask if the young person has thought through how to do it. Contrary to how this may sound, you are not planting the idea. If the youth has such an intent, it will surface. If not, the young person most likely will respond quite clearly that he or she does not intend to commit suicide. Then you can help the young person look at possible ways of dealing with the problem. But, please, be ready to refer. All of us need to recognize (1) when professional help is essential and (2) when and how to refer a young person to a trained counselor or other professional.

Ask Your Young People:
1. What do you think causes teenagers to think about committing suicide?
2. Do you have friends who have talked about suicide?
3. If you were depressed or had thoughts of suicide, who would you talk to?
4. What can the church do to help teenagers with depression?

Eating Disorders

Teenagers, like many of us, are preoccupied with how they look. Thin is still in. Overeating was the problem for children and young people in previous decades, but today, undereating, anorexia, and bulimia are serious health problems for many teenagers.

There are many underlying causes of eating disorders: loneliness, insecurity, depression, constantly worrying about what other people think, stress, pressure to measure up to a certain standard, the need to be popular, the need to be attractive, and problems with relationships.

Ask Your Young People:
1. Have you known teenagers with eating disorders? What do you think causes eating disorders?

Codependency

Codependency is a new term for an old problem. It refers to unhealthy relationships, in which one person takes on the responsibility for another person's life and problems. Most people are familiar with spouses of alcoholics who, in trying to take care of the alcoholic, actually keep the alcoholic from dealing with the problem. But codependency takes other forms as well.

Many teenagers are in codependent boyfriend-girlfriend relationships. It starts out with one of the pair trying to please the other person, to the exclusion of their own needs. It ends up with the pleaser, or codependent, being caught in a sick relationship. The codependent is afraid to break up, because the other person may have threatened suicide or threatened to hurt the codependent. Codependents have the illusion that if they stick with the person, they can change him or her; things will get better. But the truth is, of course, things get worse.

Ask Your Young People:
1. Do you know any teenagers who are in unhealthy, codependent dating relationships? Describe the relationship.
2. How might you help someone who is in a codependent relationship?

Violence

Violence has taken center stage in both the adult and the teenager's world today. No longer can we excuse the violence in movies by saying, "Everyone knows it's not real." It is real. The real violence young people encounter can be worse than what they see on television. Young people experience violence either as victims or as perpetrators.

And most shocking of all, violence often has no impact on them. On an episode of the television show "Picket Fences," the parents are appalled that their son and his pre-teen friends have beaten swans to death by bagging the swans and using them as hockey pucks. Their son's reaction to the parents' question, "Why didn't you stop them?" is "I didn't know it was a felony." This is not just television; rather; it represents a frequent response to horrible behavior. Sensitivity is gone, drilled out of young people by overexposure to violence. Young people are numb to it.

Another tragedy young people face is the amount of physical abuse inflicted on them in their homes, on the street, and in their schools. There are now metal detectors in schools, because young people are bringing guns and knives to school—for protection. Our young people have witnessed shootings and beatings. They have been beaten up in school bathrooms. Fortunately abuse prevention networks are on the rise. But the problem is immense.

Ask Your Young People:

1. Does your school have a metal detector? Are there youth who bring guns or knives to school? Describe the situation in your community.

2. How do you feel about the violence in movies? Do you think young people have gotten used to seeing brutal killings, maimings, and meanness?

3. Someone once said that you could enjoy the movie *Pulp Fiction* if you just didn't take it too seriously, that it really was funny if you didn't think about what actually was happening—referring to the killings. How do you react to that statement?

How Can the Church Respond?

We have touched on three major issues of youth today—stress, brokenness, and loneliness. What is the church's response to these issues? What is our role as adults and young people involved in youth ministry? These issues relate to the very basic nature of who youth are and how we approach them as children of God, loved by God.

In response to all three issues, the church can be a safe place where young people can find significant adult friends who will listen, support, and help them develop coping skills. The church can provide a good foundation for faith formation and point young people to healing and wholeness.

Responding to Stress: Helping Young People Find Coping Mechanisms

The church can help young people find ways to alleviate stress. When young people and adults develop caring relationships, they listen to each other; they try to help each other find coping mechanisms. The church should be the place where young people can experiment with new ways of coping. Significant adult friends can help young people make choices about their busy lives. They can help them develop their values and priorities. They can talk over the pressures young people face.

Responding to Brokenness: Helping Young People Find Healing and Wholeness

Finding wholeness and healing for brokenness is fundamental in our faith. As Christians we believe that brokenness is sin and that God has offered healing for this brokenness through Jesus Christ. God has conquered sin and has made possible a reconciliation—of all people to God and of people with one another. This is the good news of the gospel. This is what we're all about as a church and as those called to do youth ministry.

Responding to Loneliness: Helping Young People Find a Healthy Intimacy with a Loving God and Loving Friends

An adult leader told me about the changes in her church's young people over four years, since she had begun working with an expanded team of adults and youth. Young people who were now college students were maintaining contact with their adult leaders. When they came home on break, these youth planned both social get-togethers and service-oriented experiences. They wanted to spend time with one another and with their adult leaders doing the kind of caring and serving that they had done in high school.

She said that up until the new era of youth ministry, young people had not experienced healthy relationships with adult leaders. Five years ago these young people were made to go to church. It became a game with them to hide from Sunday school teachers before class started, and to see if they could do whatever they could get away with on Sunday night. They saw the adult leaders as policemen, giving them the eye, just waiting for them to do something out of line.

Gradually, over the next four years, the young people came to see that adult leaders really cared about them. The change came as adults leaders spent more time listening to the young people. These leaders chose to spend time with the youth because they truly wanted to be with them. They loved and accepted the youth as they were.

This is a description of a healthy intimacy. The relationship creates an atmosphere that says to the young person, "I'm there for you, no matter what you do. I'm not judging you. I'm not going to put you down." The result is that the young people trust these adults. The young people feel safe. They can be themselves. They know their self-esteem won't be trampled.

In our church, healthy intimate relationships have developed among young people as well. It's hard for young people to trust one another. That's why many friendships are fickle during the teenage years. But we are seeing young people in our churches become significant friends for one another.

For us it all started with that catchword of the nineties, "bonding." We took a group of senior highs to a huge youth conference. Several of the young people were concerned whether or not everyone would get along, since it was such a diverse group. But something happened on that week-long trip. Young people began to see one another with new eyes. They risked being themselves. They risked caring about one another. And when they marveled at how unbelievable it was that such bonding could

happen, they were ready to hear how God's love works in the world. They shared in small groups, in worship, and in prayer. They experienced the grace and love of God bringing them together in true community.

The good news is that through healthy relationships with significant adult and youth friends in the church, young people gain a new understanding of what church is all about, of what God's love is all about. Church should be a safe place where young people can be themselves, warts and all, and encounter a loving God, a God who loves them first. They cannot and need not earn that love.

All of us, young people and adults, are looking for a relationship in which we can be assured that we will truly be cared for and accepted as we are. That's the kind of relationship God offers. We, in youth ministry, are trying to point young people in the direction of a relationship with God through Jesus Christ. We are trying to create an environment in which young people can develop a healthy intimacy with God.

We have a mission here. Young people today need what the church has to offer. We need to reach these young people and let them know that God cares and so do we. No matter how stressful or broken or lonely their lives have become, they can find healing and reconciliation within the community of the Christian faith.

NOTES

1. *The Religious Life of Young Americans,* with commentary and analysis by George H. Gallup Jr. and Robert Bezilla (Princeton, N.J.: The George H. Gallup International Institute, 1992), 8.

THREE

The Essentials of Youth Ministry

We go to youth ministry workshops and we buy books on youth ministry, hoping to find the right "program" or "structure" that will give us the solution to all our problems with youth. Or at least we hope to find the right approach to help us deal with the issues mentioned in chapter 2. But the truth is, we won't find a ready-made solution. We need to stop looking for programs. That should not be our top priority. Instead, what we need to do is look at the basics. We need to put the horse before the cart, get our ducks in a row, or whatever metaphor works for you. There are some things we need to think about and talk about before we plan programs or undertake any changes in the direction of our youth ministries.

The most important of these "things to think about" stands alone. It precedes the eight essentials presented later in this chapter. It is a basic assumption of youth ministry. It is the foundational premise on which we base all that we do with young people. It is a belief that everyone who is involved in youth ministry has been called by God to do this ministry.

The Calling

We believe that all young people and adults who are involved in youth ministry have been called by God. If your young people or your adult leaders seem less than enthusiastic, perhaps it is because they do not see what they are doing as a "calling" from God. Explore the concept of being called by God with your young people and adults. Ask them:

What are we called to do?
• God has called us to do youth ministry.
• We are called to be faithful disciples of Jesus Christ.
• We are called to engage young people in the same calling.

We are to help all young people see that they too are called to do youth ministry and to be faithful disciples of Jesus Christ.

The idea that involvement in youth ministry is a calling may be a missing link in your program. Stop and think about why you're doing youth ministry. Is it because you feel obligated? Is it because no one else will do it? Is it because you like young people (not a bad reason)? Is it because you worry about the teenagers of today and want to help out? Whatever the reason, it may not be enough when the going gets rough and you're ready to throw in the towel. It may not be enough when you're faced with discipline problems and all you can see is brats and monsters. The call of God enables you to see children of God instead.

> You are called by God to do youth ministry.

God has called you, whether you are a young person or an adult, into a special relationship with teenagers. God has called you to take care of these children of God—the youth. God has entrusted you with a ministry with young people. God has called you and will help you develop the love and the skills needed to reach out to young people. It's an awesome calling, but you needn't be scared. You are not alone. God is calling the young people and some special adults to share in this ministry with you. And God is with you.

Robert and I marvel at how, after thirty-six combined years of doing youth ministry, we feel more strongly than ever the presence of God in the midst of our youth ministries. We are increasingly sure that this is what God has called us to do. And we have seen many adults and young people grow in their faith and knowledge that God has truly called them too. We have seen their excitement.

What you are doing with the young people in your church is blessed. An acclaimed marriage counselor once said that he never saw a marriage fail where both husband and wife saw their marriage as a calling from God. We have seen exactly the same in youth ministry. Those young people and adults who see their involvement with youth as a calling from God do not fail. Sure they have failures, but they do not fail.

The Eight Essentials of Youth Ministry

We have come up with eight essentials for building a youth ministry, each discussed below. Spend some time with these ideas. Share them with someone who shares your dream for the young people in your church or with those who may be considering becoming leaders/sponsors/advisors. Share them with your youth council or youth ministry committee. Share them with the young people, perhaps in small groups. Share them with whatever staff you have at your church—director of Christian education, pastor, youth director. Share them with parents.

Ponder these eight essentials. Pray about them. Evaluate your youth ministry in light of these basic principles. (On page 199 is a handout that can be photocopied and used for rating your youth ministry based on these eight essentials.) This is where you need to start.

1. Youth Ministry Must Be Christ-Centered

Being Christ-centered is what makes us different from all other youth clubs and organizations. It's what makes our activities different. What does being Christ-centered mean? Does it mean having a prayer before we go on a trip or having devotions every night?

To answer this question, we adult leaders decided to ask our young people. We were getting ready to go on a ski retreat. I was concerned, since we were able to arrange accommodations at a lower rate,

that the young people might be using the church as a cheap way to get to the slopes. I wondered how we could make the trip Christ-centered. Should we have small-group time, Bible study, a guest speaker?

So we asked the young people: (1) What does it mean to be Christ-centered? (2) How should being Christ-centered affect our planning of the trip? The young people's answers were most helpful. One said that being Christ-centered means we treat each other differently. Another suggested that we needed to have group time, for group building, sharing, "bonding." One suggested that we have a theme. Another thought we ought to gather at night to reflect on the day, to share how we experienced God's presence, and to pray.

Oh, you may say, that your young people would never come up with answers like these. Remember a critical point about doing youth ministry: Forget the negative: "It won't happen with our group." Or "we've tried that already; it doesn't work." People who always have a reason why something won't work are the ones who are least open to being surprised by the Holy Spirit.

To be Christ-centered means you (young people and adults together) are continually opening yourselves to what God can do. It means being hope-filled. To shut down suggestions with negative answers will get you nowhere. If you say it won't work, it probably won't. That's called a self-fulfilling prophecy.

We can grow a Christ-centered youth ministry by including the young people in the process at every level. "Asking the youth" lets them know that you value them and their opinions. Approaching them with the expectation that together we will find out what it means to be Christ-centered means much more than if you, the adult, *tell* them what they have to do to be Christ-centered. Young people do not respond well to being preached at. But they will respond to leaders who demonstrate Christ-centeredness.

Look for ways to affirm Christ-centeredness. We see a hunger for the spiritual among our young people. They are looking for places and rituals that can be sacred to them, because it is there that they encounter God. Sometimes these encounters are planned. Sometimes they are spontaneous.

Our young people have discovered two sacred spaces. The first is the carpeted three steps in the front of our sanctuary. We gather there for spontaneous worship experiences and for short special services, such as on Palm Sunday or Good Friday. It all started when a planned moonlight service during Easter week had to be moved inside because of a near-hurricane storm. It may have been because of the awesomeness of the storm, but being together, worshiping in the dark, became a special Christ-centered event for us.

The second sacred place is one of the most trafficked spaces in our church, the entryway. Before every trip or outing, we gather just before we leave and sit on the carpet in the entryway. We talk over expectations, make sure everyone knows everyone else, and pray. We talk about being a family of God. We say: We have a chance to be who Christ wants us to be for this three-day trip. If WE can't do it for THREE days, how can we expect the world to do it?

Look for the sacred in your situation, the places and rituals, that can become part of your tradition. Ask your young people and adult leaders: Is our youth ministry focused on Christ? We are called by Christ to be in ministry to and with each other. How are we doing? What needs to happen for us to continue to be Christ-centered?

2. You Have to Love the Youth

One of our adult leaders came up to me last fall and said that he had made up his mind not to come back this year—his third year on the youth ministry team. "But I just can't give it up," he said. "I love these kids." I remember when I first asked him if he might be interested in youth ministry. He wasn't sure, since he had never worked with young people. He wanted

to check it out. After only one leadership training session he was convinced that youth ministry was for him. The other adult leaders made it sound like so much fun. Their enthusiasm as they told stories about the young people impressed him. He was expecting stories of discipline problems, but instead he heard endearing stories, funny stories. He saw a group of adults who really loved young people.

This particular year, however, his workload at his job had increased, and he had become a deacon of the church. He wasn't sure he could do it all. I told him we hated to lose him, but we understood. Well, he just couldn't quit. He said he'd miss everybody. He had developed relationships with these young people. They loved him, and he loved them. The young people were a priority for him, so he decided he would manage his other commitments to allow time for his young people.

After all our years of working in youth ministry, Robert and I can say without exception, if you don't love your youth, it just won't work. It's the missing link in many church's youth ministries. So many adult advisors are fed up with behavior problems. They are tired of the lack of respect today's young people have for adults. It is true that the atmosphere in schools and churches has changed over the years; there *is* less respect from young people today.

But we believe that the only way young people will respect adults is for the adults to respect the young person first. That may sound crazy. We're taught the reverse of this as children, of course: Young people have to behave first in order to earn the respect of the adults. But think about it. It's the adults who know what respect is. So the adults should be the ones modeling it by respecting the young person first.

As strange as it may sound, this works. Young people are not used to being treated with respect. For us to give youth the kind of love and honor that goes with respect; for us to listen to them, take them seriously, treat them as intelligent, mature people, can have revolutionary effects on our teenagers. Respect does wonders for self-esteem. That's why we adults want respect so badly. Respect identifies you as a person of worth.

Teenagers today do not have strong self-images. They are handed put-downs almost daily from peers, families, and teachers. What better gift can we give them than respect? And, at the same time, we end up teaching them to respect others through our modeling. It's a win-win situation.

When asked what adult leaders want for the

young people in their churches, many respond that they want the church to touch the lives of their young people, so that the youth may know who Jesus Christ is and choose to follow Him. This is a good goal. In order for the church to touch the young people, we adult leaders need to touch their lives in significant ways. And in order to touch their lives, we need to know them, and know them individually.

Getting to know the young people seems to be the hard part of youth ministry. It shouldn't be, because it's probably the most rewarding. But it takes time. It takes adults who are willing to make phone calls, attend school functions and extracurricular activities, and hang around with the young people after church functions.

Getting to know the young people is part of this essential. Knowing them leads to loving them. It doesn't happen overnight. It takes about three years to feel that you know and trust the young people and vice versa, which is why we encourage adult leaders to commit to more than one year of youth ministry. The first year will not be your best experience. The third year will. It is so sad that the average tenure of a youth minister is sixteen months. But the good news is, we don't need professionals to make it work. Lay people can be educated in youth ministry. They are the ones to provide the continuity. It is helpful if at least two adult leaders stay with youth ministry for at least three years.

As you work toward adult-youth partnership and developing young people as leaders, you'll see the need for knowing your young people and loving them. You'll know how much responsibility each young person can handle. You'll be more at ease turning over aspects of youth ministry to them. As adult leaders and young people grow confident in mutual trust and mutual respect, there will be a whole new atmosphere about your youth ministry. Young people and adult leaders become free to be about the real business of youth ministry, being faithful to Jesus Christ.

3. You Must Build Relationships

Think back to your years as a teenager. If you were involved in a Sunday school class or youth group, think of one or two of the most meaningful classes or programs you had. Now think of adult leaders, Sunday school teachers, adult friends you had.

Which is the more vivid memory, the program or the person? Most people cannot remember a specific program, but they can remember a significant adult in their faith journey. One leader put it this way, "I can't remember what she taught me. I just remember that she loved me."

Another leader recalled having a Sunday school teacher who was an insurance salesman. They had a good relationship throughout this leader's high school years. Later on, when the leader was in college, he went back to this Sunday school teacher to talk about the insurance business. We know of numerous cases of young adults and their former youth leaders who connect as these young adults are looking at careers.

The term we use to describe the role of the adult leader in youth ministry is *significant adult friend.* Adult leaders should become significant adult friends to the young people in the church. Taking the time to work on relationships with the young people is essential, as we firmly believe that relationships are more important than program. You could have a year full of excellent programs, and it still would not compare with an hour of time spent with one of your young people.

> Relationships are more
> important than the program.

Instead of driving yourself crazy trying to find programs for your youth group, switch gears and focus on your young people. What are you doing to build relationships with these young people? Hopefully, you have instituted some form of the team approach in your program. Get together with your team and brainstorm what you need to do in the area of relationship building. At the beginning of the year, all the adults on the team should give as much time as possible to getting to know the young people. If you are having a fall retreat (and we hope you do), encourage all your adult leaders to attend.

Adult leaders are not the only ones to build relationships with the young people. The young people need to work on relationship building among themselves. To achieve a more youth-driven ministry, young people must buy into the need for relational ministry. For example, cruelty among them is a common problem. As youth begin to take ownership and work on relationships, the problem decreases. It decreases because the young people themselves are dealing with the issue, which is much more effective than constant lectures by adults on how to treat one another.

There is help for both adult leaders and young people as they try to build a relational youth ministry. Group-building activities are crucial at the start of each new year, when you have a new class of young people coming on board. There are many youth ministry resources that contain icebreaker ideas and group builders (see appendix 5).

It takes fourteen contact hours to build a group. This means that, whatever your structure for youth ministry, whether it's a Sunday night youth group, or small groups, or mission groups, it will take fourteen hours of time together for the youth to begin to bond as a group. So you need time for group-building activities.

Youth ministry is much bigger than good programs. It's much more comprehensive. It has a vision of what life in the church can be when adults and young people are given opportunities to grow and work together in partnership. It puts people ahead of programming. Church becomes a safe place where youth know they can go and find people who care about them.

4. Youth Need Ownership

You walk into a Sunday night youth meeting. There is an adult standing in front of the group, leading the program. Along the back wall of the room are several parents who have volunteered to help out with the youth. They decided to volunteer this year because their own sons and daughters are in the group. The young people are sitting on sofas and chairs, and a few are on the floor. They look a little bored, but it's hard to tell. They don't say anything, but then they aren't used to speaking up in a group. Anyway, if they don't speak, it'll be over sooner. It's 7:30 P.M., the adult leader says a prayer, and they're out of there.

What's wrong with this picture? You ask one of the adults how they plan their programs. You find out that the leaders, who all happen to be parents—in fact the youth refer to them as "the parents," instead of the "advisors" or "leaders"—get together once a

month and decide who will take each Sunday night. They share program ideas to help those who are having a hard time coming up with a program. The leaders feel pretty good about the group, for they have a fairly good turnout each week. But then, parents make their young people attend.

What's missing from this picture is youth ownership. The young people have no investment in their program. This is a picture of adult-driven youth ministry. The adults run it, plan it, lead it, and control it. It's a grim picture. Let's hope that most of us can say we've seen better. But something in this picture may strike a familiar chord. It could be that the adults don't

> Youth ministry should be youth-driven.

know any other way to do it. And it may be that the adults have put together a good program for the young people.

Good programs, however, don't make good youth ministry. Even with good programs, if there is no youth investment, there won't be much excitement among the young people. Adult leaders need to work toward sharing youth ministry with the young people. When there is ownership by the young people, the picture is entirely different:

You walk into a Sunday night gathering and you see a group of young people finishing their plans on a "fun night" that they will be leading for a congregational dinner. Another young person is meeting with an adult leader to go over a prayer she has written for worship Sunday morning. Two of the youth are up front getting ready to announce upcoming events. They are passing around a sign-up poster for a retreat. The adults are mingling with various young people while they wait for the announcements to start.

After the announcements, a young person from the planning team that planned the program stands up and opens with a scripture reading. He then introduces the program on "faith for tough times" and explains that everyone is going to get into smaller groups and come up with a list of tough issues facing teenagers. One of the planning team members is in each group.

Toward the end of the program, several young people are talking about how tough it is to live in a single-parent family. This leads one to ask about the work Big Brothers–Big Sisters does. Another young person asks if they could help out with Big Brothers–Big Sisters. The adult leader mentions the name of the local director of that program. Next thing you know, the youth have contacted the director and are planning a Christmas party for the Big Brothers–Big Sisters children.

That's youth ownership. That's youth-driven youth ministry. It's a picture of young people who want to be there because they have an investment in it. They are willing to work toward their goal of providing a place where everyone can feel welcome and included. It's a picture of young people working alongside adult leaders. They enjoy the adult leaders, who in addition to being their friends, are the ones who encourage them to drive their own youth ministry.

One way to think of ownership is to consider how you treat something you own, such as a car. You take care of it. You protect it. You fix it when it's broken. You use it, not abuse it. You polish it, vacuum it out, tune it up. But with something you don't own, you would hang back and let the owner take responsibility for it.

Both young people and adults need to explore the concept of ownership. How much ownership do your youth have? The more ownership the young people have, the more committed they will be. The more they give, the more they will receive from the church.

To help you work constantly toward youth-driven youth ministry, keep asking: Can a young person be doing this? As adult leaders who find it easier to do things ourselves, whenever we are getting ready to do something, we need to ask: Can a young person be doing this? Leading a game, planning, making a poster, handing out pencils—can a young person be doing it? You'd be surprised how many times the answer is yes.

5. Commitment Is Critical

One of the problems many of us face is asking for commitment. This is ironic, for commitment is basic to the nature of who we are as Christians. But we find ourselves sensitive to demands on people's time, and we can be timid when it comes to making demands on young people's and adults' time. When recruiting volunteers, we find ourselves trying to make the job sound easy or saying that it won't take up too much time.

We are selling youth ministry short if this is our approach. Instead, we should be getting people fired up about the vision of what youth ministry can be and the part they can play in it. We should not only be asking for their support and their commitment but be inviting them to help shape the vision. In other words, ownership works at all levels. If you want adult leaders, parents, the church, and the pastor to be committed, share the dream with them, listen to them, and constantly keep promoting the dream.

The youth, adult leaders, parents,
the church, and the pastor
must be committed to the youth ministry.

Commitment of the Young People

As we mentioned before, youth ownership is the key to increasing the commitment level of young people. As young people take ownership, they become more involved in planning and leading. This requires commitment. They get excited when they see their ideas take shape.

Robert's and my young people join together each June to do a mission in Mexico. All during the year, the young people are involved in making it happen. They work together on fund-raisers. They give talks to Sunday school classes. They do slide presentations. They do creative work on huge promotional displays. As the time nears, they form committees to get supplies together, to write notes to those who have supported the mission, to make banners for the sanctuary of the local church in Mexico—whatever is needed that particular year. Since the young people have ownership of this mission, they are committed to it. On the day we leave, it's impressive to hear the list of jobs read, and to hear a young person yell out "taken care of" or "it's on the van" as items are checked off. That day is the culmination of many hours of hard work by many young people. That's commitment.

Commitment of the Adult Leaders

Adult leader commitment seems to be proportionally related to whether or not the adult feels needed. Like the young people, if adults feel like spectators at youth activities, or if you recruit people who say, "I don't want to lead, I just want to help," chances are they will never get on board. Their commitment level will be low. They will never have ownership. And they won't find youth ministry fulfilling.

The leaders who take on the most responsibility are the ones who get the most out of youth ministry. They are the ones who spend time getting to know the young people. On a retreat they are the ones who, during meals and free time, choose to be with the young people instead of getting together with other adult leaders. Youth ministry is a priority for them. It's a joy to see these adults get excited about the young people.

Our youth group has a tradition of taking a ski retreat over the Martin Luther King, Jr. holiday. It was not an activity for which adult leaders were beating down the doors to chaperon. It's a ten-hour drive. We spend four nights at the slopes. There were stories about all kinds of behavior problems in past years.

When I started going on the ski retreat, we had already begun the expanded team approach. Now, each year, the young people are involved in shaping how we spend our time together on the retreat. A few years ago a group of boys who had gained a reputation as troublemakers had signed up to go. I got lots of advice and cautions from parents. I was not worried, though, for I was taking three of the finest adult leaders. First of all, they were regular leaders and not just chaperons for the ski retreat. They truly loved the young people and were committed to the expanded team concept of youth ministry. They were committed to building relationships, youth ownership, and partnership in leadership. They loved these boys and did not view them as troublemakers.

The result was: It was one of the best ski retreats ever. It was one of the worst for skiing, but that didn't matter. The young people and adults bonded. When we arrived home, it was like breaking up a family, because such community had developed in just four days. Two days later, at a fellowship dinner, one of the leaders was sitting at the other end of a long table. In earshot of everyone, he yelled down the table to me, "I miss it. I want to go back. I miss the kids." There were several surprised faces at that table. I don't think they believed we could have had that good a time with that particular group of young people. It was the best promotion for youth ministry ever.

This is what we're looking for: adults who are committed to and passionate about youth and youth ministry.

Commitment of Parents

A parent came up to one of our adult leaders to express concern that the young people were being rowdy during their Sunday school class, which met next door to this parent's Sunday school classroom. The parent insisted that the young people couldn't be learning anything if they were loud and unruly. In actuality, the young people were role-playing a lesson on temptation. It's unfortunate that I did not follow up with that parent. I missed an opportunity to explain what the young people were doing and to point out how wonderful it is to have teenagers who are enthusiastic about their Sunday school class.

Parents need to be committed to youth ministry. But in order for them to be committed and to support youth ministry, they need to understand what we're trying to do. That puts the responsibility on adult leaders and young people alike to communicate with parents our dreams, vision, and goals for youth ministry. We need to invite parents into conversation. We need to listen to parents. They have concerns. This type of conversation will open the door for parents to lend their enthusiasm and support.

We are seeing a healthy movement in many of our churches, a new emphasis on ministries to families. We talk about this in chapter 12.

Commitment of the Church

The commitment level of the church is another critical issue. Many youth leaders do not get support from their churches. Maybe there's a pat on the back now and then, with a patronizing "good job." But when it comes to money in the budget, or advocating for the young people, or involving youth in worship or in other areas, the church is just not supporting youth ministry.

Look for ways to increase the visibility of your young people. In one church the monthly report on youth ministry to the church board is done by a young person. That's a good idea. Check the appropriate channels to find out how to increase church support. It's usually best to accomplish change by working through the system. Have a brainstorming session with young people and adults. It's hard for the "powers that be" to ignore young people who are growing in faith and developing a passion for their church.

Commitment of the Pastor

Sometimes it's the pastor who is not supportive. It's an uphill battle to develop a strong youth ministry if you don't have the pastor's support. There is power in the pulpit. What the pastor promotes from the pulpit is an indication of what he or she is excited about. It helps if they have a commitment to youth ministry.

If you feel like you're off on your own doing youth ministry, and have little or no connection to the ministry of the church, then seek ways to gain the pastor's support. Studies show that active youth programs are a factor in a family's decision about church membership. So pastors *should be* interested. Share with the pastor your commitment. The young people too can share their vision, enthusiasm, and hopes with the pastor.

It's impossible to have youth ministry without commitment from a lot of people. Take a look at your situation. What are the barriers keeping your youth ministry from happening, from taking off, or from receiving new life? Talk to somebody about it. Don't let the church let you down.

6. Program: Think Big

After years of working with youth groups, an essential hit me like a ton of bricks one afternoon after school. I was pulling up to the front of the middle school to pick up my daughter when I noticed Ted, one of our eighth-grade church members who never came to youth group, standing on the steps. I thought of how I wished I knew how we could get him to come to church. I was about to wave, when I noticed he saw me and was turning his back to me. I felt bad, because I figured he was thinking, "Uh oh, youth director; she's probably wondering why I haven't been to church"—feeling guilty.

And then it hit me. I was asking the wrong question. My query was, How can we get him to come to us? What I should have been asking was, How can we go to him? Here was a boy I did not know. I should be interested in getting to know him. Ideally, when he sees me coming, he shouldn't feel guilty. He should feel, "Here comes Ginny. She really likes me, even though I don't go to church."

That incident changed my ministry. My definition of outreach had been to get young people to come to us. And I had been guilty of writing off those who didn't want to be a part of youth group.

It's More Than Sunday Night

Your program—what you actually do in youth ministry—should be multifaceted, not limited to Sunday night programs. It should be geared to the needs of young people, your young people in particular. Rodger Nishioka, one of our mentors in youth ministry, who stays on the cutting edge of what is happening with teenagers today, has said to us: "Youth ministry for the future must be flexible enough to happen when and where young people are available." This is good news for all those who are frustrated in trying to get young people to come on Sunday nights or to a midweek Bible study. We were basing our youth programs on young people coming to us, instead of us going to where they are.

By "where they are" we mean more than just place. We need to know our young people well enough to know where they are in their interests, their needs, their emotions, their relationships, and their faith.

There are young people out there who don't want to be a part of your group—and for various reasons. Their friends don't go to your church. They don't feel accepted by those who do attend youth group—a common problem in many churches. It could be that they don't like the adult leaders. Or it may be that Sunday night is not a good time for them. A lot of young people are returning home on Sunday night from a weekend with their noncustodial parent.

Don't leave out these young people. Adult leaders and young people should be connecting with them in various ways. These youth are often willing to do special things, like participating as worship leaders, or helping build a Habitat house, or going on a mission trip or work camp, or working in the church kitchen or nursery, or using their individual talents: designing a T-shirt or bulletin cover, being in a play, helping "behind the scenes" with a play or musical. They may be interested in special programs, such as career counseling or church league basketball.

We make a big mistake when we equate youth ministry with youth group. Youth ministry is so much more than a Sunday night meeting.

7. Program: Here's the Beef

Despite the need to think of "program" as being broader than Sunday nights, most of us do have Sunday night "programs" or weeknight "programs." These programs are the "beef" of youth ministry. Often the Sunday night program is a young person's introduction to youth ministry. For some it may be the only activity in which they participate. So there is a responsibility to make it good. What you do with program time is critical. Group building—working on relationships—is part of the Sunday night program. But then, what do you do after that?

Program is the meat on the bones of whatever structure you have set up for youth ministry. What kind of meat are your young people feasting on? How do you design the program time to fulfill your goals? Are your programs faithful to your vision of youth ministry? Are your programs well-integrated into your total youth program? We will discuss designing programs in chapter 9.

> Program is the meat on the bones.

Your programs should reflect all the essentials discussed in this chapter. Programs should be Christ-centered. They should be relationally based. They should deal with the needs and issues of the young people. They should be youth-led as much as the young people are willing to lead.

8. Promote! Promote! Promote!

At a youth ministry workshop, I was working with a church that had good leadership and good program planning in both their junior and senior high groups. The senior high ministry team was having a good year, as young people were coming out to activities in increasing numbers. The level of youth ownership was high. The junior highs, however, had a lot of young people on the roles, but not in attendance. It should have been a strong year, since most of the junior highs were from active church families. They had a core group of four junior highs who helped plan youth ministry and who had a high level of commitment. The adult leaders felt they were letting these four enthusiastic youth down, even though no one could figure out why attendance was low.

The problem was quite simple, once we uncovered it. The coordinator of the senior high ministry team was very organized. She encouraged the senior highs to publicize and promote activities way in advance. She shared leadership responsibilities with the young people and the other adult leaders. She liked to make phone calls, so she called young people to remind them of responsibilities.

The coordinator of the junior highs hated to make phone calls. He had planning sessions with the young people. They scheduled a variety of activities. He said he would send out a calendar. He never did. Hardly anyone showed up for anything. They had planned a retreat but had to cancel because the coordinator couldn't find a retreat site. Only three young people came to a lock-in. They were sent home, and the lock-in was canceled.

The solution surfaced when one of the other junior high leaders offered to make phone calls. The more we talked, the more they recognized that they needed a role change. The junior high leader who offered to make phone calls became coordinator, and the coordinator decided to use his gifts as a member of the team. Both adults were happy with the switch, as it better suited their personalities and their leadership skills.

Publicity is so important. The junior highs at that church had a great program, but how was anyone to know? Assess the personality styles of your leaders. If all your leaders hate to make phone calls, you are in trouble. People say they will phone people and then they don't. Encourage all team members to be honest about what they are willing to do.

Keep a publicity calendar. On it note dates to send out mailings. Note people who should receive phone calls to remind them of responsibilities. Also note inactive young people who should be invited to an activity.

Make it a priority to stay in contact with inactive youth. It's easy to talk to your friends, but we all, adults and young people, need to consciously reach out to others. We all need to invite other young people. Robert asked one of his college students who had been very active in the church in high school why he came. His answer was simple: "You invited me." Many of us know what it's like to be shy and to fear that people will think you're weird if you invite them to church. But it's worth the risk. Take the risk and invite.

Help each other with publicity and promotion. Robert believes you ought to put something in the youth members' hands each week, something that tells what's coming up. Then they can plan for it, put it on their personal calendars, and make sure they sign up. When you send fliers or postcards, send them to both active and inactive young people.

My budget tells me I can't send mailings every week, but I usually can send a flier once, sometimes twice, a month. We have a "Youth Corner" in our church newsletter. We're working on getting all young people and adult leaders to read the newsletter. Parents read it. In fact, lots of church members read "Youth Corner" and tell us how delighted they are to see what the young people are doing.

It's important to promote youth ministry to the entire congregation. It gives visibility to your youth program. It helps in advocating youth concerns. And it helps integrate youth ministry into the life of the community of faith.

Make use of bulletin boards in your church. Keep them current. Make posters. Put youth stuff in the bul-

letin. Make youth-related announcements at Sunday morning worship. It's wonderful when young people do these announcements; this lets the congregation see who the young people are. The pastor should make some of the announcements and talk about youth ministry. This gives youth ministry a strong endorsement.

> So what if your program is great,
> if no one knows?

Young people and adult leaders can make announcements in skit form at various congregational functions, like church suppers and adult Sunday school classes.

Make youth ministry a personal priority. Bring it up in conversations. Get used to "stumping" for youth concerns. Talk about the young people every chance you get.

Conclusion

In our church, we go over these essentials many times throughout the year, especially when things are not going well. At those times when you're beating your head against the wall, or when you're ready to quit, then pull out these essentials, and ask, What's

missing from our youth ministry, from our youth program? Where's the missing link? It's likely to be one of these eight essentials. Then you'll know what needs attention. It's hard to build a youth ministry without a solid foundation. These essentials are essential.

FOUR

Images and Imagination: The Bible Speaks

The first essential listed in chapter 3 is that youth ministry must be Christ-centered. To be *Christ-centered* means we, young people and adults together, are continually opening ourselves to what God can do. One of the ways we do this is through studying God's Word, the Bible. Through Bible study, we can discover images of youth ministry that confirm our beliefs in what God is doing through Jesus Christ and in the lives of the faithful. Hearing the Bible speak, as it were, involves our imagination. As we listen to what God's Word has to say, we imagine and envision our world, our lives, and our youth ministries through the eyes of faith.

Imagination and God's Word

God's Word should be what shapes us and shapes our youth ministry. It provides a foundation for all that we do. It helps shape our dreams, our vision, and our imaginings of what the future can be. It gives us a different slant on what reality is. God's Word can be the glasses through which we see, or perceive, our reality.

Let's look at the concept of imagination for a minute. The way we look at our future, in a sense, is through our imagination—how we imagine it to be. We can imagine optimistically or pessimistically. For example, you may have to move to another town because a member of your family has taken a new job. Even though it is painful to separate from friends and home, you have a choice as to how you will view what's ahead. You can perceive the move as awful: you won't like the people in the new town; you'll be stressed by having to find a new job or go to a new school. Or you can perceive the move as a chance to start over, to make new friends, to take on new challenges that will help you grow.

The optimist imagines the future to be an exciting challenge; the pessimist imagines it to be dreadful. The future is as unknown to the optimist as to the pessimist. So how can the optimist be so upbeat? The pessimist wonders if the optimist has inside information about the future. Is the optimist wearing special glasses through which the future is seen differently? In a sense, yes. Like the optimist, we Christians have what could be called special glasses through which we can see the world in a new way.

These special glasses are God and God's Word. God and God's Word can shape your imagination. Instead of thinking about your life and future with fear and self-doubt, you think about it as guided by God, by divine love and anticipation of good.

The result is that you can move beyond preoccupation with self—for you no longer view self as negative—toward a passion for others, which leads you to loving, caring, and serving. You can approach life, your life, with passion.

What does this deep concept have to do with youth ministry? Most important, it has to do with the way we approach our young people. If we "imagine" them, perceive them, to be loved by God and given worth by God, then we will approach them with the kind of love they need—unconditional love. If we imagine them to be wonderful, lovable human beings, then we will be excited about being with them. But if we imagine them to be rude, disrespectful troublemakers, then we will not love them as God has called us to.

Put on these glasses and let God and God's Word shape your imagination. Look at the following passages from the Bible. Use your God-given imagination and discover images that relate to young people and to youth ministry. Discover how God wants you, adult leaders and young people, to approach youth ministry. As you read, consider how you might use these passages with young people and adults.

Images from the Bible for Youth Ministry

Many Bible passages can relate to youth ministry. We have chosen seven that offer clues about what God is calling young people and adults to do in youth ministry. We invite you to study these passages and find images to guide you in youth ministry. Look at the passages with several groups: with your young people, with adult leaders, with parents and step-parents, with the youth ministry committee or youth council.

We all need to be biblically grounded and informed in order to do faithful youth ministry. But more than that, we believe that God will speak to you, your young people, and your adult leaders through these passages and will begin to shape your imagination, so that you will approach youth ministry with passion. We hope you will recognize that God has called you into an exciting ministry that has an exciting future.

These passages relate to the themes of caring, reaching out, acceptance, invitation, community, faith, challenge, and leadership.

Jesus and the Woman at the Well
(John 4:3–30)

Jesus speaks to a Samaritan woman. If you were a Jew, which Jesus was, you just didn't do that. You didn't associate with Samaritans. Jesus makes a request, "Give me a drink." How puzzled she must have been. Why does he give her the time of day?

Jesus and the woman talk. He offers her something strange, but something very special—living water—which will cause her never to be thirsty again. She wants what Jesus has to offer.

As the passage goes on, Jesus suggests she call her husband. But, of course, Jesus knew she didn't have a husband. In fact, he knew a lot about her and her "undesirable" background. He shouldn't have been associating with her, yet he did. He reached out to her, undesirable though she was, and offered the best he had to offer. He accepted her as she was. He didn't even tell her to go and repent. He accepted her, as the saying goes, warts and all.

Questions for Discussion

1. What do you know about the Samaritan woman?

2. How did Jesus treat her? What did he say? What did he do?

3. What is the living water?

4. How do you think she felt after the conversation?

5. Who are the Samaritans in your school or community? Who are the people you're not supposed to associate with?

6. What does this passage have to say about youth ministry? about adult leaders?

7. How are we supposed to treat people who are unacceptable?

8. Have you ever felt like the Samaritan woman? In what way?

Some Thoughts

Adult leaders are to accept young people as they are, meet them where they are, love them, and offer them the living water, which means, point them to Jesus Christ. The hard part for adults and young people alike is accepting people as they are and loving them. Sometimes, adults talk about a young person's potential. The call is to love people as they are, for who they are, right here and now.

The Call of Andrew and Simon Peter
(John 1:35–42)

As Jesus walked by, John the Baptist announced, "Look, here is the Lamb of God!" Two of John's disciples heard this and followed Jesus. They asked Jesus where he was staying. He replied, "Come and see." They came and saw and remained with Jesus. One of those disciples was Andrew, Simon Peter's brother, who then went to his brother Simon and brought him to Jesus, saying, "We have found the Messiah."

Questions for Discussion
1. What made the two disciples follow Jesus?
2. Jesus said, "Come and see." Expand this invitation. Come what? See what? If Jesus said this to you, today, what would he say?
3. This passage is referred to as the call of Andrew and Simon Peter. What were they called to?
4. What does this passage have to say about youth ministry? About one's calling?
5. List ways to invite people to your youth group. To your church.
6. What makes it hard to invite? What keeps you from extending an invitation?
7. Talk about inviting someone to follow Jesus Christ. Share experiences, both of inviting someone to follow Jesus and of being invited.
8. Role-play inviting someone. (a) to church, (b) to youth activities, and (c) to follow Jesus.

Some Thoughts

The phrase "come and see" points to the way we should be inviting young people to be a part of what's going on in the church. Instead of a hard sell of youth ministry, we are to gently say "come and see" for yourself.

When our junior highs have just had a good retreat experience, we say to them, "You think this was great, just wait till next year. Just wait until you can experience what's ahead in your senior high years. It's even better." In a sense, we're saying, "come and see." It's important to remember to say this at the end of the experience. How often, at the end of a retreat, do we just pack up and go home and forget to reinforce the significance of the event? Talk with the young people about what made the event special. Reinforce the experience or the learning that took place.

Robert asked one of his college students what caused him to be active in high school youth activities? The student's response was: "You invited me" (come and see) "and then you taught me how to invite others" (come and see).

In our youth ministries we want to provide an environment that points to Jesus Christ in such a way that young people will want to follow him.

The Parables of the Prodigal Son and the Lost Sheep
(Luke 15:11–24; Luke 15:3–7)

Both of these parables, which Jesus tells to the Pharisees and tax collectors, show God's unconditional love for each and every person. In the prodigal son story, the younger son insults his father by asking for his inheritance. In those days, such a request was equal to wishing your father dead. The son then squanders the inheritance, hits bottom feeding pigs, and decides to return home to ask his father to take him back as a hired hand. He knows he is not worthy to be called a son.

The Bible paints an exciting reunion scene. "While he (the son) was still far off, his father saw him and was filled with compassion; he ran and put his arms around him and kissed him." The father throws a party to celebrate, saying, "for this son of mine was dead and is alive again; he was lost and is found!"

In the lost sheep story, Jesus poses the question, "Which one of you, having a hundred sheep and losing one of them, does not leave the ninety-nine in the wilderness and go after the one that is lost until he finds it?" When the lost sheep is found, "he lays it on his shoulders and rejoices," and goes home and calls friends and neighbors together to rejoice with him, "for I have found my sheep that was lost."

Questions for Discussion
1. How do you think the son felt when his father came running to him? What was he expecting to happen?
2. How is the father like God? What does the story tell you about God's relationship with us?
3. What does the lost sheep parable tell you about God?
4. Why did Jesus tell these parables? See verse 2.
5. What do these stories have to do with youth ministry?
6. Share a time when you felt left out or lost. What helped you get through the experience?
7. Some people think you have to earn God's love

and earn the love of other people. In light of these parables, what's the real story?

8. What changes could you make in the way you treat individual youth, especially those who feel left out, and those who never attend?

Some Thoughts

The parable of the prodigal son shows us the kind of love we should have for our young people, love that exudes compassion, acceptance, and restoration, no matter how "bad" they have been.

In the parable of the lost sheep, we are reminded that every single young person is worth the effort. When the shepherd finds the lost sheep, he lays it on his shoulders (he treats it gently). Then he rejoices (worships). And when he comes home, he calls together his friends and neighbors, saying to them, "Rejoice with me, for I have found my sheep that was lost" (community). Both young people and adults can get excited over the young person who seemed lost and unreachable, but who, because of the diligence of some shepherd (youth or adult) is found and restored to the community with a celebration.

Jesus the True Vine
(John 15:1–5)

"I am the true vine, and my Father is the vine-grower. He removes every branch in me that bears no fruit. Every branch that bears fruit he prunes to make it bear more fruit. You have already been cleansed by the word that I have spoken to you. Abide in me as I abide in you. Just as the branch cannot bear fruit by itself unless it abides in the vine, neither can you unless you abide in me. I am the vine, you are the branches. Those who abide in me and I in them bear much fruit, because apart from me you can do nothing."

Questions for Discussion
1. Who is the true vine? Who is the vinegrower? Who is the branch? What is the relationship among these?

2. How does the vinegrower take care of the vine?

3. What does it mean to "bear fruit"?

4. How does this passage relate to youth ministry? How would your youth ministry be different if you took this passage seriously?

5. What does this passage tell you about your relationship to God and to Jesus Christ?

6. What does it mean to "abide in me"? Why did Jesus say it three times?

7. What would happen if the branch were cut off from the vine? What would life be like if you were cut off from Jesus Christ?

Some Thoughts

This particular passage relates to three aspects of youth ministry: (1) Christ-centeredness, (2) relationships, and (3) service.

Christ-centeredness. We can do nothing without being centered in Christ. Unless he abides in us, we cannot bear fruit, which means we won't be able to do much in any aspect of our youth ministries.

Relationships. This passage offers a powerful image of how we are related to Christ and to God. We are included. We are connected. We are wanted. God does not leave us alone. God prunes us, which means God tends to us and fusses over us, to get us into the best possible shape to bear fruit, meaning, to do God's work in the world.

When young people recognize this image, it can be the greatest of affirmations. God wants them and will take care of them. God will refine their gifts, talents, and skills to prepare them for God's service.

Service. This passage tells us that we need to bear fruit, which means we need to be doing God's work in the world, loving and serving. In order to produce, we must abide in Jesus Christ. Apart from him we can do nothing (v. 5). This is good news to the teenager who feels inadequate in so many ways. It's as if Jesus were saying: "Hey, I know you feel inadequate. That's okay. If you and I stick together, we can do wonders!"

Jesus Calms a Storm
(Mark 4:35–41)

Jesus had been teaching large crowds of people. He had been speaking to them in parables. To his disciples, though, he explained the meaning of the parables. It was on that day, when evening had come, that Jesus and the disciples got into a boat and headed to the other side of the sea. A great storm arose and was beating the boat. Jesus was asleep in the stern. The disciples woke him, saying, "Teacher, do you not care that we are perishing?" Jesus rebuked the wind. The wind ceased, and there was a dead calm. He said to the disciples, "Why are you afraid? Have you still no faith?" The disciples were awestruck, saying, "Who then is this, that even the wind and the sea obey him?"

Questions for Discussion

1. Why did the disciples wake Jesus?

2. Why did Jesus question their faith? What is faith?

3. Why were the disciples surprised that Jesus calmed the storm? What did they know about Jesus?

4. If you had been one of the disciples, how would you have reacted to the whole situation?

5. How does this passage relate to youth ministry?

6. Was there a time when you felt that you were perishing, dying inside or out?

7. Have you ever cried out to God with a similar plea—God, don't you care that I'm falling apart?

Some Thoughts

So many of us in youth ministry get the feeling of exasperation, that we're drowning down here. Our efforts don't seem to be working. The youth aren't responding. We spend hours planning an event, and it fizzles. And so we cry to God, who we know has called us to do this, Do you not care that we are perishing?

Many times in youth ministry I feel discouraged and that I haven't done enough, or I haven't said the right thing, or if I don't call six more young people, they'll forget their responsibilities. I get frantic, perhaps feeling a little like those disciples. And then it seems God finally gets through to me with a calm that says, "Let it go, and trust me to reach these young people." This is a humbling and very needed experience.

Teenagers also feel abandoned in times of great stress. This passage assures them that God is always with them. It's OK to cry out to God, "Don't you care?" When they do cry out, they will find God waiting to calm the storm within, or without, or both.

The Body of Christ
(1 Corinthians 12:12–26)

Paul is writing to the church at Corinth, which had experienced rival factions within its membership. Some members thought they were more spiritual than others. In this passage, Paul emphasizes unity and the importance of all members.

"For just as the body is one and has many members, and all the members of the body, though many, are one body, so it is with Christ. For in the one Spirit we were all baptized into one body—Jews or Greeks, slaves or free—and we were all made to drink of one Spirit. Indeed the body does not consist of one member but of many." Every part of the body is important and needed. No one part of the body can say to the other, "I have no need of you." "On the contrary, the members of the body that seem to be weaker are indispensable, and those members of the body that we think less honorable we clothe with greater honor, and our less respectable members are treated with greater respect."

The members of the body should have the same care for one another. "If one member suffers, all suffer together with it; if one member is honored, all rejoice together with it."

Questions for Discussion

1. Why do you think Paul compares the church body to the body of Christ?

2. What is Paul telling the Corinthian church members to do?

3. Do you think this is a good description of the way the church should be? Why (or why not)?

4. How does this passage relate to youth ministry?

5. Do you ever feel like an inferior member?

6. If you were to take this passage seriously, what changes would you need to make in your church's youth ministry? In your church?

7. What one verse speaks to you personally as to how you are to live as a Christian?

8. What does this passage have to say about leadership?

Some Thoughts

The good news that young people need to hear is that God arranged all the members in the body. Each has a function; each is needed. And even better than that, if you're feeling inferior, there's more good news. "Those members of the body that we think less honorable we clothe with greater honor, and our less respectable members are treated with greater respect."

God has arranged the body in such a way that all the members have the same care for one another (v. 25). Verse 26 could be a slogan for a retreat or a year's theme: "If one member suffers, all suffer together . . .; if one member is honored, all rejoice together . . ."

The Bible on Leadership

Because developing young people as leaders is an important part of our vision of youth ministry, let's see where in the scriptures we can find illustrations of leadership.

The best illustration of leadership is not found in a single passage. Rather it is found in the person of Jesus Christ. In his life, teachings, and actions, Jesus exemplified the kind of leadership we hope to employ. If you want to find out what a good leader does, look at what Jesus did. The foremost thing he did was serve. Leaders serve their followers.

Jesus taught that people should be servants. "Whoever wishes to be great among you must be your servant, and whoever wishes to be first among you must be your slave; just as the Son of Man came not to be served but to serve, and to give his life a ransom for many" (Matt. 20:26–28).

Jesus' life was lived in service to others. He healed. He drove out demons. He restored life. He saved a woman from stoning. He taught people to care, to love, and not to judge. Even through his miracles he served. He turned water into wine for the wedding at Cana. He fed five thousand people on a hillside where he was teaching.

He served his disciples. The best picture we have of Jesus' servantlike leadership is his washing the disciples' feet (John 13:1–17). He taught his disciples the vision of God's kingdom. He mentored them by spending three years with them, preparing them to be "fishers of people," to go "and make disciples of all nations, baptizing them in the name of the Father and of the Son and of the Holy Spirit, and teaching them to obey everything that I have commanded you" (Matt. 28:19–20).

One attribute of leaders is that they are people with a vision. They know how to create visions and how to invite people to share their visions. Jesus spent his life focused on the vision of the kingdom of God. That vision transformed people's lives, as do the visions we embrace in youth ministry.

The Healing of the Paralytic
(Luke 5:17–26)

This passage is not often thought of in the context of leadership. It's the story in which Jesus asks the Pharisees, "Which is easier, to say 'Your sins are forgiven you,' or to say, 'Stand up and walk'?" However, we would like to look at the role of the friends and how they exemplified leadership.

In this passage, Jesus was teaching in a house full of Pharisees and teachers of the law. "Just then some men came, carrying a paralyzed man on a bed. They were trying to bring him in and lay him before Jesus; but finding no way to bring him in because of the crowd, they went up on the roof and let him down with his bed through the tiles into the middle of the crowd in front of Jesus" (Luke 5:18–19).

Questions for Discussion

1. How would you describe the friendship between the paralytic and the men who brought him to Jesus?

2. In your own words tell exactly how you think the men got the paralytic up on the roof, then through the roof, and down on the ground in front of Jesus. How do you think they got through the tiles?

3. How would you describe the friends?

4. What qualities or attributes of leadership did the friends have?

Some Thoughts

One characteristic of leadership is the ability to create a vision. The men envisioned Jesus healing their paralyzed friend. Leaders have a purpose. The friends' purpose was to get their friend to Jesus.

Leaders take a stand for what they believe. They are courageous and willing to take risks. Coming through someone's roof was risky. But they did it because they were firm in the belief that they needed to get their friend to Jesus.

Leaders are determined. These guys certainly were determined. They did not give up easily.

Leaders are creative. The house was packed. There was no way to get their friend in to see Jesus. They had to be creative. Coming through the roof and lowering their friend on his mat was creative indeed.

Leaders serve. They put the needs of others before their own needs. These friends risked their safety to tend to the needs of their paralyzed friend.

The Bible on Team Leadership

Look at three occasions where team leadership is mentioned in the Bible. First, look at Moses. When God called Moses (Exodus 3 and 4), Moses had major doubts about his ability to lead. He felt he had no authority, and thus people would not listen to him. He was not good at speaking. So God provided a team: Moses and his brother Aaron. God told Moses: "You shall speak to him [Aaron] and put the words in his mouth; and I will be with your mouth and with his mouth, and will teach you what to do" (Ex. 4:15).

Second, look at the ministry of Jesus. Jesus had a team of twelve. He trained them—three years of live-in, on-the-job training (travel included).

Third, look at the book of Acts, where you will find several examples of team leadership. The disciples and other followers were sent out to the New Testament churches in teams—Peter and John, Paul and Barnabas, Paul and Silas and Timothy.

Explore Other Passages

Don't stop here. Explore other passages. Surely you'll discover some that you never thought would have a relationship to youth ministry or to leadership. It is exciting to read and reread, to study familiar passages and discover new insights into the ways God is calling us to seek wisdom within God's Word, wisdom for our journey as young people and adults who are seeking to be faithful servant leaders.

FIVE

Developing
Youth-Owned Youth Ministry

What do you want for the young people in your church? When asked that question, youth leaders and parents alike most often reply: We want our youth to *want* to be involved in the church. We want them to willingly participate in their youth group. And we want young people to grow in faith in Jesus Christ. They know that in order for that to happen, the young people need to have some kind of positive experience with the church. So the logical next question is the following: How do we motivate young people to come to church? How do we get them to participate in youth activities?

Youth Must Have Ownership

Experience has shown that young people will be actively involved in youth ministry if they have ownership in it. They need to feel that youth ministry is theirs, that whatever happens at their church belongs to them. They need to own it, drive it, and care for it.

To help you get a picture of what ownership is like, we suggest using the image of a car. Suppose you own a car. What are some things you can do with your car? You use it to go to work or school. You drive around with your friends, to go places when you want to, instead of depending on someone else. You go on a date, take a trip in it.

Next, What do you need to do to take care of this car you own? You buy fuel and oil. You keep up a maintenance schedule. You clean it.

Note that since it is your car, you like spending time with it and you are willing to do what is needed to take care of it. The same goes for youth ministry. If young people feel that they own their own program— by program we mean the entire youth ministry of your church, not just a Sunday night program—then they will spend time on it. They will decide what they want to do with it. And they will do what is needed to take care of it. The program will be youth-driven and youth-owned. As a result, you will see enthusiastic young people who are willing to participate. You will see youth who are taking on leadership responsibilities.

In order to have ownership, young people must feel needed and wanted. They need to be listened to. They need to be in on decision making. They need to work as partners with adult leaders. They need to be given opportunities to be creators of the vision, so that together in partnership with adult leaders, they can design and shape youth ministry. Once the young people have ownership, then they are willing to go out and invite other young people to come and participate. When you own it, you share it.

Contrast this to adult-owned youth ministry. The adult leaders make the decisions. They decide what the young people need. They plan the activities. They are responsible for taking care of youth ministry. As a result, the young people are spectators. They attend rather than participate. They sit passively. They wait until they are told what to do by the adults. They simply aren't as enthusiastic.

In adult-owned youth ministry, the youth don't have much responsibility and don't need to be responsible because the adults will take care of everything. It's the "I'm the adult and I know what you young people need" attitude. The youth don't feel needed. They have no ownership in the program, so why would they want to take care of it?

Many adult leaders are familiar with adult-owned youth ministry. If you are an adult and were active in your church's youth program when you were a teenager, most likely it was adult-owned and adult-driven. If adult-driven youth ministry is what is familiar to you, how are you supposed to do it any other way? Answering that question is the reason for this book.

In chapter 3, we described two very different Sunday night youth groups. In the first picture, a group of young people sits relatively quietly at their regular Sunday night meeting. An adult is up front leading the program. Several parents are lined up in back of the group, trying to blend in with the back wall, because they know their own sons and daughters don't want them there. As soon as the up-front adult finishes, the young people bolt out the door.

This is a picture of adult-driven youth ministry. The leaders, who happen to be parents, get together and plan the programs. They are in charge of everything that happens in youth ministry. The programs are not bad, but the young people aren't at all enthu-

siastic. More than half the youth are there because their parents make them attend. Parents know how hard the leaders are trying, so they want to help by making sure their young people attend. And everybody wonders why the young people don't seem to like youth group.

The second picture is of a group of very active, involved young people. You can tell that by their body language. Several are working on a fun night for a congregational supper. An adult and a young person are working together on a prayer. Two youth are standing up front, ready to make announcements. The adult leaders are mingling with the young people. At the end of the meeting, some young people stay to talk with an adult leader about the possibilities of their youth group helping out with Big Brothers–Big Sisters. Two other young people are chatting with another leader.

This is youth-driven youth ministry. The young people own it. It is a picture of healthy youth ministry. It's what all of us wish we had, a group of young people who really want to be there, who like being a part of their church, who are enthusiastic about activities and service projects and worship services.

Developing an Adult-Youth Partnership

Youth-owned youth ministry is not achieved by adult leaders turning everything over to the young people. That would be "abandon-the-youth" youth ministry—and definitely not what any of us want. The secret to developing youth-driven youth ministry is adult-youth partnership.

The young people in the second picture did not get to the stage of youth ownership by having the adults bow out of the picture. The adult leaders did not say: "Okay, what do you want to do?" They spent time developing relationships in which both young people and adult leaders shared ideas and dreams. They shared values and beliefs. They talked to one another about what's important. They talked about how they might respond faithfully to what God is calling them to do as the church. Youth ownership was achieved by adults who were willing to engage young people in a partnership venture of developing youth ministry together.

In such a partnership, adults and youth challenge

each other. For instance, if several young people were to say that they didn't want Bible study, the adult leaders would not just quietly say, "Whatever you want to do." They would not simply scratch Bible study from the list of activities. Rather, they would raise questions: Why don't you want Bible study? Can we be true to our vision of ministry and not have Bible study? How will we fulfill the "nurturing faith" part of our youth ministry? In this way, the adults challenge the young people to think through why they don't want Bible study.

> The secret to developing youth ownership
> is adult-youth partnership.

It's not always the adults who do the challenging. At a recent youth ministry committee meeting in our church, one of the young people did the challenging. "We haven't been doing much serious discussion of faith stuff lately." Merely bringing it up challenged the committee to look for ways to nurture faith.

In adult-youth partnership, both young people and adults have a responsibility to challenge each other to stretch, to move beyond the ordinary—what they're used to doing, or what's easy. Both young people and adults must look beyond what they did last year, especially if it was narrowly focused, as in a program limited to recreation and topic discussions. Both young people and adults take responsibility for bringing up ideas, questions, and concerns.

Portrait of an Adult-Youth Partnership

So how does this transformation from adult-driven to youth-driven youth ministry happen? How do you achieve an adult-youth partnership? Let's begin with a saga, a true story of "How Ginny learned the hard way." I had a crisis with my junior highs, a crisis for which I am grateful, because it forced me to face the issue of youth-driven youth ministry.

I had just moved to a church where I was the director of youth ministry. The first event of the year, a senior high fall planning retreat had been wonderful. It was followed by a junior high planning retreat the next weekend, which was my usual way of starting off a new year of youth ministry. This was not a big deal, except that I had been forewarned that this was the year the "boys" would be in junior high. We all know how one or two classes of young people seem to be trouble all the way through school. When they were in preschool, these boys were trouble. As they advanced through the elementary grades, you heard about them from each Sunday school teacher. And everybody dreaded the day when they would be in junior high, because younger adolescence carries its own set of unique challenges.

Alas, the "boys" were in seventh and eighth grade. They dominated the group that year, outnumbering the girls. The girls would roll their eyes in disgust at the immaturity of these boys. As the junior high retreat approached, the adult leaders were nervous. So, making the first of many mistakes, we adult leaders decided we were going to take charge, be in control, keep these boys on a short leash.

As soon as we got out of the cars at the retreat site, we insisted everyone go straight to the recreation room, where we told them they could not go anywhere unless accompanied by an adult. Now there's a great way to start a retreat!

The boys rebelled immediately. Several took off running before we started the first activity. Adults scattered to find them. After corralling them, we started a game. The boys refused to play. After being sternly told they must play, they decided to make fun of the game by playing it wrong. Throughout all the activities, the adult leaders were preoccupied with placing themselves strategically in the group in order to control the boys.

Anything the boys were told not to do, they did. And what they were supposed to do, of course, they didn't. Adult leaders lost their tempers and did lots of yelling. The rest of the junior highs were tired of the whole mess.

By lights out, everyone was worn out, but the boys were not finished. The next morning, the male leaders reported having little sleep due to spending the night chasing boys who were sneaking out. Two of the boys had gotten into a fight. Trying to have devotions was a complete disaster. Instead of the kind of personal sharing and insights one hopes to hear in the late night hours of a retreat, the adults reported the worst language ever heard on a retreat.

I was stunned. How could I have experienced one of the worst retreats ever just a week after one of the best senior high retreats ever? How could such a disaster happen when we thought we knew what we were doing?

What we were doing was treating these boys with no respect, no trust. We're supposed to love young people, right? If you had asked the boys, they would have said the adult leaders didn't even like them. We treated them as if we expected the worst from them. So of course they weren't about to disappoint us. I think we lost three, maybe four, adult leaders because of that weekend. I really don't want to remember, because they were dedicated leaders, and I hated to see them go. We simply were taking the wrong approach. We had made a judgment before the retreat started. We had decided we would experience the worst, and that's exactly what we got. There is a truth in all this, and that is, that young people will live up—or down—

to your expectations of them. If you expect great things, you will get great things.

You may be wondering how the year went. Well, it got worse before it got better. The climax came at a Sunday night junior high meeting. The junior highs found out the adult leaders had canceled their upcoming lock-in. The reason given was the junior highs were not responsible enough to handle a lock-in—too many behavior problems. What the junior highs perceived was that they all were being punished because of "the boys." To be honest, they were being punished simply because they were normal junior highs.

Needless to say, that Sunday night meeting got off to a shaky start. The activity for that night was making goody bags for nursing home residents in preparation for a visit the following Saturday. The junior highs had chosen this as a service project; it was not something the adults were making them do. Fourteen young people were there, in the fellowship hall, assembling the items. Several of "the boys" were running around the hall, throwing a football, not responding to the beckoning of their leaders. A few others were complaining that making goody bags was stupid. And more than half the junior highs said they weren't coming on Saturday to visit the nursing home.

One of the leaders had had about all he could take. He lost his temper. He said, quite directly, "You are going to be there. You've committed to this. The nursing home is expecting us. And you will be there!"

The following week was one of those that keep people from going into the profession of youth ministry. I must have had eight calls from parents and visits from six. "Our kids are quitting youth group." "My son won't be back." "My son wants to start going to another church."

As we had time to think and cool down, out of the crisis emerged a call for a new day, a clean slate for everybody. Lots of phone calls were made—to young people, to adult leaders, to parents. We said, "We're starting over. We need everybody's support and willingness to buy into a new deal." Then we proposed our next steps: (1) We would carry out the Saturday service project, since we were committed to it and it was happening that Saturday; (2) We would reinstate the lock-in; (3) I would meet with the junior highs on Sunday morning during Sunday school to hear their concerns and assure them that the adult leaders were ready to listen to them that night at youth group; and (4) The leaders would really listen to the young people and stay cool and not be defensive during the youth group meeting.

All of the above happened. Eleven junior highs, including the nine "boys," went to the nursing home that Saturday. The young people did believe that the leaders would listen to them, and they came out in full force that Sunday night. And the adult leaders did listen to these junior highs.

At that point junior high ministry completely turned around. The young people and adults worked together reshaping the calendar for the remainder of the year. Adult-youth partnership was emerging. A newly configured youth ministry committee was formed with more junior high representation. We sent copies of the new calendar and a letter to parents informing them of the progress we were making. This was a good public relations move.

Youth ministry did not become youth-driven immediately as a result of the crisis. But the groundwork was laid. We found ourselves responding to the needs of our young people and to the particular flavor of youth group that year. We were willing to make adjustments in the way we did things. One thing that is certain about youth is that nothing is for certain. Adults and young people alike need to be flexible and willing to change and grow where and when needed.

Two positive things happened in the next couple of weeks. Our church had an Ash Wednesday service. A lot of our junior highs were there. They went forward and received crosses that they wore on leather strings around their necks. Several wore their crosses all during Lent. The rewarding part was that a couple of the adult leaders said that, as a result of that service, they saw those junior highs in a different light.

The second positive thing has become my favorite story for describing what youth-driven youth ministry looks like. It happened at the first meeting of our newly formed youth ministry committee. It was Sunday night, around nine o'clock. We had just finished our meeting, and the junior high members were hanging around. One of them asked, "Can we have a prayer breakfast?" I said, "Sure. What day should it be on?" They decided on Mondays. I asked where. They said "Bojangles." I said, "Great. Let's plan for a week from tomorrow. Who should lead . . .?" They interrupted and said they wanted to start tomorrow. I reminded them it was almost 9:15 P.M. How would people know to come? One of "the boys" said he would call everybody. I asked him if he meant he would call everybody or just his friends. Another of "the boys" said he would help make the calls to everybody. "Who's going to lead it?" I asked. Macie said, "I will." I was amazed at what was taking place.

I asked her what she would do. She said she didn't know but would think of something, and she would lead in prayer.

I tried to hide my skepticism. I pictured Macie and me, just the two of us, at Bojangles at seven o'clock the next morning. But these young people were enacting my vision of youth ministry; they were in the driver's seat. It was their idea. And I certainly wasn't going to squelch their enthusiasm.

The next morning Bojangles was packed. Twelve junior highs were there.

Please understand the significance of this story. If I, the adult leader, had suggested and planned a prayer breakfast, perhaps half the number of junior highs would have been there. But since it was youth-driven—that is, the idea came from the young people, and they planned it, notified everybody, and led it—it took off. The young people continued faithfully to come to prayer breakfast for the rest of the school year. They shared leadership. They prayed. And these are the same junior highs who drove us crazy at that fall retreat.

Methods for Developing an Adult-Youth Partnership

That's a glimpse of youth-driven youth ministry. Now, how do you get there? How do you make the move in your church toward youth-driven youth ministry, toward youth ownership, toward adult-youth partnership, and toward developing youth in leadership?

Let's say, right here at the start, that we are aware that leaders and youth programs come in all different shapes and sizes, have various structures, and are at many different levels of youth involvement. Some who are reading this book don't have a youth program and want ideas on how to get started. Some of you would like to see your adult leaders take some ownership of youth ministry. You are tired of pulling the load all by yourself.

And some of you have been doing the team approach for years now but sense your adult leaders are losing their enthusiasm. Things are dragging. Your youth ministry needs something, a new spark, a new direction, a shot in the arm, as it were.

We believe that youth-owned, youth-driven youth ministry that is carried out in partnership with adult leaders is what is needed, no matter where you are or what your program is. Even if you are just starting out, your adult leaders and your young people need to work together to build a youth ministry.

Look at the story about the junior highs. What happened that enabled youth-driven youth ministry to happen? You could say it just happened. No one planned for the young people to design a prayer breakfast or to partner with the adult leaders in planning the rest of the year. In this instance, a crisis triggered it. But surely no one wants to wait for a crisis to happen.

However, if you happen to be in the midst of a crisis, use it. Take a good look at it. Let crises teach you about where you need to go. We all fear failure and mistakes. We fear that we will look like incompetent fools or that the young people and adult leaders will disappear. But what often happens with failures is that a wake-up call reaches everyone involved. New energy and compassion emerge as everyone pulls together to work through the crisis. We need to learn to welcome mistakes. Crises and failures can be a bonding experience within a group.

If you are not in a crisis situation, there are four steps you can take to move toward youth-driven youth ministry and adult-youth partnership:

1. Assess the level of involvement of your adult leaders and your young people. The diagram on page 44 shows the levels of involvement of adult leaders and of youth. The discussion of these levels may help you identify where you are in youth ministry and where you need to be heading.

2. Assess your adult leaders' ideas about youth ownership. How would the adult leaders describe their own style of leadership? Are they open to working in partnership with the young people? What barriers might keep them from moving toward youth ownership? Moving away from adult-driven youth

ministry requires commitment and work from adult leaders.

3. Assess your situation in relation to developing young people as leaders. Do you have young people who are very active? These are the ones to help you get started on developing youth in leadership. Do some of your young people serve in a leadership capacity? Do you have a youth council or committee? Developing youth as leaders is the focus of chapter 6.

4. Assess the way you plan youth ministry. Are the young people involved in planning and carrying out their own program? How will young people and adult leaders work together in creating the vision (dreaming), doing the planning (developing), and carrying out the plans (delivering)? In chapters 7, 8, and 9, we will look at youth ministry in 3-D: dreamed, developed, and delivered.

For the remainder of this chapter, we will focus in more depth on points one and two above (as noted, points three and four are discussed fully in later chapters).

Assess the Level of Involvement of Adult Leaders and Youth

Looking at the diagram on page 44, assess your present situation. You are striving to move up to new levels. You may find that you're not even on the steps yet. That's OK.

Share this diagram with both adult leaders and young people. They should decide at what level their youth ministry is currently functioning. It helps to see how far one has to go. This diagram should also help readers see which parts of this book will be helpful. For example, the young people may not be ready for the leadership lock-in (see chapter 6) if they are on one of the bottom two steps. If the young people barely know that their church has a youth program, then they are not ready for a full-blown leadership lock-in. Or if the majority of the young people attend youth group because they are made to go, then they would not be motivated to commit to a lock-in of this type.

Your immediate goal should be to move up a step from your current level. How quickly you move will depend on your young people and your adult leaders. It may take a year; it may take three years. In some groups more than one level could be achieved simultaneously, as your people work toward new goals in youth ministry. For example, on the levels for youth involvement, level three (youth coming because they want to), may be achieved by working on level four (involving youth in planning). The top levels are the ultimate goals of adult-youth partnership.

The Levels of Adult Leader Involvement

Level 1: One or two adults do it all.

Here, adult leaders plan and lead the youth program. There are several problems with a youth program at this level.

- The young people do not get to meet and develop friendships with other adults in the church.
- The young people get to do only what that one adult leader is willing to do in terms of program.
- The church risks losing its youth program once that leader leaves.
- The likelihood of leader burnout is high.

If you're at this level, what should you do? You need to get help. Try getting together a team of adult leaders. The team can be as small as three or as large as twelve or more in larger churches. Size is not what's important. What is critical is that this group of adults works together as a team. Working as a team does not mean, "Carla takes the first Sunday of the month, Fred the second," and so forth.

The team works together to identify the purpose and the goals. It involves the young people in the dreaming stage. The team concentrates on building

Adult Leader Involvement

Level 5 — Adults are in partnership with the youth.
They are supportive and encouraging of young people as leaders.

Level 4 — Adults are in good relationships with youth.
They ask young people to help.

Level 3 — Adults work well as a team. They take responsibility.

Level 2 — Adults help the adult leader or youth director/youth minister.

Level 1 — One or two adults do it all.

Youth Involvement

Level 6 — Youth are championing youth ministry (youth-driven).

Level 5 — Youth are involved in leadership (partnership with adults).

Level 4 — Youth are involved in planning (partnership with adults).

Level 3 — Youth are coming to activities because they want to.

Level 2 — Youth don't know what's going on. Many attend because their parents make them.

Level 1 — Youth are not involved. There is no youth ministry.

relationships with the young people and on developing a balanced program of ministry that fits the goals and the needs of the youth in their church.

Down the road the church can begin to develop young people in leadership.

Level 2: Adults help the adult leader or youth director/youth minister.

At this level, adults are willing to help the main leader, but they have little or no responsibility for programming. If this is your situation, you must decide: Should these adults remain mere helpers? Or is it time to give them responsibility and engage them as full-fledged members of the team? Are these adults willing to make the shift to team leadership? Maybe not. There are adults who don't want to be in leadership positions. They just want to help.

What everyone needs in this situation is some education as to what a leader actually does. These folks need assurance that, as part of the leadership team, they will be trained and supported, and they will play an important role in the young people's lives. If their leadership experience in the past has been one of sink or swim—"here are the kids; now do something with them"—then they won't be eager to be thrown to the wolves again. Everyone involved in leadership needs to see that they are involved in an exciting ministry, a ministry with a vision and a plan. They need assurance that they will not be left alone.

All leaders should share in the dream of developing an adult-youth partnership in leadership. Developing youth in leadership may be down the road, but to catch a glimpse of the possibilities might inspire adult leaders to a new level of commitment.

Level 3: Adults work well as a team. They take responsibility.

If this is your situation, then you are ready to take full advantage of the ideas in this book. Invite the adult leadership team to look at the concept of developing youth in leadership. Share the vision of adult-youth partnership. Work out a strategy for sharing the vision with the young people.

If the young people are actively involved in their youth ministry, then they are ready to work on youth leadership. If they are not, then your adult team needs to focus on involving the young people in planning and carrying out their program. Everyone needs to work on moving away from adult-driven youth ministry.

Level 4: Adults are in good relationships with youth. They ask young people to help.

In this situation, adults and young people are ready for adult-youth partnership in leadership. They are ready to move into the dreaming, developing, and delivering stages discussed in chapters 7, 8, and 9. Adults and young people should consider the possibilities of having a leadership lock-in (see chapter 6).

Level 5: Adults are in partnership with the youth. They are supportive and encouraging of young people as leaders.

If this is your situation, bravo! You already know the rewards of seeing young people grow in confidence, in ownership, and in their faith. We encourage you to share what you are doing with other churches. Your youth and adults may find ideas in this book for doing things a little differently each year. Variety is good.

Sometimes, after you reach this level, you find youth ministry seems to be slumping into a routine. If this is the case, youth and adults together should evaluate where you are and where you need to be going. Changing the way a retreat or leadership event is done may be what's needed. Or perhaps you need to restructure the way activities are planned and led. Don't be afraid to try something new, to do it differently this year.

The Levels of Youth Involvement

Level 1: Youth are not involved. There is no youth ministry.

If your young people are not involved in church activities, or if there is no youth ministry, then you are starting from scratch. Get some adults and young people together to talk about the possibilities. Together look at the essentials of youth ministry described in chapter 3. Look at the church membership list. Who are the young people? What do you know about them? What do they need? Share dreams and hopes of what can be. Decide how to begin. Will you have a youth council? What adults need to be recruited to form a leadership team? What kind of structure will you have? Stay enthusiastic and positive, pray for God's leading, and talk to every young person personally.

We talk with many people about how they got

their youth ministry started. Almost without exception, they began by visiting individual young people in their homes. The same was true for recruiting adult leaders. Just a forty-five minute visit in someone's home or at work can do wonders for engaging people's enthusiasm for youth ministry.

Level 2: Youth don't know what's going on. Many attend because their parents make them.

In this situation, there are youth activities, but it's a struggling youth ministry. The young people don't know what's happening on Sunday night, or whenever youth group meets. A few come, but they're not enthusiastic. Or perhaps quite a few come, but they come because their parents make them. It seems that the young people just don't care.

If this is your situation, see our suggestions under Level 1 of youth involvement: "Youth are not involved." In a sense, that's your situation too. Your best bet may be to start from scratch. Begin by finding one or two adults who care about young people. Have them get together with several young people and explore the possibilities.

Your goal is to involve the young people, to enable them to gain ownership of their youth ministry so that they *want* to be involved . . . of their own free will. Have patience. It takes time to develop a youth ministry that young people want to be part of and that parents no longer make them attend. It usually takes three years to develop a program in which youth have ownership and take leadership.

Youth ministries are grown. We advise people to put lots of effort into their junior high/middle school programs. When you're starting from scratch, it's difficult to get eleventh and twelfth graders involved. They often have formed opinions about their church's youth program that are hard to change. For instance, we were in the third year of a revamped youth ministry. We had lots of enthusiastic youth and adults doing many wonderful activities, trips, service projects. And yet, I was told that a junior who hadn't been around in a couple of years told a new student that we didn't do anything at our church. We had tried to reach this junior, but he chose not to give it another chance.

Level 3: Youth are coming to activities because they want to.

You must be doing something right if this is your situation. Perhaps your adult leaders have developed good relationships with the young people. Perhaps the young people feel loved and affirmed. Perhaps the programs have been exciting, geared to youth needs and interests, or just plain fun. Or perhaps everyone experiences a challenge to grow in faith.

Nevertheless, it seems your youth ministry needs something more. Perhaps it has hit a plateau. Perhaps you're recognizing the need to increase the level of youth involvement, to get them interested in service, or in reaching out, or in participating more in the life of the whole church. Perhaps you're sensing the need for the young people to play a stronger role in the development of their youth ministry.

If you have an active youth ministry with youth who are willing to participate, then the young people should be ready to make decisions about their youth ministry. Look at the suggestions in chapter 7 for the dreaming stage. There are suggestions for a youth council day retreat and for a total-group planning session (see appendix 2). The youth council or the whole group could do the "Toy Exercise," on ownership (see p. 170), or the young people could, "dream," or brainstorm, about the activities they could do in the areas of worship, explorations, ministry within the congregation, service, and fellowship (see p. 80 for help with brainstorming).

Level 4: Youth are involved in planning (partnership with adults).

Youth involvement in planning and adult-youth partnership are the two ingredients for youth ownership. It sounds like you're ready for the next step—developing youth as leaders. Explore the idea with the adult leaders and the young people. Consider using the leadership lock-in (see chapter 6) as a tool for developing young people's abilities and skills and identifying their gifts in the area of leadership.

Look at the spiritual nurture aspect of youth ministry. One of the principles behind adult-youth partnership is that both adults and young people are called by God to do youth ministry. Look at the scripture passages in chapter 4. Choose one to study with the young people and the adult leaders.

Level 5: Youth are involved in leadership (partnership with adults).

If this is your situation, then this book will reinforce what you are already doing. It may give you ideas on new ways to do dreaming and goal setting and ideas and exercises for educating youth as leaders. We hope you can use the leadership lock-in (chapter 6). Remember that, due to the variety of personalities involved in youth ministry, every year is different. Each year decisions must be made as to how leadership will be constructed. In some years only a few young people may be willing to take leadership roles. Keep in close communication with your young people. Listen to them. They'll tell you what needs to be done differently each year. Don't be afraid to try new things. At the same time, build on traditions that are becoming a meaningful part of youth ministry. Your efforts are commendable!

Level 6: Youth are championing youth ministry (youth-driven).

If this is your situation, congratulations! Isn't it exciting? You need to be out teaching other churches how to develop youth ministry. (See appendix 4 for a model that you can use to teach another church.) It wouldn't be appropriate to say "you have arrived," for there's always room for growth. But you are experiencing the fulfillment of some of the goals of youth ministry.

At this level, the young people are inviting other young people to participate. They are excited about the church and what God can do in their lives. They tell adults how wonderful the youth program is. They see needs in their church and in their community, and they get the rest of the young people to respond. They are movers and shakers.

In such a wonderful situation, what is there to do?

As we said in the level 5 discussion, stay close to your young people. They may need to revise aspects of the program to keep it fresh. Be aware of the personalities of those who are graduating and those who are coming up. You may lose a whole class of enthusiastic youth through graduation and be a bit thrown by the differences that result. Remember, those who remain have seen youth-driven youth ministry modeled. Encourage them to be models for the new class coming up.

Reach out into new areas. Consider special ministries that your young people could start. If you've never had themes for the year, the young people can work on a theme, complete with T-shirt design, promotional skit, jingle, poster, banner, and so on.

Add a new aspect to the dreaming stage. Study one of the Bible passages from chapter 4 with the young people. In fact, anytime during the year may be a good time to assess the present situation in light of a Bible text.

It's great to be at this level, but that doesn't let any of us off the hook. We have to keep challenging ourselves, our adult leaders, and our young people to be faithful and to make youth ministry special.

No matter where you are on these levels, the essentials given in chapter 3 apply. The need to increase the involvement of youth in the life of the church applies. The need to develop a youth ministry that is focused on relationships more than program applies. The need for a biblical base (see chapter 4) applies. And dreaming, developing, and delivering a youth ministry, which is discussed in chapters 7, 8, and 9, applies to all the levels.

Assess Your Adult Leaders' Ideas About Youth Ownership

After deciding which level of adult and youth involvement best describes your situation, look at the adults who are involved in youth ministry. What is their thinking about youth ownership and adult-youth partnership?

Adult leaders usually approach youth ministry with an attitude of "What do I need to do to help the youth of our church?" rather than "What do we—young people and adults together—need to do?" That's only natural. Even before they start, adults take ownership. That's why many adults are

reluctant to do youth ministry. They don't feel equipped to "lead"—they think they don't have the skills; they fear they don't know enough; they are afraid young people won't listen to them. They

> What are the barriers that might keep you from moving toward youth-driven youth ministry?

have a preconceived notion of a youth ministry driven by adults. They are not familiar with any other way to do it.

Because of this preconceived notion, adults can be a barrier to youth-owned youth ministry. You may have a lot of work to do with your adults before launching a new approach based on adult-youth partnership. Adults can be barriers to youth-owned youth ministry:

1. By not being committed to developing youth ownership, sharing leadership, and being in partnership with the young people.

2. By not believing young people are capable of the responsibilities associated with ownership and leadership.

3. By being set in their ways and not willing to try something new.

> Adult leaders need to be committed to developing youth ownership, sharing leadership, and partnership with the young people.

The first step in developing youth ownership and adult-youth partnership is to assess the commitment of adult leaders. The adult leaders must buy into it. That's not always easy. It is one thing for adult leaders to *say* they want the young people to have ownership. It's quite another to *do* what is needed to make it happen. It may require a major change in the way adults relate to young people.

It's often hard for adults to give up control. Adults are used to running things that concern young people. Sometimes, it's because adults don't believe young people are capable of taking on the responsibilities. Other times, adults find it easier to do things themselves than to take the time and make the effort to teach other people. Many adults feel inadequate when it comes to teaching young people leadership skills.

In this book we offer tools for developing young people as leaders. However, adult leaders will need to help one another work on and resolve the control issue. They'll need to discuss what youth-driven youth ministry might look like in their situation.

Since you are striving for adult-youth partnership, gather all adult leaders and young people together and talk about your present situation. Encourage the adults to listen to the young people. As you discuss

these questions, assess the adult-drivenness of your youth ministry:

- Who plans what the young people will do?
- Who plans individual programs and events?
- Who leads the meetings and programs?
- Who makes decisions?
- What kind of youth participation do you have?

What has been the history of participation by the young people? If you are just starting out and don't have much history, then it may take a little longer for young people to develop ownership and to partner with adults in developing and leading youth ministry. Then again, maybe it won't: there are no bad habits to break. Your young people are not accustomed to adult dominance, so it just might be easier to generate a partnership than in a program with entrenched traditions.

Ask your adult leaders how they feel about young people in leadership. Encourage them to be honest about any reluctance or perceived inability to let go of control. Suggest to them the image of a high school yearbook staff. Who does the yearbook? The young people. The students decide what pictures will be taken and used. They decide what will be written—what stories and quotes. In many cases the students choose the format of the yearbook. Where are the adults? They literally are advisors. They are there to help, to suggest resources, to clarify ideas. The adults do not create and design the yearbook. The adults do not do the work. The young people do it. As a result, the young people have ownership in the product and are proud and excited when the yearbook comes out.

Youth ministry can happen in exactly the same way as the development of a yearbook. Adults need to see the significance of giving young people the kind of support that encourages them to take ownership and drive their youth ministry. Adult leaders are more than mere advisors, though. They are partners in ministry.

In chapter 11, in the adult leadership sessions, you'll find a section on leadership style. Each of us tends to operate from a specific style. As you discover your style, you may find, for example, that you are a strong manager or boss. Therefore, you may have a tendency to take over, to direct and "lead" too much. Or you may discover that you like to get things done quickly and efficiently. Understanding your style can help you see why it may be hard for you to share leadership with the young people.

> Adults need to believe that young people are capable of ownership and taking leadership responsibilities.

Ask adult leaders: What is your view of young people today? If adults see young people as children who are incapable of taking responsibility, they will have a hard time believing that young people can take on leadership roles.

Sometimes adults are not even aware of how they treat young people. Robert tells the story of a youth council meeting, a council composed of adults and young people. All the adults believed in youth-driven youth ministry. An advisor was leading the meeting. As the advisor was talking, Robert noticed that the youth council president and a senior representative had moved out of their chairs and were sitting on the floor, coloring on the back of a sheet the advisor had distributed.

He looked around the room, and the symbolism of the whole picture hit him. The two young people were acting like children. They were not trying to act like children; it just happened. When he thought about it, he realized that the adult advisor was taking over the responsibilities of the president, who should have been leading the council meeting. Why? Didn't the advisor believe the youth president could handle the meeting? The advisor obviously was not expecting much from the young people, so the young people met his expectations. They sat on the floor and colored.

The adult advisor had not realized that he was usurping the young people's responsibilities. He barely noticed what the two youth were doing. It wasn't until Robert called it to their attention that the adults on that youth council realized how easy it is to slip into the "taking over" role.

Like Robert's adult leaders, those of us who believe we treat young people as equals will find that there are times when we undermine our efforts to give young people responsibility and leadership. We set up a structure in which youth can take on lead-

ership roles, but then we take over. We don't mean to. Time gets away from us. The task needs to be done. We don't have time to call the young people together, so we do it ourselves. It's a common problem among adult leaders.

All too often adult leaders view young people as less than responsible, less than capable. They really don't believe young people can pull it off. Perhaps they have a perception of adolescence as an irresponsibility age. Perhaps they have never been around responsible teenagers.

One antidote for this perception is a visit to a church or a district youth event where the young people exercise leadership. Once you see responsible young people in action, your attitudes change. Remember: *Young people live up to the expectations adults have of them.* In churches where young people are accustomed to taking responsibilities, you will find adults who believe in young people and expect the best from them. The young people then live *up* and act *up* to what's expected of them.

> Adults can be set in their ways. If they don't know any other way to do it, they will do it the old way.

Many adults go through teacher training to learn how to use age-appropriate methods for teaching junior or senior high Sunday school. Yet when they get in the classroom, these "trained" adults resort to lecturing, because it's the method with which they are familiar and most comfortable. For example, role-play can be taught as a method to use in the classroom, but if Sunday school teachers have never experienced role-playing, they are not likely to try it in their classrooms. The same goes for leadership. If an adult has never seen young people in leadership roles, that adult will continue to take over.

Find out where young people are taking leadership roles. You may have to look beyond your local church. Look for those retreats or events in your district, presbytery, state, or conference which are led by young people. Make plans for your adults leaders to attend one with your young people. It is a marvelous experience to see youth in action.

Hold On to the Vision
of Youth-Owned Youth Ministry
and Adult-Youth Partnership

Once you have assessed the situation with your adult leaders, you can begin to explore the possibilities of developing youth in leadership. You can move toward an adult-youth partnership in planning youth ministry.

As you read on, keep before you the vision of youth-owned youth ministry and adult-youth partnership. Remember that adult leaders are called by God to do youth ministry. What you are doing with your young people is a calling. Believing this can transform your ministry with youth. How you perceive that call is crucial. If you perceive that you are the only one to tell them everything they need to know about the Christian faith, and you have only so many Sundays to do so, then your vision of youth ministry is short-sighted, and you'll likely be frustrated.

If, however, you perceive that you are called to love the young people unconditionally, to listen to them and take them seriously, and to respond to the gifts God has given them, then you will be able to

catch sight of the vision of youth-owned youth ministry. You will have a vision that is focused first on God who has called you and second on the young people. You will still share the Christian faith with them, of course, but the important thing is you will be modeling the unconditional love of God. God does not wait for teenagers to love God first. We—young people and adult leaders—love because God first loved us.

We hope you are getting a sense of why ownership and partnership are so important. In the next chapters we will discuss developing young people as leaders. We will also be looking at how to develop youth-owned, youth-driven youth ministry, which is based on adult-youth partnership.

Here is one more story of youth-owned youth ministry. Robert had been talking to all the young people about youth ownership. As a result, one seventh-grader took it upon herself to write the following letter on behalf of her class.

Dear Robert:

Today, I, along with the rest of the attendees of 10 A.M. Sunday school in 7th grade came up with a list of things we enjoy doing and things we don't enjoy doing in Junior High Fellowship (J.H.F.) on Sunday nights. We want to discuss this list with you to try to make J.H.F. a place that everyone enjoys coming to and no one tries to "skip." Our goal is to have our J.H.F. program be the best that it can be, while having fun and learning about the Bible and Jesus, but doing so in a safe, healthy environment where everyone can feel welcome. We hope this is to your satisfaction as we have put a lot of thought into it, but we understand that we can't do these things every Sunday because we'd put our parents in debt. Because of this we'd also like to discuss what our options are for the Sundays we're meeting at the church and have nothing else planned. One more of our concerns though is to "own" our group, and to do so we think we should have more say in what is being planned for us on Sundays therefore, making the members of the 7th and 8th grade committees the leaders and letting the adults be advisors and helpers to what we want to do and what we have to say. And we think that having these committees is a great way to start.

Thank you,
On behalf of the rising 8th grade 10:00 Sunday School class
June 11, 1995

We marvel and rejoice at how amazing young people are!

SIX

Developing Youth in Leadership

What is Leadership, Anyway?

Leadership is "in." Young people today are finding that colleges and universities are interested in the leadership experiences that students list on admissions applications. Businesses are interested in hiring people with leadership qualities, as many companies move away from the hierarchical model of management. Many companies are embracing forms of the team approach, where employees share the company's vision and have power to make an impact on the workings of the organization. Workers gain a sense of ownership, as they see their contributions to the company appreciated. Workers are encouraged to use their leadership abilities.

What do we mean by leadership? Is it just having the ability to stand up in front of a group and lead a meeting or give instructions? If it were, then perhaps only a few people would be candidates for leadership. On the contrary, it's a lot more! Leadership involves many varieties of qualities, abilities, and styles, which we explore in this chapter.

> Ask both young people and adult leaders: What is leadership? What do leaders do? See what kinds of answers they give.

Leaders? Yes!

James

James is one of those people you might not readily identify as a leader. He's kind of quiet, but he is willing to do whatever you ask him to do. Serving others seems ingrained in his personality. He's keenly aware of what other people need. He offers suggestions that make whatever you are doing easier. If you're lost on a trip, he's the one to find the right road.

Is James a leader? Definitely.

Leaders serve. They put the needs of their people first. They listen to their people. Leaders are servants first. "Servant leadership" is becoming a popular design for management. It may revolutionize companies and organizations. Servant leadership has been popular in the church for a long, long time. Jesus Christ was a servant leader who called twelve others to be servant leaders. Jesus gave them ownership of the church. He modeled ownership and leadership and then sent his followers out to do the same.

Becca

Becca is a member of the youth council. She's willing to take a stand, like the time she said, "I think we need to do more Bible study." Not everyone jumped to applaud her suggestion. But the more she talked about the total program, the more everyone came to see that she was right.

Is Becca a leader? Yes.

Leaders take stands for what they believe. Leaders are courageous. They take risks and welcome failures and mistakes.

Becca is also a patient person, who listens well and thinks about what others have to say. She has an ability to take people's ideas and pull them together into the creation of a vision. She embodies some of the following descriptions of leaders:

Leaders are learners. They don't have to know it all, nor give the impression that they know it all. Rather leaders are constantly asking questions. They learn from observing, listening, and exploring.

Leaders are followers. They are listeners. They seek to discover the needs and will of the group. They empower the group to lead.

Leaders are visionaries. They create visions and are able to inspire people to adopt the visions. They engage people in shaping the vision, so that the vision becomes the vision of all. This enables ownership.

Leaders can take visions and translate them into action. They see possibilities and can engage people in designing ways to put vision into action. Leaders are determined. They do not give up easily.

Lin

Lin is our cheerleader. She's excited about God, about our church, about youth group, and about getting new people involved. The level of enthusiasm automatically rises when Lin's in the room. She has a talent for getting people involved and for recognizing the talents of others. She says things like, "Ask Mario. I think that's something he'd be good at." She's also our biggest promoter. Whatever activity is coming up, she spreads the word at school.

Is Lin a leader? Of course.

Leaders embrace the talents of others. They are not threatened by others' gifts. Rather, leaders encourage people to discover their talents and abilities.

Leaders empower others. You know you have a good leader when those who "follow" are excited about what they are doing. They feel important, because they have a say in decisions and outcomes. The leader makes them feel that they can make a difference. A leader's enthusiasm and passion should be contagious.

Leaders are communicators. They must be, in order to help people adopt the vision and see what needs to be done.

Matt

Matt is a good listener. He is shy and says he will never get up in front of a group. He has a lot of confidence, though, and a good grasp of what he is capable of doing. He will listen to all sides of a dilemma and come up with a creative solution.

Is Matt a leader? Yes.

Leaders are creative. They are able to figure out new and different ways to accomplish a task.

Leaders know who they are. They know their strengths and weaknesses. They are learning how to build on their strengths and minimize their weaknesses. They know what they want and why they want it.

Whit

Whit is another one who will not get up in front of a group. He's cool, very cool. You might think he's too cool to go over and talk to the less "popular" young person who is sitting alone on the sofa. On the contrary, Whit is the one who plops himself down and says, "What's up?" or "How did practice go last night?"

Is Whit a leader? Oh, yes.

Leaders are role models. They may not be aware of the effect they have on other people. But people do watch them. People observe their lifestyles, the way they carry out their jobs, and the way they treat people. People want to emulate them.

Identifying Leadership

All the young people described above—James, Becca, Lin, Matt, and Whit—are role models of leadership. Sometimes it's just a matter of calling attention to what young people do and naming it as leadership. It's a matter of broadening our concept of leadership. Most likely, you would not find descriptions of leadership such as those above on a student's resume. The old concept of leadership is being president of an organization. It's easier to list titles than descriptions. However, once we broaden our concept of leadership, we can see the need to affirm the leadership qualities we recognize in our young people. Of course, first we have to learn how to recognize leadership.

All young people do not have all the qualities of leadership just described. It's exciting that there are so many, varied qualities and that each young person can claim to be a leader as she or he recognizes any of these qualities within. That's why we can say every one of our young people is a leader. In some way, every one *is* a leader.

With this broadened definition of leadership, young people and adults together can begin to identify the qualities and then work on developing leadership potential. This process takes time. Everyone possesses talents, abilities, and values that can be considered attributes of leadership. It's often just a matter of recognition and development.

Think about the individuals in your youth ministry. Can you begin to see qualities in them that can be identified as leadership? What gifts do you see?

What values? As young people grow in faith, they adopt values that fit this expanded understanding of leadership. Both young people and adults need to be open to seeing how God is leading them to "lead" in new and different ways.

Adult leaders have a wonderful opportunity to play a part in the development of leadership in young people. Adult leaders can open doors to new ways of living, caring, and serving, if they treat young people as capable people.

In this chapter we describe a leadership lock-in, which offers young people an opportunity to explore leadership. Remember that leadership development takes time. The lock-in is just a beginning. Every experience a young person has can contribute to her or his leadership development. Young people need to learn to be alert to what their experiences teach them.

Experiences of leadership in the church prepare young people for leadership as adults in the church. Our churches need strong leadership. So let's begin developing youth as leaders.

Developing Youth Leaders

As you think about the following questions, think not only of traditional leadership roles but also of ways young people have been creators, visionaries, and role models; how they have influenced or persuaded others; and how they have used their enthusiasm to "lead." It may not be easy to broaden the concept of leadership. But once we do, we can see how all our young people can be leaders. We can begin to recognize leadership potential and gifts that might have gone unnoticed.

> Evaluate your youth ministry in terms of young people in leadership.

Discuss the following with your young people:

1. What leadership opportunities do young people have in this youth ministry?

2. What leadership opportunities have young people had in the church?

3. What about in school and in other clubs?

4. Talk about gifts the young people have. (Check the list of gifts on page 150 of the leadership lock-in notebook in appendix 1.) How might we encourage one another to discover and use these gifts?

5. Where do you see youth ownership? Look hard. You may see glimpses. Look for the times young people have gotten excited about an activity or project and encouraged others to buy into whatever was going on.

Can a Youth Be Doing This?

If developing youth in leadership seems overwhelming, consider this little step. If you find that the old adult-oriented patterns are hard to break, try asking: *Can a youth be doing this?* Adult leaders, at every turn, ask yourself this question. It's a simple way to start on the road to youth-driven youth ministry.

• You find yourself making posters for an upcoming event. Can a youth be doing this? Of course.

- You're planning the devotions for the retreat. Can a youth be doing this? Absolutely.
- You're trying to figure out what to do about the rowdy ninth-grade boys. Can a youth be doing this? Yes. Ask the youth what to do about the boys.
- The adult leaders are trying to decide how much planning should be done at the fall retreat and whether some of it should be done on Sunday nights. Ask the youth!

It's not easy breaking out of old patterns. But if you recognize that you have old patterns, and if you are committed to the concept of youth ownership and youth-driven youth ministry, then you will get there. Adult leaders will need to keep encouraging one another.

How Can We Do It More Creatively?

A second question that is effective for drawing out youth leadership is: *How can we do it more creatively?*

- Your young people are serving a spaghetti supper for the congregation. Ask the youth: How can we do this more creatively?
- Your youth are to meet the family with whom they will be building the Habitat house. Ask the young people: Instead of just shaking hands and saying hello, how can we do this more creatively?
- Sunday night devotions: How can we do this more creatively?
- Announcements: How can we do this more creatively?
- A leader makes the annual report on youth ministry to the church board: How can we do this more creatively?
- It's the annual senior send-off: How can we do this more creatively?

Remember, developing youth in leadership takes time, more time than developing adult leadership. When you are working on developing young people as leaders, you cannot expect meetings to go as quickly as they would with adults leading them. Meetings will last longer, especially in the early stages of youth leadership.

It also takes constant effort. Don't give up. Resist the urge to take over. Ultimately, your goal is adult-youth partnership in leadership, but getting to that balanced relationship may take some consciousness-raising on the adults' part. Adults need to get used to the fact that young people are capable. Keep asking: *Can a youth be doing this?*

What Can Young People Do?

If you're still not convinced that young people can take leadership roles, ask your young people and your adult leaders to list leadership opportunities available in your church. You could do this exercise with parents as well. Encourage everyone to think broadly. Some opportunities are easily overlooked because people don't think of them as leadership roles. What can the young people do?

If answers are slow in coming, you might try rephrasing the question: How are young people involved in the life of the church? What are ways young people could be involved in the life of the church? Sometimes we don't identify as leadership things young people do. Singing in the choir is a form of worship leadership. Think broadly.

Just so you'll have an idea, the following is a collection of answers from several occasions when we asked this question.

Youth Involvement in Leadership

Be an example

Be a role model

Model Christian behavior

Lead in prayer

Teach songs to people of any age

Lead meetings

Create games

Design programs

Come up with ideas

Promote youth

Be in service to others

 build houses

 serve at soup kitchens

 teach vacation Bible school

 tutor

 lead fun days

 teach crafts

Lead children's worship

Facilitate group interaction

Ask questions

Speak out for what you believe

Affirm others

Give demonstrations

Lead small groups

Teach games to people of any age

Lead singing

Teach Sunday school

Make announcements

Create themes/songs/slogans

Create the vision

Share ideas and activities

Promote youth ministry

Be in worship

 read or act out scripture

 lead in prayer

 do liturgical dance

 carry banners in processional

 be an acolyte

 give the children's sermon

Welcome new youth

Lead discussions

Be good listeners

Encourage someone else

Levels of Leadership Development among Youth

Young people do not develop their leadership gifts, skills, and abilities at the same pace. Some blossom immediately, with leadership ability screaming to be noticed. They are the naturally outgoing and enthusiastic ones who can probably lead the group in any direction. Most young people, though, need adult leaders working side by side with them as the young people discover who they are, what they value, and what they can do. Again, here is where adult-youth partnership comes in.

Treat each young person and each task individually. In some cases, the adult may need to do the task while the young person watches and/or assists. In some cases, the adult and the young person will function as partners in leading. And in others, the youth will be able to do the task, needing only words of encouragement and support from the adult. In every case, adults and youth are working together in partnership.

Affirm the young people, even in the little things. You are their cheerleaders. Encourage them. Help them build confidence. Sometimes it's simply a matter of letting a young person know that something he or she considers insignificant is actually leadership.

We had a young person who was convinced that he couldn't do anything. As he saw it, he was surrounded by talented teenagers who could sing, speak, play sports, make friends, make good grades. We asked him if he would carry a banner in a worship service. He agreed, though he was not very excited about it. What's carrying a banner? Big deal. We made sure he knew how important his role as a worship leader would be. We talked about processions of all kinds, from a royal wedding to the servant Jesus entering Jerusalem on a donkey. We talked about how his walking down the aisle would set the tone for the worship service, and about that action as leadership. We talked about how God calls us to do things we humans consider insignificant.

> Youth are at different levels of development when it comes to leadership.

It was a joyous occasion. All eyes were on him. He carried the banner with joy and grace. He carried it as one who was called to do exactly that. To a rather shy and seemingly unhappy boy, this was a moment when he knew God smiled on him. You could tell he felt important, included, and that he understood his role as a worship leader. He asked if he could do it again the next year. Four years later, when he left for college, many people said they would greatly miss this particular boy who carried the banner. He was an important part of their worship experience. And of course we told him what they had said.

Once again, our job as adult leaders is to help the young people gain confidence, to help them identify their abilities and their gifts, and to affirm these gifts as leadership. In addition, we need to teach them leadership skills and give them opportunities to practice these skills.

The Leadership Lock-In

How do you develop the leadership potential in your young people? How do you help them discover their abilities and gifts? How do you teach what leadership really is—that a leader is not just someone who stands up in front of a group? How do you teach leadership skills?

The lock-in (see pp. 61–63) has been developed in an attempt to answer these questions. A lock-in is a miniretreat held at the church, with all the young people "locked in" for the night. Given the relatively confined area, a lock-in offers more concentrated program time than a retreat. This lock-in offers a place to start in leadership development with young people. It is just a start, though, and further leadership development needs to take place throughout the year.

It's called a leadership *lock-in,* but the three sessions would also work well in a retreat setting. A lock-in is a jam-packed format. For some churches it works well. We use the lock-in format because our young people love lock-ins. Our youth and adult leaders together, in partnership, decided on the lock-in format. A retreat may be a better setting for you. Retreats offer more relaxed time between the sessions. Our young people do not like retreats that are work-oriented. For our particular situation, a work-oriented lock-in works, but not a work-oriented retreat. Because this leadership event works at both a lock-in and a retreat, we provide sample schedules of both.

Another option is to do Sessions 1 and 2 at a retreat or lock-in, and Session 3 a week later. Or the activities from all three sessions could be scheduled over a period of several weeks. Ask your young people. They may tell you that doing leadership training for several weeks would get old. It takes approximately eight hours to complete the three sessions.

Choosing the format is not an adult leader's decision. As with everything we talk about in this book, make the decision in partnership with the young people. They are more likely to buy into the concept of leadership training if they have a say in its structure. They can tell you which format will work best. Get them involved in designing the leadership lock-in. It's the youth ownership principle again. If they own it, they will support it.

When to Have a Leadership Lock-In

The beginning of a year is a logical time to have a leadership lock-in. It's a good time to gather the group together for a common purpose. Besides teaching skills, the lock-in is an affirmation event. The young people's gifts, skills, and attempts at skills are affirmed by the entire group.

If you have a fall retreat in late September or early October, late October or early November may be a good time for this lock-in. Or your group may be interested in an August lock-in, to get themselves ready for leadership in youth ministry.

Consider how you will change the leadership lock-in from year to year. You may not choose to do it every year. With your young people, consider a long-range plan. For instance, the first year you could have a lock-in on a Friday night, the third week in October. The sec-

ond year, you could have an August preparation for leadership. The third year, you could have a Saturday-Sunday lock-in in November, which includes teaching Sunday school on Sunday morning. And the fourth year, you could have a leadership retreat in February.

The decision depends on the nature of your group—which changes from year to year. Some years you'll have young people who are gung-ho, ready-to-go leaders with a passion for leadership. Other years, leadership development may be slow. It also depends on where your young people are in their involvement with youth ministry. The decision will be different for those of you starting out, building or rebuilding a program, than for those who already have a tradition of young people in leadership. *The leadership lock-in is for both.* You'll need to decide how this leadership event can best serve the needs of your group. That's why it's essential to make the decision with the young people.

How Many Young People Can Participate in This Lock-In?

Twelve to fifteen is a good number of participants for the lock-in. Twenty-one is the maximum. If you do it as a retreat, twenty-five can participate. At a retreat, you have a little more time for everyone to practice the various skills.

Should you have more than twenty-one who wish to participate in the lock-in, consider having more than one leadership lock-in.

Option for a Saturday-to-Sunday Lock-In: Teach Sunday School

A Saturday-to-Sunday lock-in provides an opportunity for the young people to try out their teaching, discussion-leading, and teamwork skills. They could teach Sunday school for their own Sunday school classes on Sunday morning of the lock-in. Arrange ahead of time for the teachers to take a break that Sunday and to share the curriculum with the young people.

The decision about doing this should be made by the young people as they plan the lock-in. Some young people would be more comfortable than others taking on the teaching task. Remind them that they would work in teams, which should increase their comfort level. They would not have as much preparation time as teachers should have, but still it would be a good experience to lead at least a part of the class time.

Talk with your young people. If they are willing, go for it. There is time allotted in Session 2 (see p. 69, Activity 3) and in Session 3 (pp. 71–76) for preparing to teach Sunday school.

If your group chooses not to teach as part of the lock-in, they could make plans to teach Sunday school at a later date. It would give the young people a chance to try out some of the skills they learned at the lock-in. Consider team teaching with adults and youth in partnership.

A Saturday-Sunday lock-in with Sunday school teaching built in is a good way to do this lock-in the second or third year.

Purpose of the Leadership Lock-In

This lock-in is designed to give young people opportunities to acquire and practice leadership skills, to identify their leadership gifts, and to discover how the Holy Spirit empowers them to use these gifts which have been given them by God. They will explore various learning styles and leadership styles. They will look at Jesus as a model for leadership. They will learn how to lead games, a discussion, a small group, a meeting, how to work as a team, how to use resources, and how to evaluate.

This is not just a leadership event. The design gives you an opportunity to promote your church's approach to youth ministry, your goals, your traditions. The intention is that your young people will come away with not only leadership skills but also a renewed enthusiasm for their youth ministry. Throughout this event, they should gain enthusiasm for the vision of your particular youth ministry. This event can be a critical step toward youth ownership. Once young people buy into and have ownership in their own program, your problems of apathy are gone. You are on your way to youth-driven youth ministry.

Leaders for the Lock-In

If this is your first year working on developing young people as leaders, you'll need to have two or three adults leading this event. After the first year, young people and adults could lead it together. Either way, it's good modeling of team leadership. For us the adult/youth ratio for this event works best at one adult leader per seven youth participants. For the activities in which participants are divided into smaller groups, it is not essential to have an adult in each group. The young people should be able to handle their own small-group tasks—that's good leadership practice. The adult leadership should be composed of adults who work with the young people regularly. If you have other adults with particular expertise in leadership, you could invite them to be a part as well.

Leaders should prepare by going over each session in detail. They should discuss the content to make sure everyone understands what's going on and to decide who will lead which activities. Each leader should check the "Preparation" list in each session. Reading one or more of the following resources may be helpful for leaders: *Youth Ministry Leadership Skills,* by Scott C. Noon (Loveland, Colo.: Group Publishing, 1990), has helpful information on leadership style, dealing with disruptions, and leading discussions; *Creative Crowd Breakers, Mixers, and Games,* by Wayne Rice and Mike Yaconelli (Winona, Minn.: Saint Mary's Press, 1991), has an excellent introduction on cooperative gaming; *Why Nobody Learns Much of Anything at Church: And How to Fix It,* by Thom and Joani Schultz (Loveland, Colo.: Group Publishing, 1993), includes discussion techniques (see chapter 5) and information on active learning (chapter 6) and curriculum (chapter 8).

Setting

You'll need a big room with chairs, tables, floor space for games, a rug for floor sitting if possible, and break-out rooms or areas for small groups.

Think about where you could have the evening worship experience. Look for areas that have special significance to the young people. Some of our best worship experiences have occurred at night on the carpeted steps in the sanctuary, so we have our lock-in worship in that same spot. Be on the lookout for places and situations that could provide the start of a tradition for your group.

You'll need to check: If you do a Saturday night lock-in, is it acceptable for the young people to wear casual "retreat" clothes at church on Sunday morning? Is there an early or less formal worship service that the young people might attend? Or should they bring a change of clothes for worship? We don't recommend skipping worship, for two reasons. First, youth ministry should affirm and support worship participation. Second, it's great public relations for the rest of the church members to see the young people in worship at the conclusion of their leadership lock-in, especially if the service includes an announcement about what has been going on with the young people at the overnight event.

Food Arrangements

For a Friday-to-Saturday lock-in at the church, have a parent bring in sandwiches, pizza, taco salad, or such for supper on Friday, or for lunch and supper if it's a Saturday-Sunday lock-in. Parents could come in and cook breakfast. If a restaurant or fast-food place is nearby, you could go out for breakfast. In any case, delegate the food responsibilities. If you are at a retreat center, make arrangements for food. Leaders of the lock-in should not be responsible for food preparation.

Resources

Newsprint
Colored markers—one for each participant
Videotape of *Sister Act*
VCR and TV for viewing *Sister Act*
Construction paper
Masking tape
Salt and pepper shakers (one set per eight participants)
Baggies with eight gum drops, twelve toothpicks, and four marshmallows (one baggie for each participant)
Prepared newsprint sheets and signs (directions under "Preparation" or "Activities" in each session)
Copies of a lesson from the young people's current Sunday school curriculum

Bibles
Paper
Pencils—one for each participant
Resources (see resource list in appendix 6)
A leadership notebook (see below, also appendix 1) for each participant

The Leadership Notebook

Having a notebook gives the young people the feeling that they are part of something important. Provide a half-inch binder notebook for each participant. You'll need to figure this into your budget. You can create your own title page and put it on the front of the notebook or use it as the first page. One of our young people created ours. Material for the complete notebook is found in appendix 1. You may reproduce it.

"Steps for Planning" (p. 160) is used only briefly in this lock-in. It is included in the leadership notebook because planning requires leadership skills. Because the lock-in is so full of learning activities, we felt that planning could be saved for later. Use this in connection with planning your youth ministry and for planning specific activities and events.

One Last Word

This lock-in is jam-packed. It includes a lot of learning, a lot of discovery, and a lot of practicing new skills. If the participants are losing steam, and you sense the need to eliminate one or two of the activities, that's fine. Use the eliminated activities at a later date.

Session 1.
What's a Leader?
(1 hour, 40 minutes)

In this session the participants begin to explore the concept of leadership. They should gain a broad understanding of what it means to be a leader. They are introduced to their leadership notebooks, which contain lots of information and tips on all aspects of leadership. They play two games that, in addition to being fun, are good teaching tools. In their discussion of the games, they discover the relationship of the games to leadership and teamwork.

Friday-to-Saturday Lock-In: A Sample Schedule

Friday
SESSION 1: WHAT'S A LEADER
  4:00—Making Name Tags and Key Words on the Wall (Activities 1 and 2)
  4:25—Explanation of Agenda and Expectations (3)
  4:35—Discussion on Leaders and Leadership (4)
  4:45—The Leadership Notebook (5)
  4:55—Working as a Team: Machines (6)
  5:25—Leading a Game: A What? (7)
  5:45—Supper

SESSION 2: HOW WE LEARN AND HOW WE LEAD
  6:30—Communication Exercise: Gumdrops (1)
  6:50—How People Learn: A Discussion (2)
  7:05—Learning Styles and Sunday School: A Look at Teaching Activities (3)
  7:20—Discovering Your Gifts (4)
  7:35—Discovering Your Leadership Skills (5)
  7:50—Finding Out about Your Personality Style (6)
  8:05—Break and Refreshments
  8:35—What Would You Do? Leadership Styles (7)
  8:55—*Sister Act* Clip: A Look at Good Leadership Techniques (8)

SESSION 3: TOOLS FOR LEADING
  9:10—Leading a Game (1)
  9:50—Leading a Group Discussion (2)
10:05—Break
10:20—Practicing Leading a Discussion (3)
11:05—Game/Free Time/Video
  1:00—Quiet Down/Sleep

Saturday Morning
  8:00—Breakfast and Cleanup
  8:45—Wake-up Game
  9:00—Working as a Team (4)
  9:15—Using Resources (5)
  9:45—Delegating (6)
10:15—Leading a Meeting (7)
10:25—Discovering Other Areas of Leadership (8)
10:35—Break
11:00—Evaluating (9)
11:15—Taking It Home (10)
11:25—Closing Worship (11)

Saturday-to-Sunday Lock-In: A Sample Schedule

Saturday
SESSION 1: WHAT'S A LEADER
11:00—Making Name Tags and Key Words on the Wall (Activities 1 and 2)
11:25—Explanation of Agenda and Expectations (3)
11:35—Discussion on Leaders and Leadership (4)
11:45—The Leadership Notebook (5)
11:55—Working as a Team: Machines (6)
12:25—Lunch
12:55—Leading a Game: A What? (7)

SESSION 2: HOW WE LEARN AND HOW WE LEAD
1:10—Communication Exercise: Gumdrops (1)
1:30—How People Learn: A Discussion (2)
1:45—Learning Styles and Sunday School: A Look at Teaching Activities (3)
2:00—Discovering Your Gifts (4)
2:15—Discovering Your Leadership Skills (5)
2:30—Finding Out about Your Personality Style (6)
2:45—Break and Refreshments
3:30—What Would You Do? Leadership Styles (7)
4:00—*Sister Act* Clip: A Look at Good Leadership Techniques (8)

SESSION 3: TOOLS FOR LEADING
4:20—Leading a Game (1)
5:00—Leading a Group Discussion (2)
5:15—Practicing Leading a Discussion (3)
5:30—Break for Supper
6:15—Practicing Leading a Discussion (3)
6:45—Working as a Team (4)
7:00—Using Resourses (5)
7:30—Break and Refreshments
8:00—Delegating (6)
8:30—Leading a Meeting (7)
8:40—Discovering Other Areas of Leadership (8)
8:50—Evaluating (9)
9:05—Break
9:25—Taking It Home (10)
9:35—Closing Worship (11)
10:00—Video/Free time/Games (If the participants will teach or lead discussions in Sunday school, preparation could be done at this time.)
1:00—Quiet Down/Sleep

Sunday Morning
8:00—Breakfast and Cleanup
8:45—Worship with Congregation
9:45—Attend or Teach Sunday School

Retreat: A Sample Schedule

Saturday
SESSION 1: WHAT'S A LEADER
11:00—Making Name Tags and Key Words on the Wall (Activities 1 and 2)
11:25—Explanation of Agenda and Expectations (3)
11:35—Discussion on Leaders and Leadership (4)
11:45—The Leadership Notebook (5)
11:55—Working as a Team: Machines (6)
12:30—Lunch
 1:15—Leading a Game: A What? (7)

SESSION 2: HOW WE LEARN AND HOW WE LEAD
 1:30—Communication Exercise: Gumdrops (1)
 1:50—How People Learn: A Discussion (2)
 2:05—Learning Styles and Sunday School: A Look at Teaching Activities (3)
 2:20—Discovering Your Gifts (4)
 2:35—Free Time/Outdoor Games
 5:00—Discovering Your Leadership Skills (5)
 5:15—Finding Out about Your Personality Style (6)
 6:00—Supper
 6:45—Singing
 7:05—What Would You Do? Leadership Styles (7)
 7:25—*Sister Act* Clip: A Look at Good Leadership Techniques (8)

SESSION 3: TOOLS FOR LEADING
 7:40—Leading a Game (1)
 8:20—Leading a Group Discussion (2)
 8:35—Practicing Leading a Discussion (3)
 9:20—Break
10:00—Night Game/Campfire/Devotions

Sunday Morning
 8:00—Breakfast and Packing up
 8:45—Wake-up Game
 9:00—Working as a Team (4)
 9:15—Using Resources (5)
 9:45—Delegating (6)
10:15—Leading a Meeting (7)
10:25—Discovering Other Areas of Leadership (8)
10:35—Break
11:00—Evaluating (9)
11:15—Taking It Home (10)
11:25—Closing Worship (11)

Through the game, A What? they get a glimpse of the world of communicating and giving directions, as you will see from reading the complicated directions for this game (see Activity 7 below).

Agenda

1. Making Name Tags
2. Key Words on the Wall
3. Explanation of Agenda and Expectations
4. Discussion on Leaders and Leadership
5. The Leadership Notebook
6. Working as a Team: Machines
7. Leading a Game: A What?

Preparation

• Cut sheets of colored construction paper in half for name tags (for Activity 1). Place them on a table with markers and a roll of masking tape.
• Prepare a newsprint sheet with instructions for making the name tag (see Activity 1 below).
• On four newsprint sheets print the following words, one in the center of each sheet:

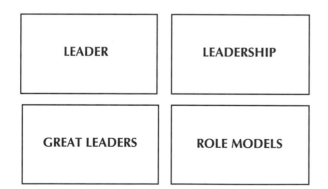

LEADER	**LEADERSHIP**
GREAT LEADERS	**ROLE MODELS**

• Prepare a newsprint sheet with instructions for Key Words on Wall (see Activity 2 below for these instructions).
• Prepare three newsprint sheets, each with the agenda for one session. An agenda is listed for each session.
• Prepare leadership notebooks, one for each participant, by photocopying the material in appendix 1. Obtain a half-inch binder notebook for each

participant. Using a hole punch, put a set of photocopied material in each binder notebook.
• Provide a pencil for each participant.
• Provide a set of salt and pepper shakers for each eight participants to use in the Activity 7 game.

Activities

As participants arrive, encourage them to begin doing Activity 1 and then go right on to Activity 2.

1. Making Name Tags
(15 minutes)

DIRECTIONS:

Provide a table and half sheets of colored construction paper and markers. Display a newsprint sheet on which you have prepared the following instructions:

1. Choose a piece of construction paper and a marker.
2. Write your first name in the center of the name tag.
3. Write answers to the following four questions in the appropriate corners:

For upper left corner: Who is someone you admire?

For lower left corner: What is one gift or talent you have?

For upper right corner: What is one adjective people might use to describe you?

For lower right corner: What is your favorite movie? (See the illustration, below, for an example.)

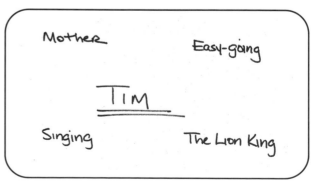

4. Put on your name tag with masking tape.

2. Key Words on the Wall
(10 minutes)

DIRECTIONS:

As the participants finish their name tags, encourage them to move on to this activity. On the walls you have displayed five newsprint sheets, four of which have one of the following words printed in the middle: *leader, leadership, great leaders, role models;* the fifth sheet contains these instructions:

- Add words to each sheet in response to this question: What words come to mind when you see the word printed on the sheet?
- Write your answers anywhere on the sheets. As you are roaming about the room, read one another's name tags.

The participants are to read the instruction sheet and follow its directions. Each should take a marker and write words on the four sheets, as directed.

3. Explanation of Agenda and Expectations
(10 minutes)

Everyone gathers where each can see the newsprint sheets with the agenda for all three sessions.

DIRECTIONS:

Begin by telling them that they have been called to this event. They have been called by God and by their church to develop their gifts and abilities in the area of leadership. The Holy Spirit has given them gifts that, during this lock-in, they will identify in themselves and affirm in one another.

Introduce the leaders. Explain what will happen. Go over the agenda. Be upbeat. Make it sound like fun. Share your enthusiasm with the participants. Tell them that not only will they be learning and practicing leadership skills but they will be preparing themselves to take on important leadership roles in their church. And they can become the cheerleaders for their youth program.

Explain that the aim for youth ministry is to have young people and adults working together in partnership. The hope is that youth ministry will move from being adult-driven to being youth-driven. This group can make that happen.

Explain that the pace may be different from that of other lock-ins. If any young people have come to the lock-in mistakenly expecting free time and recreation, they need to be told now what is going to happen. Otherwise, you'll have some unhappy youth who won't benefit at all from this experience. The adage "you get what you expect" applies here. If you expect participation, learning, and work from the participants, you'll get it. The word "work" might scare them, so you'll want to let them know that school and homework is not what's happening here. The kind of work they will be doing will be fun and active. It's also a good selling point to tell them how colleges and businesses are looking for young people with leadership training and experience. This event can be listed on their resumes and applications.

Explain that they will have an opportunity to practice leadership in a safe setting, with adults and young people who won't ridicule them, but who will encourage them. The ground rule is that put-downs are not allowed. Remind them that everyone is in the same boat here. They'll be trying new things that might be difficult to try at school or elsewhere, because of the pressure to get it right or worry about what other people might think. Let everyone know that the church is there for them.

Consider initiating a group response. Whenever someone feels he or she has messed up, the entire group could say "That's okay." Group responses can be a good bonding technique. I realized this one summer at a youth conference where, whenever someone yelled out "God is good," a thousand youth and adults would respond in unison "All the time." It was a good bonding experience.

4. Discussion on Leaders and Leadership
(10 minutes)

DIRECTIONS:

Ask the participants the following questions:
   What is a leader and what does a leader do?
   What makes a good leader?
   What skills do leaders need?

For each question, encourage lots of responses. List all answers on newsprint. These newsprint sheets can be taped to the wall next to the newsprint sheets from Activity 2. Participants may refer to responses listed for Activity 2.

Note: Here are some ideas you may want to add if the young people do not think of them: Leaders serve the followers. Leaders are followers, in that they follow the will of the group. Leaders appreciate their followers. They know how to delegate and share responsibilities. Good leaders can build the morale of the group. They know how to lead differently in different situations. Good leaders are dreamers and visionaries. Leadership characteristics include being responsible, creative, diplomatic, assertive, dependable, enthusiastic, confident, and caring. Leadership skills include being good listeners, delegators, organizers, and team builders.

5. The Leadership Notebook
(10 minutes)

DIRECTIONS:

Distribute the leadership notebooks and ask the participants to look at the first page, "A Leader," and add to this page some ideas listed on the newsprint sheets. As participants look through the notebook, explain that it has tips on leading games, leading discussions, leading a meeting, and so on. It's a quick reference for ideas for dealing with future situations of leadership. Encourage them to take notes in their notebooks as the lock-in continues.

6. Working as a Team: Machines
(30 minutes)

If you have more than nine participants, divide into smaller groups of five to nine each. This first exercise is from the realm of drama and pantomime.

DIRECTIONS:

Each group is to create a machine with movable parts. The parts of the machine are the members of the group. Everyone should be included. The machine can be a real object, like a pinball machine, an airplane, or a cuckoo clock, or it can be a conglomerate of levers and moving parts. Creativity is what you're shooting for. Each group has fifteen minutes to decide what to do and how to do it. Each group will then demonstrate its machine. Everybody cheers the accomplishments of each group.

After the demonstrations, bring the groups together to discuss the following questions:

How did your group decide what machine to create?

What role did you play in the creation of the machine? Examples are as follows: came up with the idea, affirmed other people's ideas, made suggestions, clarified what someone was supposed to do.

Which of these roles can be considered leadership roles? Encourage participants to think broadly of leadership. The one who affirms or clarifies is performing a leadership function, just as is the one who tells everyone what to do.

What did you like about the way your group accomplished its task?

What didn't you like about it? How might it be improved?

In what ways is this a good exercise to get a group to work together as a team?

7. Leading a Game: A What?
(15 minutes)

Participants will experience some confusion and difficulty playing this game. They will explore game leading as well as face challenges in order to accomplish a task.

Have the participants form new groups of seven to ten people. Each group sits in a circle. Give one person in each group a set of salt and pepper shakers. As everyone listens to the instructions, they are to listen for two things: (1) how to play the game, and (2) how the directions were given. Part of leadership is learning how to give directions.

DIRECTIONS:

The starter person in each group has the salt shaker in her or his left hand and the pepper shaker in the right hand. The starter turns to the person on his or her left and says, referring to the salt shaker, "This is a dog." That person asks the starter: "A what?" The starter responds, "A dog," and gives the salt shaker to the person on the left. Then that person turns to the next person on the left, saying, "This is a dog." "A what?" he or she responds. "A what?" back to the starter. "A dog." "A dog." And so forth around the circle. Before the "dog" is given to the next person, it must be confirmed all the way back to the starter that it is a dog. So you have, "A what?" and from the next person, "A what?" relayed back to the starter. And the starter replies to his or her left, "A dog," and the next person, "A dog," and so on.

Just after starting the salt shaker to the left, the starter turns to the person on the right and says: "This is a cat," referring to the pepper shaker. The person on the right says back to the starter, "A what?" and the starter responds, "A cat," and gives the person the "cat," who then passes it on to the next person on the right with the same drill.

The fun comes when the person half way around the circle receives a dog from the right, a cat from the left, and hears from both sides: "A what?" It is a fun game filled with lots of laughs and, of course, lots of confusion. The object of the game is to get the dog and the cat around the circle and back to the starter.

Have several different people be the starter, so that several will get the challenge of getting the dog and cat to cross and get on "home."

After about fifteen minutes of playing the game, bring the groups together and discuss the following:

What helped you understand how to play the game?

How might the directions have been given more clearly?

What did the leader (the one who gave the directions) do when things got messed up with the dog and cat crossing? Why was that part of the game frustrating?

What does this game demonstrate about working together on a task? What does it demonstrate about communication?

Session 2.
How We Learn and How We Lead
(2 hours, 10 minutes)

This is the discovery session, as participants discover that they are unique individuals, created by God with special gifts. In the first activity they will discover a frustrating and fascinating side of communication: Everybody isn't alike. People have different learning styles, personality styles, and leadership styles and different gifts and skills. In the process of exploring all these differences, participants will identify what's unique about themselves.

Agenda

1. Communication Exercise: Gumdrops

2. How People Learn: A Discussion

3. Learning Styles and Sunday School: A Look at Teaching Activities

4. Discovering Your Gifts

5. Discovering Your Leadership Skills

6. Finding Out about Your Personality Style

7. What Would You Do? Leadership Styles

8. *Sister Act* Clip: A Look at Good Leadership Techniques

Preparation

• Prepare a baggie for each participant. The baggie should contain eight gum drops, four marshmallows, and twelve toothpicks (for Activity 1).

• For Activity 2, write the following words, each on an 8½ × 11 sheet:

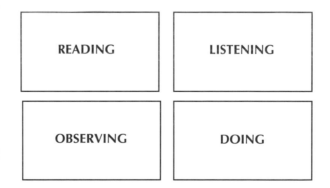

| READING | LISTENING |
| OBSERVING | DOING |

• For Activity 3, obtain copies of the young people's Sunday school class curriculum. Make copies of the lesson to be used on the Sunday that follows this lock-in.

• On seven sheets of 8½ × 11 paper, write the numbers 1 through 7, one number on each sheet (for Activity 7).

The Ultimate Authority	Chief	Consultor	Democratizer	Hands Offist
Makes the _____	Works out _____	Consults the _____	Encourages _____	Gives _____
_____ _____	_____ _____	_____ _____	_____ _____	_____ _____

- Prepare five newsprint sheets: Write on each one of the five leadership styles and its description, as shown in the illustration above (see appendix 1, p. 153).
- Obtain a videotape of *Sister Act,* the film starring Whoopi Goldberg. Find the scene where Sister Mary Clarence (Whoopi) is walking into the choir rehearsal. She has been told she is to sing in the choir. Stop the tape at that point, so that you can begin with this scene when you show the tape to the participants. Set up the VCR and TV, making sure all the wires are connected properly.

Activities

1. Communication Exercise: Gumdrops
(20 minutes)

This exercise is done in pairs. To avoid awkwardness about pairing, you could ask all the participants to line up according to their birthdays and then to pair up with the person next to them in line. Then they are to find a place where they can sit back to back.

Give each person a baggie with the gumdrops, marshmallows, and toothpicks (see "Preparation").

DIRECTIONS:
Tell the participants the following:

1. In this next exercise you will discover interesting things about your ability to communicate, about leading, about following, and about listening. This exercise focuses on one particular learning-listening style. Not all of us learn best by listening. Some of us are visual; we learn best by observing. Others learn best by doing, experimenting. We'll discuss these differences a little later.

2. Start this exercise by deciding who in each pair will be the leader, the communicator. The partner is the follower, the one who follows the directions. At no time is the follower to peek at what the leader is doing.

3. The leader is to build something out of the contents of the baggie. The leader must describe every move, because the follower will be trying to build an identical structure. The follower may ask the leader to repeat a direction he or she has just given. The leader may repeat it only once. The follower cannot ask questions about the direction. The follower just interprets it and does it.

4. You have ten minutes to work on this.

After ten minutes, the paired participants compare their creations. Some may be quite similar. Others will cause everyone to have a good laugh.

In the full group, discuss the following questions:

What did you learn about yourself as you did this exercise?

What surprised you?

What would happen if you switched roles? (You might want to try that later on.)

2. How People Learn: A Discussion
(15 minutes)

DIRECTIONS:
Tape the four signs (*reading, listening, observing, doing*) on the walls around the room (see "Preparation"). As a full group, talk about the different ways of learning. Use as an example learning how to use a computer or word processor, and explain that there are four ways of attacking the learning process:

Reading—Some people prefer to read the manual to learn how to work the computer.
Listening—Some prefer having an instructor explain it. They might even take notes.
Observing—Some people learn best by watching someone else do it, by observing.
Doing—And then there are those who would rather sit down with the computer, play with it, and figure out what they need to know.

Point out the signs on the walls. The participants are to stand next to the sign that they feel best represents their learning style, how they learn best. The people at each sign should discuss with one another why they feel this is their learning style. Encourage them to share experiences of how they learned to do something.

While they are still standing by their signs, ask several to share with the full group why they chose that particular learning style.

Gather everyone back together. Point out that no one learns by only one method. People could stand by any one of the styles, depending on the particular subject of learning. But it is true that most people have a dominant style.

3. Learning Styles and Sunday School: A Look at Teaching Activities
(15 minutes)

For activities 3, 4, 5, and 6, participants should be in small groups of six or seven.

For this activity, hand out copies of the participants' Sunday school lesson for the Sunday that follows this lock-in. .

DIRECTIONS:
Tell the participants the following:

1. Since people have different styles of learning, we want to look at ways to approach teaching and leading. We need to be aware that any one method, like lecturing, may not reach all the learners. If you were teaching a Sunday school class, what would you do, what methods would you use, to appeal to all four styles of learning?

2. To answer this question, in small groups, you'll be looking at your Sunday school lesson for Sunday and at the list of teaching activities in your notebook (see p. 149). Discuss the following questions within your group:

For which learning style is each activity in the lesson geared?

Look at the list of teaching activities in your notebook (see p. 149). What activities could you use to teach the lesson?

Tell the participants that they will discover good ideas to pass on to their Sunday school teachers, as well as good tips for a time when they might teach Sunday school or lead a Bible study.

4. Discovering Your Gifts
(15 minutes)

This is a good exercise for building self-esteem, because young people usually are impressed that they can mark so many items on the list of "gifts" they will use. If you gave them a blank piece of paper and suggested they list their gifts, they would have trouble. They would list a few and would feel a little low. The explanation is that they probably never thought of their attributes—things like being a friend, being easy-going, paying attention to details, humor, courage, and honesty—as gifts.

The scripture used in this exercise, 1 Corinthians 12:7, reminds everyone that the Holy Spirit is at work in each person, and that the Spirit is manifest in each of us in a particular way, for a particular purpose. This exercise will give participants an opportunity to confirm the gifts that the Spirit has given them and to affirm the gifts they see in each other.

DIRECTIONS:
Still in small groups, everyone should turn to "Discovering Your Gifts" (see p. 150). They should take a few minutes and mark all the characteristics that apply to them.

Then they should discuss the following questions within their groups:

What did you learn about yourself?
Which of the gifts would you like to develop or work on?
Look at the quote from 1 Corinthians 12:7. How does the Holy Spirit work in a person's life?

Next ask them to place an X next to the gifts they think a leader should have, and to discuss why they feel leaders should possess the gifts they marked.

When everyone is finished, they should put their sheets back in their notebooks. They will need this gift list at the worship service later.

5. Discovering Your Leadership Skills
(15 minutes)

DIRECTIONS:
Still working in small groups of six or seven, everyone is to turn to "Leadership Skills" (see p. 151), and read the instructions. They are to place a number between 1 (lowest) and 7 (highest) after each item to indicate how they feel about their ability to do each item.

While they are filling out their forms, put the seven sheets of paper (numbered 1 through 7) on the floor in a line, each about four feet from the next.

Explain that when they complete their forms, they should take their forms and stand on the appropriate number for each skill. There will be a lot of moving around here, and it is both fun and interesting to see the range of self-evaluated skills of the whole group.

When everyone is finished, call out the first skill, and ask them all to stand on the number they wrote on their sheets for that skill. After everyone has had a chance to see where everyone is, call out the next skill. Many will move to another number. Continue this for all the skills.

Remind everyone to keep these sheets in their notebooks. Consider making a tally chart for the whole group or making a copy of everyone's form for the files. Their forms could be helpful when you are looking for people to lead certain activities throughout the year.

6. Finding Out
about Your Personality Style
(15 minutes)

DIRECTIONS:

Still in small groups, the participants should look at "Four Personality Styles" (see p. 152), and at the descriptions of these four personality styles:

party person
go-getter
boss
loyal supporter

Each should decide which description best fits the type of person he or she is.

Ask if anyone has taken the Myers-Briggs Type Indicator, which identifies sixteen personality styles, or the Keirsey-Bates Personality Sorter (short form of Myers-Briggs). The result of both tests is a four-letter personality type, for example, ENFP, ESTJ, INFJ (*E,* extroversion; *N,* intuition; *F,* feeling; *P,* perceiving; *S,* sensing; *T,* thinking; *J,* judging; *I,* introversion). Some may have taken the Myers-Briggs in connection with career counseling. Ask how many know their four-letter type.

In their groups, they are to discuss what they have discovered about themselves as a result of examining their personality style. Discovering personality type or style can help people understand why some tasks are harder for some people than others. Some people are better suited to making phone calls than others. Some people are more detailed-oriented. Some are more aware of people's needs and feelings. Some are outgoing and not afraid to get up in front of big groups.

7. What Would You Do?
Leadership Styles
(20 minutes)

Put the five sheets of newsprint with the descriptions of the five leadership styles on the walls in five different parts of the room.

DIRECTIONS:

Point out the five styles of leadership on the sheets of paper posted on the walls (The Ultimate Authority, Chief, Consultor, Democratizer, and Hands Offist). Read the descriptions out loud.

Read out loud one of the sample situations which can be found at the bottom of page 153. Give the participants three minutes to decide individually—no discussion—what they would do in that situation. Then they are to decide which style best matches their decision.

Each participant should go and stand under the style she or he chose. With those others who have chosen the same style, they are to discuss what they would do in that situation and why they chose that style.

Ask one person from each group to report on the group's discussion. After each group has reported, go on to the next situation. You should have time for three situations.

Gather everyone together and discuss the following questions:

Did you discover any similarities in your personality style (previous exercise) and your leadership style in this exercise?
What did you discover about the way you approach problems?

It helps to point out that everyone has elements of the five styles, and people vary style and responses depending on the situation. And there is no one right answer. It is important for young people to understand this, since they often feel that there is only one right way to do things. This exercise helps broaden their perspective.

8. *Sister Act* Clip:
A Look at Good Leadership Techniques
(15 minutes)

The *Sister Act* videotape should be cued to the scene where Sister Mary Clarence (Whoopi) is walking into the choir rehearsal (see "Preparation").

DIRECTIONS:

Play the scene for the full group and then discuss the following question: What did you notice about Sister Mary Clarence's leadership technique?

List on newsprint things she did that participants cite as good leadership.

Session 3. Tools for Leading (4 hours)

In this session participants will have a chance to practice some leadership skills. They will take turns leading a game and leading a discussion. The morale of the group is very important at this point. They have been together for several hours. They have shared, explored, asked questions, and made discoveries. There should be an atmosphere of camaraderie and support. Support and affirmation are necessary in this session, as the young people will be trying out new skills. Emphasize the importance of cheering each other on and giving emotional high fives.

Participants will have a chance to explore resources that they may use in the future as they plan their youth ministry program. Exploring teamwork, delegating, evaluating, and other areas of "leading" is part of their leadership training to become responsible members of their youth ministry and of their church.

In the closing worship experience, they will have a chance to affirm one another's gifts and to offer one of their gifts to God to be used in service to God's people.

Agenda

1. Leading a Game
2. Leading a Group Discussion
3. Practicing Leading a Discussion
4. Working as a Team
5. Using Resources
6. Delegating
7. Leading a Meeting
8. Discovering Other Areas of Leadership
9. Evaluating
10. Taking It Home
11. Closing Worship

Preparation

- Provide young people's Sunday school curriculum.
- Gather youth resources—books on games, topics, worship, devotions, retreats, programs for youth meetings, Bible study, service projects, drama, music; also curricula and youth magazines. Provide at least one resource per participant. Don't have more than thirty resources; that would be overwhelming. Display them on one or two tables. Leaders of this event need to become familiar with the resources in order to talk about them.
- For Activity 6, make copies of four months of a calendar, starting with the month of this lock-in. The participants will be simulating planning a retreat scheduled in four months. Make copies of this four-month calendar for each participant.
- For the closing worship, read 1 Corinthians 12: 12–27. This passage lends itself well to being acted out. Check out the worship setting. Is there a cross where the participants can bring their offerings of "gifts"? Everyone needs a Bible, a slip of paper, and pencil.
- For the worship, find two people, young people or adults, who will do the opening prayer and the closing prayer.

Activities

1. Leading a Game
(40 minutes)

DIRECTIONS:

Ask the participants to turn to "Tips for Leading a Game" (see p. 154). Spend a few minutes reviewing the tips on how to lead a game.

Divide the group in half. Ask for one or two

volunteers in each of the two groups to teach a game to their group. Yes, two can teach one game. We call it team teaching. The volunteers think of a game and proceed to teach their group how to play. The group then plays the game for ten minutes.

After the game has been played, the group evaluates, using the following questions:

What did the leader/s do that was helpful in teaching the game? Refer to the tips in the notebook.

Which tips might help the leader in teaching the game?

Ask the leader/s how it felt to lead the game. What was difficult? What was helpful?

Ask for another volunteer or two to teach another game. After each group has played three games, gather everyone together. Ask the group: What did you discover about leadership?

2. Leading a Group Discussion
(15 minutes)

Tell the group they will now try another form of leadership: leading a discussion. The most challenging thing about leading a discussion is asking good questions and being able to take responses and form further questions from those responses.

DIRECTIONS:
Everyone should turn to "Leading a Discussion" (see p. 156). Review each of the guidelines in the notebook for leading a discussion. Use the corresponding questions below.

1. Give an example of a yes-or-no question. Give an example of an open-ended question.

2. Why are the "w" questions good questions?

3 Suppose we were talking about Jesus telling the parable of the lost sheep. Think of a question that could relate that story to a person's life situation.

4. Give an example of an easy question and a deeper question on the same subject.

5. What should leaders do when they ask a question and no one has an answer, at least not immediately? Is silence really that deadly?

6. Think of a time when you asked a question, and someone looked puzzled, so that you had to rephrase the question.

7. Would you be offended if the leader started humming the "Jeopardy" tune?

8. Create a list of affirming comments a leader can make after one person has answered a question, but the leader wants others to add their answers.

9. What are other ways to encourage participation by more people?

10. Try repeating what you just heard someone say, by saying: "So you're saying that . . ." or "You think that . . ."

11. Create a list of comments a leader can make if a person's answer is not on target. You're trying to affirm the person, while at the same time you are seeking other answers.

12. What kinds of things help you to be a good listener?

13. In this discussion have you noticed anyone encouraging group members to talk to one another? How did that person do it?

14. Respond to this guideline. Is it easier to share if the leader shares first? What do you think?

15. In any situation of leadership that you have experienced—here at this lock-in or previously—how would you rate yourself on enthusiasm on a scale of 1 to 10, with 10 being maximum-enthusiastic and 1 being virtually lifeless?

16. What are some other ways to keep certain people from dominating?

3. Practice Leading a Discussion
(45 minutes)

For this activity, the participants work in small groups of six to eight. Within the groups, people need to pair up in teams of two, but a threesome would be fine. Each team will need a copy of the Sunday school curriculum or a youth ministry program resource. (If you are doing a Saturday-Sunday lock-in and the participants are teaching Sunday morning, they will need only their Sunday school curriculum.)

DIRECTIONS:
Within each small group of six to eight, ask the participants to form three teams of two or three people. Each team is to prepare to lead a discussion with their small group on a discussion section of their Sunday school lesson or on a topic from the youth ministry program resource. Each team should have a different part of the lesson or topic.

They will have fifteen minutes to prepare. Acknowledge that fifteen minutes is not enough preparation time, but remind everyone that this is not about polished teaching performances. Rather, this is about having an opportunity to try out leading a discussion, to see what it feels like.

After the fifteen-minute preparation, one team in each group takes the leadership role and begins the discussion. They lead the discussion for five minutes.

Tell the participants to help each set of leaders with their support and their suggestions, but especially their affirmations. Remind the group that everyone is in this boat together and needs to cheer each other on! They should have page 156, "Leading a Discussion," in the notebook available.

After the first team leads, the group discusses the following issues:

For the leaders:
• What was leading like?
• What was scary or what worried you?
• Which part did you feel good about?
• Where did you feel uncomfortable?

For the group members:
• What did you like about what the leaders did?
• Where did they make good use of the guidelines?
• What might have helped them?

Then the next team leads. The entire activity should take about forty-five to fifty minutes. The repetition should help the entire group's learning. Watch the clock. Don't let it drag. You want to give everyone a chance, but you don't want everyone moaning with boredom during the last team's turn.

After all teams have finished and the discussions are concluded, bring everyone together to reflect on the experience of leading a discussion. Ask the following:

What did you learn about yourself?
What did you learn about leading a discussion?
What was helpful from your feedback discussions?

Remind the group what a tough skill "leading a discussion" is. Not many adults are good at it. Assure them that it takes lots of practice and they should take advantage of any chance they get to practice leading a discussion. Practice will improve their leadership abilities and increase their confidence.

4. Working as a Team
(15 minutes)

DIRECTIONS:
In the full group, invite the participants to think

back to the machines they created earlier in this event. They talked about how leadership emerged. Now ask them about teamwork, using the following questions:

• How well did you work together as a team when you were creating those machines? What kinds of things happened that showed good teamwork?
• What does it take to enable people to work well as a team?

After exploring these questions for a few minutes, ask the participants to turn to "A Good Team" (see p. 157), and review the characteristics of a good team. Ask the following: What insights do you gain about working as a team?

Suggest that they keep these insights in mind throughout the year as they plan activities. It is important in teamwork to affirm and encourage each member of the team. Being aware of this should help the young people be more conscious of the needs and contributions of individuals in their group.

5. Using Resources
(30 minutes)

On one or two tables, display youth ministry resources—books on games, topics, worship, devotions, retreats, programs for youth meetings, Bible study, service projects, drama, and music, as well as curricula and youth magazines.

DIRECTIONS:
Participants turn to "Guidelines for Using Resources" (see p. 158), and read the guidelines. Point out that guidelines 3–6 are evaluation questions. Invite the participants to look at the resources on the resource table and to refer to these questions as they look.

Ask if any of the participants have used any of the resources. Give them time to look through them. Review what's in the resources and suggest how they might use them—in planning a Sunday school lesson, a youth activity, a worship service, or whatever.

6. Delegating
(30 minutes)

Everyone is in one group at the beginning of this activity. Then they divide into the same groups they were in for Activity 3, leading a discussion. Each small group will need newsprint and markers. Each participant should have a copy of the four-month calendar (see "Preparation").

DIRECTIONS:

With everyone together, note that delegating can be one of the hardest jobs for a leader. Ask why this might be so. Encourage several answers. (Possible answers: It's easier to do it yourself. Delegating means you have to check up on people to see if they are doing the job. Sometimes it's hard to explain what needs to be done. Time gets away from you.) Ask: Why delegate? What are the benefits?

After a few minutes of discussion, participants are to go to the groups they were in for Activity 3. Once in their groups, they are to read "Action Plan" (see p. 159).

Each group should practice using an action plan by simulating being the planning team for a retreat. (If you have an upcoming retreat or event, this practice could help you get ready for actual planning.) As the planning team, they are to follow the steps of the action plan. On newsprint, each group should list what it will do for each step. On the four-month calendars, group members can assign dates for the steps to be completed. Allow twenty minutes for this part of the exercise.

Bring everyone back into the total group to discuss the following questions:

How was the action plan helpful in your planning? What did you delegate?
How will you check on the progress of the tasks delegated in the action plan?
Where might the pitfalls be? What might you need to do to see that things don't fall through the cracks?

Remind the participants that delegating is difficult and takes practice. Have them turn back to "Leadership Skills" (see p. 151), and look at the number they put by number 8, "Delegating responsibility." Those with higher numbers are more comfortable delegating. Those with lower numbers will need help sharing responsibilities and sharing control.

Now ask them to turn to "Steps for Planning" (see p. 160). Review the steps and tips. These steps and tips and the action plan will be helpful when they plan activities.

7. Leading a Meeting
(10 minutes)

DIRECTIONS:

Tell the full group: As part of striving toward youth ownership and adult-youth partnership in youth ministry, you should have opportunities to lead meetings of the youth group, youth council, leadership/care groups, planning groups, and so forth. Some of you will be in a position to lead meetings at school, for clubs or organizations, and in your workplaces.

There are many kinds of leadership. Organizations and meetings need people to call everyone together, make announcements, introduce activities, give directions, call on people for reports, and be responsible for the flow of the meeting. Meetings also need people who are supportive of ideas, who encourage others to contribute, who are general morale boosters, and who, in these various ways, are also responsible for the flow of the meeting.

Ask the participants to look at "Tips for Leading a Meeting" (see p. 161). Review the tips together. Ask the following:

What do you think is the hardest part of leading a meeting?
Would you be willing to take a leadership role in a meeting? In what way? What would you be willing to do?
What can we do to help each other when one of us is leading?

8. Discovering Other Areas of Leadership
(10 minutes)

You'll need newsprint and a marker to list ideas from the participants, and participants will list them in their notebooks.

DIRECTIONS:

The entire group should turn in their notebooks to "Other Areas of Leadership" (see p. 162), and write their responses as directed below:

What are other leadership roles in which youth can participate? List these roles in the first column. Examples are as follows: leading in prayer; reading scripture from the pulpit; calling others to sign up for a mission trip.

For each of these roles, list in the second column what is needed to prepare for that role. For example, for both leading in prayer and reading scripture, the preparation may simply be practice; for calling others to sign up for a mission trip, the preparation may be making the commitment, building up enthusiasm about the mission, and setting time aside to make calls.

9. Evaluating
(15 minutes)

DIRECTIONS:

Begin by asking the participants the following questions:

Why do we need to evaluate?
What kinds of questions would be helpful in an evaluation? (Possible answers are the following: What did you like about it? What would you change if we do it again? Did we meet our objectives? How did the participants respond? How did the leaders do? What could have helped them? How are we doing?)

Tell the group that good leaders learn from mistakes, from failures. In fact they don't look at mistakes as failures. They look at them as opportunities to learn how to improve. When an activity or program is weak, it usually shows us where we need to redirect our energy. Perhaps we misread the needs of our group. Or perhaps timing was bad. If we don't evaluate, we may make a wrong judgment. We may end up giving up on something for the wrong reasons. Evaluating with a group is essential if we are going to be faithful to our calling. The primary evaluation question for youth ministry is, Are we doing what God has called us to do?

Participants are to turn to "Suggestions for Evaluating" (see p. 163), and review the suggestions. Then invite the group to use the evaluation form in their notebooks to evaluate this leadership training event (see p. 164). Participants should turn in their evaluation forms when they finish.

10. Taking It Home
(10 minutes)

With the total group, talk about ways to take the learnings from the lock-in back to your youth ministry. Ask the following questions: What will happen next? What do we need to do to encourage people to use their leadership skills? List the participants' ideas on newsprint.

11. Closing Worship
(20 minutes)

PREPARATION FOR WORSHIP:

Participants will need their Bibles, pencils, gifts sheet (see p. 150) and "Jesus as Servant Leader" (see p. 165). Each person will need a slip of paper for the offering of gifts.

Participants are to get into the same smaller groups they were in for activities 3 and 6 and do the following:

Everyone is to read 1 Corinthians 12:12–27.
Each group has twenty minutes to come up with a way to creatively interpret the scripture. Group members can act it out, sing it, dance it, whatever.
Everyone should look at their gift sheet and pick one gift to offer to God to be used in service to other people.

WORSHIP:

Gather together in a circle for worship. Break the circle to allow space for the groups to present their interpretations of the scripture.

Opening Prayer—Have the two people lead who were asked earlier to handle this responsibility.
Act Out the Scripture—Each group presents its interpretation of 1 Corinthians 12:12–27.
Offering Our Gifts—Distribute paper and pencils. Participants are to write the gift they will offer to God so that God can use it through them to accomplish God's work. They fold the slip of paper and place it in the center of the circle, or at the foot of the cross (if you have one), as an act of offering of their gifts and talents to God.
Affirming Our Gifts in Prayer—With everyone in a circle, pray an affirmation prayer in this way: Choose a person. Everyone is to focus on this person. They are to affirm this person's gifts, talents, and abilities in prayer by saying, "I am thankful for (name) for her (gift/talent)." Each person mentions a gift or ability that the person has. It is not necessary to go around the circle in order. Let anyone who wishes to speak, do so. If your group

is too large, make two circles. Everyone should have a chance to be the focus of this prayer. A designated person closes by praying that God will use each of the gifts and talents offered.

Closing Response—As a closing, use "Jesus as Servant Leader" (see p. 165), as a litany. Divide the group in half; one half is to read part 1 and the other half should read part 2.

Final Note

Remember that this is just a start on leadership development. It doesn't stop here. Adults and young people, together in partnership, need to be constantly assessing the leadership needs of the variety of young people who make up your youth ministry. Your goal is that everyone be given a chance, an opportunity to try on leadership roles at some point, in some way, and to use the God-given gifts each one possesses. As a result, young people and adults together will experience the joy, the challenge, and the passion of responding to God's call to be faithful and to love and serve in the context of youth ministry.

SEVEN

Youth Ministry: Dreamed

In chapters 7, 8, and 9 we will take you through a process for developing a three-dimensional youth ministry. We call it Youth Ministry: Dreamed, Developed, and Delivered. A solid youth ministry needs all three dimensions: (1) dreaming: of what youth ministry can be; (2) developing: the plans to carry out the dream; and (3) delivering: to the youth, the church, and the world. Delivering is doing what needs to be done to make it all happen.

This process combines things we have done at our own churches with accents from other churches. We don't want to call it a model. Although it is a model, we don't want you to feel locked into doing it one way. In this chapter we will concentrate on the dreaming stage of the process.

> Youth ministry is an art, not a science.

There's one more thing to say before we get into dreaming. Sometimes what we suggest may seem dogmatic or cut-and-dried, in that we want to give you concrete ideas, structures, and systems, the how-tos. We give you several options in the hope of hitting on something that is right for your situation. But there are limits. We can't prescribe what is right for every situation. We must leave it with you to seek God's guidance and to begin to paint a picture, a unique masterpiece, that is your church's youth ministry.

Think about the difference between painting by numbers and creating a masterpiece. We can give you a canvas with numbers. We can give you brushes and a variety of colors. The result will be a painting, but it won't be a masterpiece. Only you and other young people and adults who have the same commitment and enthusiasm can take your vision of youth ministry, your unique situation, your call from God, and create a masterpiece. Your strokes are unique; your choice of brushes and colors unique. So we encourage you to approach your canvas, ready to discover what God is calling you to do with it.

Youth Ministry: Dreamed

Let's see, you've got your essentials, your biblical basis, your goal of youth ownership, and some ideas on how to develop youth in leadership. So all you need to do is put it all together, right? If your response is, "You must be dreaming," that's a good answer. Dreaming is the place to start; it is the beginning of the creative process. Dreaming is where we need to begin with youth ministry.

We always tell people to dream big. What do you want your youth ministry to look like? What do you want for the youth in your church? Dream about what youth ministry can be. Describe it. What does your dream include? Again, dream big. Stretch your imagination and creativity. You'll be surprised at what's possible.

Spending time in the dreaming stage helps young people and adult leaders form the vision for youth ministry. It is through dreaming that groups figure out their purpose. Goals emerge from the dreaming stage.

Who Dreams?

Everybody dreams. You who are reading this book and the adults and young people with whom you will share these ideas all dream. An adult-youth leadership team dreams. An adult leadership team dreams. A youth council or youth ministry committee dreams. All the young people—those in youth group, those in Sunday school, those involved in various activities in the church, and even those who are on the membership rolls who have not been seen in a while—should have an opportunity to dream. All of these people should have a shot at doing some dreaming of what youth ministry will look like in your church.

When Do You Dream?

Groups can dream at any time during the year. There's never a bad time to take stock of where you are and where you want to go. It doesn't have to be in the fall. Ideally, if your dreams are to relate to the fall program, your dreaming stage should have occurred in the previous spring or summer. If you're on top of things, winter is a good time to dream about the next year.

But often you don't get your act together until fall. Maybe you've been busy recruiting adult leaders; maybe you're working hard to bring young people in; maybe you've just procrastinated. In any case, dreaming doesn't happen. So of course dreaming can take place in September. In fact, engaging young people in creating their own youth ministry in the fall, when the school year is fresh and new, and everyone is determined to start the year right, is not a bad idea.

You could do one of the dreaming exercises at a kickoff event, like a cookout. This sets the tone for youth involvement. It says to the youth, "We are serious about wanting input from all of you." It tells them that you are serious about moving toward youth-driven youth ministry. If not at a kickoff event, you could do a dreaming exercise at one of the first Sunday night meetings of the year.

If you are in the middle of the year, and things have gotten bogged down, do a dreaming exercise to get the youth fired up. There's never a bad time to dream.

How Do You Dream?

Suggesting to a group of youth and adults that they dream can be as disastrous as saying to a youth group, What do you want to do? You get a lot of blank stares. Young people have a hard time coming up with something from nothing. Often they'll suggest an activity they did the year before: "Well, we can go bowling," or "Let's talk about dating." Sometimes there's a broken-record response of "Let's go to the beach."

Young people and adults need help in learning how to dream. The four dreaming activities on pages 79–81 are options for getting young people and adult leaders to dream about youth ministry. Since they are options, you won't be using all four at once. You may use the second activity, the "Toy Exercise," at a retreat this year, and the fourth, "Questions to Explore," at next year's retreat.

Or you could use one activity with your youth council and another with the total youth membership. The questions in the first activity can be used in conversations with young people who have not been very active. For instance, the question, "What would a great youth ministry look like?" is helpful in talking with young people who have quit being involved because they don't like their group. Many of these youth would feel important and cared for if approached with this question.

Before doing any of the activities, talk about the importance of dreaming to help everyone get excited about the possibilities and not be limited to what has been done in the past. Dreaming also helps people shape a vision and establish goals.

Goal setting is often a difficult task, but young people can be encouraged to state goals in their own way. One group stated its goal this way: "We want our youth ministry to be: (1) youth-owned and youth-driven; (2) led by a partnership of youth and adults; (3) a safe place where youth can try on new roles, feel welcomed, and be challenged to grow in faith; (4) a caring youth ministry; (5) an outreaching youth ministry."

Adapt the suggestions in this book to your own situation. For example, if your youth ministry is focused on finding various avenues for young people to be involved in the church and not in a "group" per se, then the term "youth group" may not apply. "Sunday night" may not apply, if the main activity of your youth ministry is on a weeknight.

How to Encourage Dreaming: Four Activities

Brainstorm Needs, Wants, Vision, Themes

The questions in this exercise can help young people discover how they feel about their youth ministry. These questions encourage them to explore what their needs are, what they want, and what direction their youth program should take.

- What would a stranger say about our youth or youth group if that person walked into our meeting on a regular Sunday night?
- What do you want for the youth in our church?
- What would a great youth ministry look like?
- What themes or emphases should we highlight (or work on) this year?
- Each of you is called by God to do youth ministry. What do you feel called to do in youth ministry?
- What do you need from our church in order to grow in faith?
- What struggles do you face on a day-to-day basis?

DIRECTIONS:
There are several ways to do this exercise:

1. Write each question at the top of a sheet of newsprint and invite everyone to answer. List all answers. Discuss answers as they are given. This should be done only with smaller groups or in groups in which the individuals are used to speaking up.

2. In small groups of three or four, ask each question. One person records the answers. It is often easier for people to talk in smaller groups. Each group then reports answers to the larger group.

3. On the walls or on tables, provide newsprint sheets, each with one of the questions printed at the top of the sheet. Each participant takes a marker and writes answers to the questions on the newsprint sheets. After twenty minutes display the sheets for everyone to read. Ask if anyone would like to add to any of the sheets. Discuss the answers. In this method participants individually write their answers. If a person is not comfortable speaking, he or she does not have to.

Toy Exercise: On Ownership

The second activity, the "Toy Exercise," is a short simulation game in which the participants pretend that a toy is a real object. The participants are to act as owners of the objects. As owners, they need to decide what they are going to do with their object and how they are going to take care of it. The purpose of this step in the activity is to allow participants to experience a feeling of ownership. The hope is that once they experience ownership, they will recognize the need to take care of that which they own.

The second step in the exercise is to make the transference of the "ownership feeling" to youth ministry. The ownership principle is as follows: If you own something, then you make decisions about it and you take care of it. If you own your youth ministry, then you will decide what to do with it and how to take care of it.

This exercise works best in smaller groups that meet in one big room. It can be done in groups as small as three or as large as eight. If you have more than eight participants, divide into smaller groups. Ideally adults and young people should be in each group. Give each group a toy car, jeep, motorcycle, truck, boat, or horse, and paper and pencils. Begin by giving the following directions, without explaining the reason for doing the exercise.

DIRECTIONS:
1. "Owning the Toy": Tell the groups that the toy is a model of something they could actually own. (Their small group is the owner of the object.) They have twenty minutes to respond to the following questions:

- If you, the group, really owned the car (or boat, or horse, or whatever), what are five things you would do with it? List these.
- Since you own it, what are five things you need to do to take care of it? List these.

- Devise a system for doing the five things you want to do with it and for taking care of it. (This is the hardest question, and they will struggle with it.)

Invite each group to briefly share its lists with the other groups.

2. "Owning Youth Ministry": At this point the participants are to relate the toy exercise on ownership to youth ministry. Invite someone to record answers on newsprint. Explain to the whole group that one of the goals of youth ministry (or PYC or MYF or whatever you happen to call your youth ministry) is that it be owned by all the young people. Ask the following questions:

- As you did for your "toy," think of five things you can do with your youth ministry.
- What are five things you need to do to take care of your youth ministry? This question should draw out insightful and helpful responses. The young people may never have thought about taking care of their youth ministry. They may never have thought about what it means to have ownership.
- What kind of a system could you develop for doing both—taking care of it and for carrying out what you want to do with it?

If there is a system or structure already in place for planning and carrying out your youth ministry, this is the time for the group to evaluate that system. Does the system enable youth to have ownership? What would need to be changed in order for young people to have ownership?

The Five Areas

The third activity to stimulate dreaming uses the brainstorming technique. This exercise is based on a general goal for youth ministry: that all youth be given opportunities to be involved in the total life of the church. Total life is defined using five areas: worship, explorations, ministry within the congregation, service, and fellowship. This exercise gives young people a chance to look at—and dream about—the needs, themes, emphases, programs, events, and activities of their youth ministry.

DIRECTIONS:

1. Begin by listing the participants' answers to the following three questions, using a separate newsprint sheet for responses to each question:

- What are the needs of our youth?
- What themes and emphases should we consider for the year?
- What aspects of our youth ministry are ongoing or traditions? For example, Sunday night fellowship, Sunday school, Bible study, weeknight discussion groups, choirs, Scouts, leading worship, career guidance, sports teams, mission/service projects, retreats, Youth Sunday, confirmation.

Distribute as a handout photocopies of pages 176–177 from appendix 3, "The Five Areas" and the "Five Areas Worksheet." The suggested goals and issues to consider should help young people and adults think of what they would like to do in these areas.

2. Introduce and discuss the five-area concept, which offers a guide for developing a balanced youth ministry program. The five areas are the following: worship, explorations, ministry within the congregation, service, and fellowship. (If your church has a different set of areas already in place, use them.)

3. In groups of four or five, participants are to fill out the left side of the "Five Areas Worksheet," "What We Have Done." Ask them to list all the activities that have been done in each area in the past year in your youth ministry. On the right side, "What We Want to Do," they list all the things they would like to do in the coming year in each area.

4. Participants return to the larger group and do the following:

- Ask them, as a total group, to quickly create a list on newsprint of all the activities that have been done in each area.
- Then look at all the activities. Ask the following questions: Is this a balanced youth ministry? In which area should there be more activities?
- Ask for the participants' ideas of what could be done in each area. List all their suggestions on newsprint.

5. Still working with the larger group, ask them to do the appropriate activities:

- If this group is the decision-making group, then begin making decisions regarding theme and special emphases or goals for the year.
- Prioritize the suggestions in each area of activities for the coming year. Choose the activities.
- If this group is not the decision-making group, then discuss theme and special emphases or goals, and prioritize suggestions in each area of activities

(without choosing the activities). Send recommendations to the decision-making group (i.e., the youth council).

Questions to Explore

This fourth exercise offers the young people and adults a chance to explore needs, issues, and activities, using specific questions. The questions reflect issues that relate to the five areas of church life described on the handout (see appendix 3, pp. 176–177). This exercise offers another way to prime the pump, to get youth and adults talking about what their youth ministry will look like in the coming year.

PREPARATION:

Write the following ten questions, one each at the top of a newsprint sheet:

1. What are three questions you have about God or the Bible that you'd like to discuss?
2. What are three ways to worship God?
3. What are three topics you'd like to learn more about?
4. What are three things you worry about?
5. What are three questions you have about your church?
6. What are three ways to be a better Christian?
7. What are three issues or problems in your community or world that you care about?
8. What are three things we could do as a group to help other people?
9. What are three ways our youth could become closer as friends?
10. What are three problems group members face in everyday life?

You may want to add or substitute your own questions.

DIRECTIONS:

1. Have the newsprint sheets on the floor or tables—somewhere that everyone can stop and view them. The participants are to rotate around the room in groups of three, stopping at each sheet for three minutes to add their ideas.

2. Have the participants do one of the two suggestions that follow:

- Small groups could take two or three of the sheets and review the comments, discuss activities that relate to the comments, and then share their ideas for activities with the whole group.
- If there are enough participants to have five groups, assign each group an area (worship, explorations, ministry within the congregation, service, fellowship). Assign specific questions to each area group. Distribute the newsprint sheets accordingly: To the worship group, questions 1 and 2; to explorations, 3 and 4; to ministry within the congregation, 5 and 6; to service, 7 and 8; to fellowship, 9 and 10. Discuss activities that relate to the comments. Some activities may overlap areas. Small groups then share their ideas for activities with the whole group.

Dream Yearly

Dreaming needs to be done each year, but you don't want to do the same exercise every year. We have been pleased that in our experimentation with the toy exercise, it has worked well in every group and in each situation. However, we know that people would get sick of that exercise if it were used every year. At the same time, we don't believe it's an exercise that gets used once with a group and then discarded.

Discuss with the young people whether the toy exercise should be used again the following year, take a break for a year, or perhaps become an every-third-year event.

A Youth Council Dreams

Dreaming happens best in an organized group. Many churches are finding the need for some form of governing body for youth ministry. In small churches the entire youth membership can be that body. If you have fifteen or more active young people, however, it may be time to explore the possibilities of having a youth council.

We recommend the creation of a youth council or youth ministry committee for the following reasons:

1. Without a council, adult leadership may make all the decisions. With a council, young people are involved in all the decision making.

2. Council members are responsible and accountable for youth ministry.

3. A council gives young people opportunities for leadership.

4. A council connects youth ministry to the life of the church and to other committees. In many churches the youth council is responsible to the Christian education committee.

The following suggestions are ways to form a youth council or youth ministry committee:

• All the adult leaders and representative youth (one or two from each class)
• An equal number of youth and adult leaders, and a representative from the session or church board
• One or two youth representatives from each class and eight adults, as follows:

  the coordinator of the senior highs

  the coordinator of the junior highs

  a junior high adult leader

  a senior high adult leader

  a junior high Sunday school teacher

  a senior high Sunday school teacher

  a junior high parent

  a senior high parent

The council or committee needs a moderator or co-moderators. Co-moderators could be an adult and a youth person. Or they could be seniors. We have found that having two seniors as co-moderators is helpful, for keeping the senior class active. Many churches lose seniors because of the seniors' commitments.

The council or committee should meet monthly or once every six weeks and be responsible for:

• Looking at needs of youth
• Setting the direction for youth ministry
• Implementing the system to carry out youth ministry
• Doing long-range planning
• Evaluating youth ministry
• Advocating youth concerns
• Connecting youth ministry to other programs relating to youth—choir, Sunday school, Scouts, church sports leagues

It is important that the council be composed of either equal numbers of young people and adults, or more young people than adults. The aim is for the young people to gain ownership and develop leadership.

A youth council is the logical group with which to start the dreaming stage. We suggest that the group meet for a day retreat to dream of what youth ministry can be. After the members have worked through their vision and hopes for youth ministry, they can take their ideas to the rest of the young people. (A complete description of such a day retreat is found in appendix 2.)

Not every church has a youth council. In churches that do not, the dreaming can be carried out by all the young people together. To begin, adult leaders can recruit a couple of young people, share the ideas in this chapter with them, and together lead all the young people through the dreaming stage.

The sample Youth Council Day Retreat in appendix 2 can be used by all churches, those with or without youth councils. Churches without youth councils can have the day retreat with the entire youth membership, or with as many young people and adult leaders as possible.

Making the Dreams Come True

It's fun to dream. The dreaming stage energizes both young people and adult leaders. Everybody gets excited that a dynamic youth ministry is a real possibility. Great ideas emerge.

The next question is: How do you make the dreams come true? A structure or system is needed. During the day retreat the young people and their adult leaders explore ways to structure youth ministry. They create a system that will make the dreams come true. That system will determine how all the young people can be involved in carrying out their youth ministry.

The next chapter looks at the developing stage, how to develop a youth ministry that will involve all young people and adult leaders in making the dreams come true.

EIGHT

Youth Ministry: Developed

The day retreat is over. The youth council has dreamed of what youth ministry can be. It has defined what needs to happen in order for the dreams to come true. It has found a system that will enable all young people to own their youth ministry and take care of it. Now what? What happens next? How do the rest of the young people get on board? What's involved in developing youth ministry?

In this chapter, we follow a youth council, the youth council from Community Church, as it moves through the developing stage. We look at the council's day retreat follow-up meeting at which the council decides how it will take the day retreat ideas to the rest of the young people. We describe leadership/care groups and how they function. We look at a senior high kickoff event for youth ministry. We also look at a calendar for youth ministry and see how it was developed. And most important, we see how the youth council attempts to get the rest of the young people on board.

Getting Everyone on Board

The first step in the developing stage is to invite all youth to share in the dreaming process. All those who attend the day retreat then have the responsibility of sharing what happened at the retreat with the rest of the young people and engaging them in the dreaming process. This is an important step in developing youth ministry. In order to attain ownership, everyone needs to be "in on it" from the beginning. If youth council members merely tell everyone what they're going to do, it's the same as if an adult leader makes all the decisions and tells the youth what they're going to do. In this case, it's youth council–owned, instead of adult-owned. By including everyone from the beginning, all the young people get the chance to own the dreams and plans for youth ministry.

Day Retreat Follow-Up Meeting

Those who attend the day retreat need to have a follow-up meeting sometime between the day retreat and the first full youth group meeting of the year. What follows is a list of what needs to happen at this meeting and a description of what Community Church's youth council decided to do to bring the rest of the youth group on board.

1. *Decide how to share the goals, dreams, plans, and hopes they have for the year.* Community Church's youth council decided that the best way to give the rest of the youth a chance to own youth ministry was to lead the "Toy Exercise" (see pp. 79–80) at the fall kickoff event. There the council members would share the balanced program concept, that is,

having an equal number of activities in worship, explorations, ministry within the congregation, service, and fellowship (see pp. 80–81).

2. *Decide how to give the rest of the young people an opportunity to have input in dreaming and in choosing activities.* Instead of having the youth fill out the "Five Areas Worksheet" (p. 177), Community Church council members decided to share their ideas in each area and get comments from the group. They decided also that new ideas for activities would be welcomed and that everyone would vote for five activities in each area (to take place between September and May). The council would meet right after the kickoff to put these activities on a calendar.

3. *Examine the system to see if it is what the council wants to recommend.* Does the system cover all aspects of youth ministry? List all the programs of youth ministry: regular meetings, music, drama, Sunday school, Bible studies, mission projects, special events, and so on. Do all these programs fit into the system? What needs to be done to connect programs that don't fit? Youth ministry is more than just youth group meetings. Every church needs to figure out how all the parts of the program fit together. Identify who is responsible for what. For example, music may have its own separate structure. That's okay, as long as everyone is conscious of the need for youth ministry to be inclusive of other programs that affect and include the youth. The youth council needs to address this issue.

4. *Decide how to share the system for doing youth ministry and for caring for it.* Community Church council members decided that at the kickoff two youth members and one adult council member would describe leadership/care groups as the system they chose for carrying out youth ministry and for caring for it. Each class would be a leadership/care group. The council would then seek a consensus vote on having leadership/care groups as the system.

Robert and I have an interesting way of taking a consensus vote. We ask if group members can "live with" a decision. Unless someone absolutely cannot "live with it," the decision stands. If a person cannot live with it, we work on changes.

5. *Plan the fall kickoff events for junior and senior highs.* Using the steps in the "Action Plan," page 159, the youth council planned the kickoff event. They decided to have two separate cookouts, one for junior highs and one for senior highs on the same evening. These events would be led respectively by junior high council members and senior high council members. The cookouts would start with group builders, followed by a blessing, supper, and the meeting.

6. *Decide who will lead the activities at that meeting.* Several youth council members agreed to lead the various activities. There would be an adult-youth partnership leading at each cookout.

Leadership/Care Groups

The system we advocate is leadership/care groups. In this system the entire youth membership is divided into groups for the purposes of (1) carrying out what they want to do with their youth ministry, and (2) taking care of their youth ministry. The groups can be as small as two or as large as fifteen. If, for instance, a church has five young people on the membership roll, then two leadership/care groups can be formed. Responsibility for planning and leading activities would be divided in half.

How Leadership/Care Groups Are Structured

Leadership/care groups work well when structured in any of the following ways:

1. *Well-mixed groups.* The youth membership is arbitrarily divided into groups. Each group has relatively equal numbers of youth from each grade. Each has a balance of very active and not-so-active youth. Each has a balance of personalities—from aggressive to shy. Each has a balance of males and females.

2. *Grade groups.* The youth membership is divided by classes. Each grade group serves as a leadership/care group. Freshmen would meet together to plan and lead an activity for which they are responsible. Sophomores would meet together, and so on. (If there are more than fifteen in a grade, that grade could be divided into more than one leadership/care group.)

3. *By areas.* The membership is divided into as many groups as the church has areas of ministry. According to our team approach, there would be five

groups, to correspond to the five areas: worship, explorations, ministry within the congregation, service, and fellowship. These groups would be responsible for planning and leading activities in their respective areas. This option gives groups a chance to specialize and learn about a particular area of ministry. Membership of these area groups could be either well-mixed or grade groups. If grade groups, and there are four grades, then make some adjustment to accommodate the five areas. One option is for each grade to take one of the first four areas and all four groups to add a fellowship activity as part of their responsibility. Another option is to combine ministry within the congregation and worship, or ministry and service.

Who Leads the Leadership/Care Groups?

Whenever possible a young person and an adult should lead the leadership/care group. Or two youth and an adult, or better yet, two youth and two adults. Youth council members are logical choices for care group leaders. Or any young person can volunteer to lead their group. Ask the young people how to structure the leadership and the groups.

Who Drafts the Membership of Each Group?

Adult leaders who know the young people should start the process of assigning youth to groups. The youth council should have input and approval.

When I started using this system, I drafted the groups myself, because I was afraid that, if left to the youth council, the council members would arrange to be with their best friends and the result would be some strong groups, some weak groups, some popular groups and some unpopular groups.

After a few years, I realized that if I was to buy into youth ownership, I had to give up control of creating the groups. But I still feared turning it over to the young people. I found the answer in the concept of adult-youth partnership. I still draw up the groups initially, but the youth council co-moderators, which happen to be seniors, have been given the authority

by the council to rearrange the groups. We work on the groups together.

The beauty of this adult-youth partnership is that the council moderators own the concept of mixing the groups to avoid cliques and to make it easier for new people to feel included. They are highly conscious of wanting everyone to be comfortable with their groups. The moderators know most of the young people, so they do a good job of mixing the groups.

Every young person on your membership rolls needs to be in a leadership/care group. Include those young people you never see. Even if they never show up for a group meeting, at least they are not forgotten; someone is looking at their names regularly. And someone should be contacting them now and then. Don't give up on any young person, unless an inactive person tells you to remove her or his name.

What Leadership/Care Groups Do

The purposes of the leadership/care groups are first to plan and lead the activities of your youth ministry. The number of activities each group plans and leads depends on how many leadership/care groups and how many activities you have. The second purpose is to serve the needs of the leadership/care group. That's the caring function.

For one year the members of each leadership/care group get to know each other, pray for each other, and encourage each other to fulfill God's call to be faithful disciples by participating in the church, in youth ministry, and in leadership. This system enables young people to care for one another and to keep track of every single young person, so that no one is left out. If someone new starts coming to activities, assign her or him to a leadership/care group.

Young people can grow very close to one another in a group of this kind, which could be just what is needed in your youth ministry. Young people need to find a safe place where they can be themselves. If that place is not found in a larger group, then the leadership/care group may be the place where personal and spiritual growth occurs. Besides the planning and leading function, leadership/care groups could meet for Bible study and for the sharing of highlights and lowlights from the past week. In this case, groups would need to meet frequently.

Since leadership/care groups need plenty of time to plan, group members need to calculate how far ahead they should start planning a particular activity. Even though activities should be planned well in advance, we have found that young people are less enthusiastic when they plan an activity that is months away.

Groups should use action plans (see p. 159). Action plans make planning easier. All steps and responsibilities are listed on action plans. Moreover, people's names are on action plans, so that everyone knows who has agreed to do what. Leadership responsibilities must be clear.

When Leadership/ Care Groups Meet

Options for when and how often leadership/care groups meet include the following:

1. A designated night of the week could be planning night. Each leadership/care group decides how many nights it will need to get the planning done.

2. For churches that have midweek congregational suppers, groups could meet and eat together.

3. Groups could meet after the regular Sunday night or weekly meeting.

4. Each group could set its own planning schedule. One group might choose to meet on a weeknight, another after Sunday night activities, another after a weeknight Bible study, another after Sunday morning worship (for lunch).

5. Once a quarter, a regular Sunday night meeting could be reserved for planning. All leadership/ care groups could meet at that time. *Caution:* Don't set aside more than three Sunday nights a year for planning. The young people might see youth ministry as: "All we do is plan. We don't ever *do* anything."

6. Groups could meet for ten minutes at the beginning of every regular youth meeting to discuss a question, or to check on how things are going. They could stay after a regular meeting one night to do their planning.

Design the System to Fit Your Needs

This system of leadership/care groups is just a suggestion. You may have a system already in place. Design the system to fit your needs. It often takes trial and error to find out what that system is. Sometimes the system will change from year to year. It probably would not go through a complete metamorphosis each year, but minor adjustments may be needed. Don't feel that you should do youth ministry the same way forever.

Whatever system is chosen, it should do the following:

Give young people and adult leaders responsibility for youth ministry (a partnership venture).
Develop leadership among young people. Young people should be given as much opportunity to lead as they are willing to lead.
Provide a way for young people to care for one another.

The Kickoff Event: The Cookout

What follows is a description of the senior high kickoff meeting, planned and led by the youth council of Community Church.

1. **Sign My Card.** For an icebreaker, a council member handed out the "Sign My Card" sheets and invited the young people to mingle and get signatures (see appendix 5, p. 204).

2. **Supper.** Another council member led the group in prayer. Then supper—hot dogs and chicken breasts—was served.

3. **Introductions.** The co-moderators introduced the youth council members and the adult leaders. (Two of the adult leaders are members of Community Church's youth council.) As part of the introductions, the council members told what kind of pet they had, including the pet's name (if a person had no pet, then the most recent live animal they'd seen near their house). Adult leaders named a pet they had had when they were teenagers (or animal near their house).

4. **Toy Exercise.** A council member had everyone line up alphabetically according to first names. Small groups of five were formed by having the first five in

line become a group, the next five, and so on. A council member introduced this exercise and handed each group a toy. The groups did the first part of the exercise, on ownership (see pp. 79–80).

5. **Report of Results of the Day Retreat.** With everyone together, a council member explained how all the youth are the owners of their youth ministry. Together with two other council members (one adult and one young person), the council member shared the lists of "what to do with our youth ministry" and "how to take care of our youth ministry" (the lists were compiled at the day retreat). Council members explained the leadership/care group system and recommended that leadership/care groups plan and lead activities in five areas. Everyone was invited to add ideas and make suggestions. After working out the details, the group agreed to adopt the system.

6. **Choosing Activities.** The three council members shared the five newsprint sheets listing activities in the five areas of church life: worship, explorations, ministry within the congregation, service, and fellowship. (On each sheet the council had prioritized the ideas.) They also displayed the calendars on which council had begun scheduling activities.

   The youth were invited to add ideas. Discussion followed. The young people chose by consensus the activities they'd like to do during the year (the school year). The council members encouraged the group to work toward a balanced calendar with equal numbers of activities in all five areas.

7. **Leadership/Care Groups.** A council member explained how leadership/care groups would function. The council recommended that the groups be structured by grade. Discussion followed. A vote was taken, and grade groups approved. Council members announced that during the next week everyone would meet for group build-

ing. In two weeks, there would be a leadership lock-in. In three weeks, the leadership/care groups would meet and choose activities to plan and lead.

8. **Closing.** An adult and a young person led the group in a prayer and song, which could become a ritual closing. In three weeks, everyone would decide on the closing.

Comments on the Kickoff

Notice that the kickoff was led by young people and adults in partnership. This is good modeling.

It is important that everyone, all the young people, know how the system will work, how it will accomplish their dreams. Everyone needs to understand how planning will happen, how leadership will be decided, and how caring for one another will become a reality through the use of the system.

After the system was introduced, the young people discussed it. Again and again we have seen young people come up with the way to make a system work. If there are problems, they figure out the solutions. When they come up with the ideas and the solutions, they have ownership. That's how ownership happens.

Other Options for Activities during the Kickoff

Besides the "Toy Exercise," three other dreaming exercises described in chapter 7 can be used with the entire youth membership at the beginning of the year:

1. "Brainstorm Needs, Wants, Vision, Themes," page 79.

2. "The Five Areas," pages 80–81.

3. "Questions to Explore," page 81.

Creating a Calendar

Immediately after the kickoff cookout, the youth council of Community Church met to put additional activities on the calendar. The calendar spanned September through May.

A Full Year's Calendar?

There are two schools of thought on calendars. One is that you should plan the whole year in the fall, filling up September through May, or even September through August. If you have mission trips, choir trips, and summer conferences, then of course you need to get those on the calendar and in the works.

The other approach is to plan September through January in the fall, plan February through May in January, and plan summer sometime in the winter. The concern is that, if activities are planned too far ahead, young people may lose their enthusiasm by the date an activity is scheduled. For example, at a fall meeting, the young people may suggest exploring anger on March 13, but by the time March rolls around, anger is not a hot issue. Then it's very difficult to get the youth to plan and lead the March 13 program.

Probably the best solution is a compromise. Get as much as possible on the full year's calendar. Seasonal events, traditions, and trips need to be scheduled early. As for the nitty-gritty planning, concentrate on a quarter at a time. And always be flexible. Something may happen to one of the young people, like a death or suicide of a friend, which needs everyone's attention. Or something may happen that's in the news, like a flood or earthquake. The young people can help. Something may happen in the church, like a special celebration. The young people need to be a part of it. Be flexible enough to change plans and change the calendar.

It's good for the church, good for the young people and their families, and good for the congregation to see a calendar full of activities. It says, "Hey, there's a lot going on with the youth in this church."

A Balanced Program

Work toward a balanced program. If an activity for March 13 has not been chosen, first decide what *kind* of activity to have. If fellowship and recreation have been emphasized in February, then maybe it's time for an explorations activity. Make a note on the calendar: "an explorations activity."

Choosing Activities

Activities can be chosen in four ways:

1. Activities are chosen at a fall retreat by all the young people. At the retreat, five stations/tables, representing the five areas of church life, are set up around the room. On the first rotation, the youth, who are in groups of three or more, spend five minutes visiting each station, reading the list of ideas, and adding their own ideas. On the second rotation, the young people return to each station and vote for their top four activities in each area.

2. Activities are chosen by five leadership/care groups. Each group is responsible for one of the five areas. The members of each group come up with ideas in their area and present the list to all the young people. The youth add more. The leadership/care group then chooses the activities it recommends and presents the three or four suggestions to everyone for approval. The leadership/care groups are then responsible for planning and leading those activities. For instance, one leadership/care group is responsible for planning all the worship-related activities. Another plans and leads all explorations activities. And so on. When each group concentrates on an area for the year, it can be a tremendous learning experience.

3. This option is similar to the second option, except there are four groups. Each is responsible for one of four areas—worship, explorations, ministry within the congregation, and service. In addition, all four groups plan and lead a fellowship activity.

4. The youth council comes up with the ideas for each area and takes them to all the youth for changes and approval. Then from all the areas, the leadership/care groups choose the activities they will plan and lead. It goes something like this: All the young people look at five large newsprint lists of chosen activities under all five areas. One leadership/care group goes first and chooses an activity. Then the next group chooses one. And so on, until all activities are taken. The groups are encouraged to keep a balance in their

choices, so that one group is not planning all fellowship activities and another all explorations.

The fourth option was chosen by the Community Church youth council.

Planning Ahead

Encourage the leadership/care groups to avoid the "What are we going to do Sunday night? It's our turn, and we've got to come up with something" routine. Planning ahead gives the groups time to publicize and promote what they're doing. It keeps the groups from getting stuck with weak programs and a poor leadership experience. They should use action plans.

Identifying Potential Problems in the Calendar

Once the calendars are completed (or mostly completed), check out the questionables. If, for example, the young people want to work on a Habitat for Humanity house, someone needs to find out when the youth can work on a house. If the youth want to do a Sunday morning worship service, someone needs to check with the minister or worship committee. Can young people do this? Yes, of course. Young people can check on these details. They need to know the deadline for calendar completion, so they can report their findings.

Making Calendars Available to Everyone

Design the calendar. Can young people do this? Yes, the youth can design and produce the calendar. They can make huge calendars to put on bulletin boards, in the youth area, and in the general announcement areas. They can make handout-size calendars to mail to all the young people, and to friends of the young people, parents, and the congregation. If there is a church newsletter, the youth calendar should be in it.

Naming the Leadership/Care Groups on the Calendar

Since the leadership/care groups are responsible for seeing that the activities happen, their names should be on the calendar. The groups can be listed by group name (if groups have given themselves names), by grade (if leadership/care groups are in class groups), or by names of the adult and youth leaders of each group. Or list the names of everyone in each leadership/care group. In this way everyone gets equal billing. Everyone has a sense of ownership.

A Sample Calendar

On page 91 is the Community Church's complete senior high calendar. In this illustration, the senior highs have four leadership/care groups, which are by grades.

Note that the sample calendar is well-balanced in the five areas. The activities are fairly well-mixed, so that not all the serious explorations topics are lumped together. The leadership/care groups' responsibilities are not lumped together either.

When this calendar was planned and activities were chosen, the leadership/care groups kept tabs on who was doing what, so that each group had a balance of activities from the five areas. That balance is reflected in the lists of activities on page 92.

This very full list of activities is just an example. As we have said, you may choose not to plan your full year at one time. You might plan a half year, September through January, and then arrange extended planning time for the second half of the year. Evaluate the first half, and make needed changes. Check on how the leadership/care groups are doing. Evaluate youth in leadership. Make needed changes.

If you do plan the full year's calendar, more often than not, something will change. That's fine. Youth ministry must be flexible.

Senior High Calendar

	Who's Responsible
Aug. 17— Youth council day retreat (2–9 p.m.)	Group from Council
Aug. 24—Youth council follow-up meeting (6:30–8:00 p.m.)	Group from Council
Aug. 31—No activities (Labor Day weekend)	
Sept. 3 and 4—Adult leadership training	Senior high coordinator
Sept. 7—Youth kickoff cookout	Youth council
Sept. 9 and 11—Adult leadership training	Senior high coordinator
Sept. 14—Group building; care groups assigned	Youth council
Sept. 20–21—Leadership lock-in	Youth council
Sept. 28—Leadership/care groups meet	Youth council
Oct. 5—Polaroid scavenger hunt (fellowship)	Freshmen
Oct. 11–12—Fall retreat	Youth council
Oct. 19— "If I Took God Seriously . . ." (explorations)	Juniors
Oct. 26—Parent Night (ministry within the congregation)	Seniors
Oct. 30—Big Brothers–Big Sisters Halloween party (service)	Sophomores
Nov. 2—Games: Invite other churches (fellowship)	Juniors
Nov. 9—"Dealing with Prejudice" (explorations)	Sophomores
Nov. 16—"Rake 'n' Run" (ministry within the congregation)	Freshmen
Nov. 23—Worship hayride and campfire (worship)	Seniors
Nov. 28—Thanksgiving	
Nov. 30—Children's Advent festival (ministry within the congregation)	Juniors
Dec. 7—Adopt a family for Christmas; shop for the family (service)	Seniors
Dec. 14—Big Brothers–Big Sisters Christmas party (service)	Freshmen
Dec. 21—Christmas caroling (ministry within the congregation)	Sophomores
Dec. 27—No activities	
Jan. 4—Leadership/care groups meet	Youth council
Jan. 11—"Getting Along with Parents" (explorations)	Freshmen
Jan. 16–19—Snow skiing retreat (fellowship)	Seniors
Jan. 25—Souper Bowl lunch for local soup kitchen (service)	Sophomores
—Super Bowl party (fellowship)	Juniors
Feb. 1—Prepare to lead children's worship	Freshmen
Feb. 8—Lead children's worship (worship)	
—Ice skating (fellowship)	Sophomores
Feb. 15—Prepare to lead fun night for congregational	
Wednesday night supper (ministry within the congregation)	Freshmen
Feb. 18—Wednesday night supper	
Feb. 22—"Grief and Loss" (explorations)	Seniors
Feb. 25—Ash Wednesday	
Mar. 1—"Grief and Loss, Part 2"	
Mar. 7 and 8—Work on Habitat house (service)	Juniors
Mar. 14–15—District-wide spring retreat	
Mar. 22—College and Career Day (explorations)	Juniors
Mar. 29—open (fellowship)	
Apr. 5—Palm Sunday moonlight service (worship)	Sophomores
Apr. 12—Easter	
Apr. 19—Prepare for Youth Sunday	Juniors and Seniors
Apr. 26—Prepare for Youth Sunday	
May 3—Youth Sunday (worship)	
May 10—Progressive dinner (fellowship)	Freshmen
May 17—Congregational picnic	

Activities by Areas

WORSHIP
Worship hayride—Seniors
Lead children's worship—Freshmen
Moonlight service—Sophomores
Youth Sunday—Seniors and Juniors

MINISTRY WITHIN THE CONGREGATION
Parent Night—Seniors
Rake 'n' Run—Freshmen
Children's Advent festival—Juniors
Christmas caroling—Sophomores
Fun night for congregational supper—Freshmen

FELLOWSHIP
Polaroid scavenger hunt—Freshmen
Games: Invite other churches—Juniors
Snow ski retreat—Seniors
Super Bowl party—Juniors
Ice skating—Sophomores
Progressive dinner—Freshmen

EXPLORATIONS
"If I Took God Seriously . . ."—Juniors
"Dealing with Prejudice"—Sophomores
"Getting Along with Parents"—Freshmen
"Grief and Loss"—Seniors
College and Career Day—Juniors

SERVICE
Big Brothers–Big Sisters
       Halloween party—Sophomores
Adopt a family—Seniors
Big Brothers–Big Sisters Christmas party—Freshmen
Souper Bowl lunch—Sophomores
Habitat house—Juniors

Activities by Leadership/Care Groups

SENIORS
Worship hayride—Worship
Parent Night—Ministry within the congregation
Adopt a family—Service
Snow ski retreat—Fellowship
"Grief and Loss"—Explorations
Youth Sunday—Worship

SOPHOMORES
"Dealing with Prejudice"—Explorations
Christmas caroling—Ministry within the congregation
Big Brothers–Big Sisters Halloween party—Service
Souper Bowl lunch—Service
Ice skating—Fellowship
Moonlight service—Worship

JUNIORS
"If I Took God Seriously . . ."—Explorations
Children's Advent festival—
       Ministry within the congregation
Games: Invite churches—Fellowship
Super Bowl party—Fellowship
Habitat house—Service
College and Career Day—Explorations
Youth Sunday—Worship

FRESHMEN
Rake 'n' Run—Ministry within the congregation
Fun night for congregational supper—
       Ministry within the congregation
Big Brothers–Big Sisters Christmas party—Service
Polaroid scavenger hunt—Fellowship
Lead children's worship—Worship
"Getting Along with Parents"—Explorations
Progressive dinner—Fellowship

Conclusion

A lot of work goes into developing youth ministry. The youth council puts in a lot of time at the beginning of a year. All the young people and adult leaders, for that matter, put in a lot of time and energy at the beginning of the year. There's something about "beginnings" that encourage youth and adults to give it their best effort. At the beginning, everyone wants to create an exciting, faithful, youth ministry that has lots of young people involved in lots of ways.

A lot of time is expended in the beginning. And that's the way it should be, for the beginning of the year is when you'll find young people willing to give time. They are testing the waters to see if they want to commit time and energy to youth ministry this year. If they feel welcomed and needed in the development of youth ministry, then there's a good chance they'll commit to it.

In the next chapter we look at the critical delivery stage. It is crucial to be able to deliver the goods, to take the hard work of developing a terrific calendar and a system for carrying out youth ministry to the young people, and then see them respond with enthusiasm, ownership, and commitment.

NINE

Youth Ministry: Delivered

The delivering stage is when everything comes together. You have dreamed with adults and young people in various groupings. Everyone is excited about the possibilities. You have chosen a system to carry out your dreams. You have a calendar full of activities. Now how do you deliver? How do you make it happen?

In this chapter we look at key elements for making it happen—a coordinator, paying careful attention to how the year is started, good program planning, communication and publicity, building relationships, and being open to what God is doing in the midst of the young people and the adult leaders.

A Coordinator

As you can see from the sample calendar in chapter 8, each leadership/care group has plenty to do. Each group has a variety of activities to plan and lead. The challenge is to stay on top of the calendar and make sure the leadership/care groups know when their activities are coming up and when they need to meet to plan. Who does this? Who stays on top of the calendar? The youth council? Yes, but who is responsible for seeing that the youth council meets and does its job? The moderators of the council? Yes, but who contacts the moderators?

What we're looking for here is a coordinator—someone who has a grasp of the total picture, someone who is aware of all the pieces that make up the total picture.

Someone needs to coordinate youth ministry. That seems logical. So why haven't we mentioned it until now? We have not mentioned it because a coordinator is usually thought of as the person in charge. The expanded team approach is striving to get away from the top-down management style. If this book had started with instructions for a coordinator, the reader might get the impression that the coordinator is the most important component in this approach. Instead, this book is proposing an equality of leadership—equality among the adult leaders and equality between the adult leaders and the young people. We are striving for a partnership management style.

Reality, however, tells us that whoever is reading this book may be "in charge" of the youth program. Many churches hire or recruit youth ministers and youth directors to "run" youth programs. The churches expect these leaders to be in charge of youth ministry. Yet we are advocating that these youth ministers, directors, and leaders work on getting out of the "in charge" mode and into the shared partnership mode. We started this book by suggesting that the control and the responsibility of youth ministry be shared in an adult-youth partnership.

Having said that, we still recommend that someone serve as a coordinator. Someone needs to get the ball rolling, as it were. This someone, the coordinator, should be able to see the total picture and be skilled in delegation, so as to engage adult leaders, youth council, and leadership/care groups in carrying out youth ministry.

Youth ministers and youth directors are in an excellent position to be coordinators. In fact, that's exactly what they should be doing—coordinating, not running, a youth ministry.

What Coordinators Do

You, the reader, may be the one who should be coordinator or you may be the one to recruit a coordinator. In either case, the following list of coordinators' responsibilities should be useful.

1. *Coordinators become familiar with the expanded team approach, which is based on youth ownership and adult-youth partnership.* In other words, they read this book. They know what needs to be done.

2. *Coordinators communicate youth ministry to adult leaders, young people, parents, and ministers.* And they encourage other adults and young people to do the same. They become champions of adult-youth partnership and youth-owned youth ministry.

3. *Coordinators work closely with moderators of youth councils.* They meet with the moderator/s of the youth council to review items that need to be on the agenda of youth council meetings. Coordinators and moderators work together in partnership.

4. *Coordinators work closely with adult leaders.*

Coordinators help adult leaders develop their role with the young people. They encourage the adult leaders to be significant adult friends, to share power and ownership with the young people, and to encourage young people in planning and leading.

5. *Coordinators keep up with the calendar.* They make contacts and phone calls to leadership/care groups, to council members, and to adult leaders to remind them of responsibilities. They watch for conflicting dates that necessitate changes in the calendar.

6. *Coordinators set up leadership training of young people and of adult leaders.* The coordinator does not necessarily have to lead this training but should be responsible for seeing that such training takes place (see chapter 6, leadership lock-in, and chapter 11, adult leadership training).

7. *Coordinators coordinate publicity and communication.* Communication is often the missing link in the development of a solid, faithful youth ministry. It's a common scenario: Great plans are made, lots of energy is spent, and just a few people show up. It happens in many churches. People fail to use effective means of communicating. Publicity doesn't happen. Coordinators must have communication and publicity on their agenda. They remind leadership/care groups to develop a publicity plan for whatever they are planning.

Setting the Tone for the Year

Second Church finally had a dynamic youth council. Until this year, youth group had been considered boring: not much happened. This council was determined to change all that. They had spent months during the summer planning an excellent fall program. They planned a variety of fun, creative, and meaningful programs and a dynamic service project. They spent hours designing the fall retreat. And they suggested two trips—a college trip and a mystery trip. The council was so excited, for they knew everyone would want to get involved and bring friends.

The back-to-school kickoff was a cookout at a senior's house. The council members knew everyone would want to come to this particular senior's house. They envisioned everyone kicking back, hanging out, and maybe playing a little football in the backyard.

The cookout bombed. Everyone stood around, waiting for the hamburgers to be ready. Only two ju-

niors tossed the football. No one was "kicking back," enjoying being together as the council had envisioned. Instead everyone was bored . . . again . . . like last year.

What happened? It was supposed to be the start of something great. What happened was the council had neglected to consider the tone they wanted to set for the year. With such an energetic, exciting program, why didn't they start off with some energetic group builders? They had plenty of time to do so before the meal while everyone was standing around.

If they wanted the young people to bring friends, then they should have done something to intentionally mix people and help the friends feel welcome. There is nothing more awkward for new people than to have to stand around wondering if anyone will speak to them.

How the year starts is critical. Young people and adult leaders need to spend time discussing what kind of tone should be set for the year. By tone, we mean atmosphere or attitude. For instance, if one of your goals is to develop leadership among the young people, then the youth council should start the year by leading the initial activities. This models youth leadership.

If evangelism is an emphasis, start the year by reaching out. Put a strong emphasis on bringing friends or invite another church to join you in an activity in the fall. Choose activities that mix people. Talk about how to be inclusive. Be aware of and avoid actions and activities that are exclusive. Discuss what to do when a new person walks through the door.

If your activities have an aura of "boring" about them, then make sure the first activity of a meeting is a high-energy one. Start meetings with a game or active group builder. (There are suggestions in appendix 5.)

Group Building

Group-building activities are a must for starting a year. Young people usually come out in good numbers at the beginning of the year. It's fall, and everyone's off to a fresh start. There's the "I'm going to give it a try this year" attitude. So planners and leaders should make an extra effort to mix and mingle all these youth and make sure that each young person is welcomed. Young people will give it one or maybe two visits. If they don't feel included or feel some sense of belonging, or at least that they are noticed, they won't be back.

Group-building activities are fun, game-type exercises that enable young people to talk and get to know one another. Group builders are structured in such a way as to lessen the intimidation factor. They get everyone involved without putting anyone on the spot. Group-building activities are easy for young people to lead, which provides good modeling of youth as leaders. See appendix 5 for group-building ideas and appendix 6 for group-building resources.

Attitude of Youth in Leadership

In the expanded team approach, young people have many opportunities for leadership. Youth council members and leadership/care groups take various leadership roles. Teams of leaders are "in charge" of activities, which means young people may be standing in front of a group of peers.

The attitude of the young people who are leading is critical in setting the tone. If they give off an air of "we're *the* leaders," if they lead and don't participate with everyone else, you can quickly have a monster of exclusivity. Walls are built. Territory is established, and that's not one of your goals.

We have attended two kinds of youth-led presbytery/district retreats. At one, the district youth council did a good job of leading the activities of the retreat. But not one council member participated in any of those activities. The whole council stood in a clump up front, off to one side, while leadership rotated. As a result, leaders did not meet or mingle with any of the participants.

The participants' reaction to the youth council was mixed. Some expressed a desire to be one of them. They liked the idea of being the leader. Some admitted they liked the fact that the council was a kind of "in group." But most participants were put off by the council's aloofness.

At the other retreat, not only did the youth council leaders participate with everyone in all activities, but during free time and in line for meals, they would walk around meeting and talking with everyone. One council member became very popular with the younger youth, as he was determined to learn everyone's name . . . all ninety-three of them. He delighted the younger youth with his antics.

The youth participants loved the council members, because they sensed the council members liked them and wanted to be with them, which amazed our young people because the council members were older. Our young people loved the guy who tried to learn everyone's name. He was a good role model of leadership. As a result, all our young people wanted to be a leader at one of these retreats. And they had such fun that they wanted to make sure to attend the next district retreat.

Programs

What are we going to do Sunday night? That's the question that young people often ask adult leaders. If you've been following our suggestions on getting youth involved in planning and leading, then the young people won't have to ask that question. They will know what's happening, because they are the ones who planned it. They have the vision. They have developed a way to make it happen. They are taking responsibility for their youth ministry. They *own* it. They are excited about it. And they are leading it.

Planning a good program is more than getting a good speaker. As the young people gain confidence in leadership and as they begin designing programs, you may never again be in the position of having to find a speaker as a last resort. As we have said before, lecture is not the best method. It keeps young people in the role of spectator.

Programming Guidelines

Read the guidelines that follow before getting into how to plan a program. They are the foundation for developing programs.

1. *Programs should be Christ-centered.* This is the first of the eight essentials covered in chapter 3. Being Christ-centered is sometimes just a matter of reminding young people and adult leaders why they are doing youth ministry programs. Other times it means evaluating by asking, "Is what we're doing Christ-centered?" Keep Christ-centeredness in mind as you plan.

2. *Programs should be relational.* The activities of a program should enable participants to relate to each other. One reason young people come to youth activities is to talk to friends. Choose activities that give them a chance to talk to one another. In this way, they will make new friends.

3. *Programs should deal with issues and needs of the young people in your church.* Often programs are designed by adults who decide what the young people need. And sometimes programs are designed without ever considering the needs and issues of the youth. The program takes place just because someone thought it looked like a good program.

4. *Programs should be youth-led to whatever extent the young people are willing to lead.* Don't force leadership on the youth. Be sensitive to individuality; some youth are more comfortable in leadership roles than others. Some may not be ready yet, but may be in a few months or in the next year. Use team leadership—teams of young people and teams of adults and young people leading together. Be aware of the wider concept of leadership and affirm youth as they use their gifts and abilities in many ways.

5. *Programs should not be like school.* Remember that young people have to go to school. It is their job! Just as adults prefer that church not be like work for them, so do young people.

6. *Programs should not be dependent on previous programs.* Each program should be able to stand on its own instead of being a part of a lengthy series on a topic. A young person may feel "out of it" walking in on the third night of a topic. If you must have a minicourse or series, review the previous sessions at the beginning of each successive session.

7. *Programs should use a variety of media and methods.* Again, stay away from lecture. Not only is it the least effective method for youth ministry, it would be hard for a young person in leadership to give a lecture. Dividing a group into smaller discussion or task groups is an excellent method with youth. Young people are more likely to speak in a smaller group. However, dividing into small groups every week for every program might get old. Young people and adult leaders together should look for creative methods. The "Teaching Activities" list from the Leadership Lock-In (see p. 149) may be helpful.

8. *Programs should have an atmosphere that says "You are safe here" and "You can be comfortable being open here."* Young people are interested in talking about their feelings, thoughts, and beliefs, but only if they feel safe. The very first activity of a meeting should be inviting. Whoever leads it, in effect says, "We're glad you're here." The program leaders and the activities should affirm the participants. For example, don't play games that single out people to embarrass them.

9. *Programs should have a beginning, a middle, and an end.* Beginnings should be inviting; they should help participants feel comfortable; they should introduce the topic in a fun or interest-catching way. Endings should leave participants with something to think about or do. It's not necessary to moralize or draw conclusions for the participants. Check program resources to see how programs begin and end.

How to Plan a Program:
A Guideline for Leadership/Care Groups

Let's say, for example, it's Monday night, September 29. The sophomore leadership/care group is meeting to figure out how to plan and lead a program called "If I Took Good Seriously," scheduled for October 19. Where do they start? What do they do? The following is a step-by-step guideline for planning a program.

Step 1

The care group begins planning by thinking of questions the members have about God and about living a life in which God is taken seriously. What does it mean to take God seriously?

From these questions, they formulate objectives for the program. They list what they want to happen as a result of the program. For example, (1) Youth will identify challenges they face trying to live a Christian life in school, in families, and with friends; (2) Youth will identify one way they want to change in response to taking God seriously.

Step 2

The planners identify the amount of program time available. If your meeting customarily opens with prayer, announcements, singing, and/or a game, then figure out how much time is left for the actual program.

The care group decides on two or three activities that will develop the topic. For instance, they might develop a short survey on youth attitudes about God and then ask the survey questions as the introductory activity. Then they might divide the full group into smaller groups to look at a Bible passage, using the discussion questions the planners have prepared. The third activity could be a role-play followed by a discussion on changes people would make in their lives if they took God seriously.

Whether or not there is a devotional at each meeting, they should consider ending with scripture and prayer, since this topic relates well to worship.

Step 3

The care group members identify resources. They might look at the table of contents in youth ministry program books to find topics that relate to taking God seriously. They might check youth ministry resources and Sunday school materials for creative learning activities, and adapt the activities to the topic.

They should consider people as resources. There may be someone who would share her or his faith story or experience in trying to take God seriously.

Step 4

Care group members decide who will do what. Which young people will lead the activities of the program? Who will do the devotional, announcements, singing, game, and so on? Remember that each activity can be led by more than one person. It's more lively if two or more give the announcements, and lead the singing and games. And they should look for opportunities for adult-youth partnership in leadership. They should decide how to publicize and promote the program.

Then they should go over the details. Everyone needs to know exactly what they will be doing and when. The leaders of the leadership/care groups should arrange to mail notices or make phone calls to remind group members of what they've agreed to do.

Step 5

The care group should plan when to meet to evaluate the program, using such evaluation questions as:

Did we do what we set out to do?
What did we do well?
How could we have done it better?
What should we not do again?

When a Program Goes Sour!

One time our junior highs decided to do a scavenger hunt/relay race. The leadership/care group had spent hours coming up with creative things to do at each "station" of the race. The full group was divided into teams of four. Each foursome would go to different stations, do what was posted at that station, and move on. For example, at one station they were to sing Old MacDonald while lying on their backs with feet touching in the center. At another they were to put on a set of baggy clothes. All eight stations were zany but fun. At least the care group thought so.

It didn't work. It took the care group thirty minutes to explain the instructions, who would go to which station first, where to go from there, and so on. The junior highs were not listening, so they got confused and had tons of questions. By the time the game started, everyone was worn out. Some ran off in every direction and didn't play. Those who did play finished in eight minutes. It just didn't work.

On another occasion, our youth were practicing for a worship service that was to be totally youth-led. Practice started upstairs in the youth room, where the young people were finishing writing prayers and practicing a minidrama. They were to move to the sanctuary for a complete run through. They headed downstairs and around to the sanctuary, or so we thought. Only half of them got there. The others just left. The few that stayed practiced their parts. No one had a clue how long the service would run.

Another time the leadership/care group didn't get their plans finished in time, so the adult leader took over. The program was okay, but enthusiasm was way down. Still another time, the senior highs watched a video that the care group had not previewed. The video was inappropriate and this was a big mistake.

So what happens when the program goes sour? And it will. Sometimes there's an explanation, and sometimes there's no rhyme or reason. The reasons could be any of the following: It's January. The spring dance was the night before. There's a chemistry test the next day. Just a slump day. It's raining. Everyone's hyper. Everyone's dead.

Tips for Dealing with a Program That Goes Sour

1. Don't let it get you down. The leadership/care groups that do the hard work may take it hard. Adult leaders and youth need to encourage each other. They need to say, "It's okay, it's nothing you did wrong. It's just one of those things." Next time will be better. If youth ministry is to be faithful, it can't cave in to a setback. Keep up the enthusiasm.

2. Keep your sense of humor. Adults, this is for you. Don't be quick to blame or come down hard on the young people for not being responsive. Many times it's just an "off" night.

3. Talk about it. If behavior is the problem, talk about the disappointment of not being able to do what the group had planned.

4. If lack of commitment is the problem, as with the worship rehearsal, the care group needs to decide what to do next. In that particular instance, they called everyone and scheduled another rehearsal.

5. Have a backup plan. Sometimes what is planned doesn't work because too few people show up. The care group should take that possibility into consideration when they are planning.

6. Last, and surely not least, *be flexible*. This phrase should be imprinted on everything related to youth ministry. A familiar sight is leaders running up to each other, suggesting they try something a little different. It's amazing to see how young people can learn the skill of reading a group. There's always an element of surprise in youth ministry. Help each other get used to it. Teenagers have a phrase for it: "Get over it."

What about Canceling an Activity?

ase No. 1: The deadline for the district youth rally is tomorrow and only three youth have called to sign up. So you get on the phone and call the three to cancel, and call the district to tell them your church will not be represented due to lack of interest. Should you have canceled?

Case No. 2: Your group is going roller skating on a Sunday night. Two youth show up. Do you go?

Case No. 3: An adult leader who just moved from a church in another town suggested having a talent show as a fundraiser. It had been a big success in his former church. With great enthusiasm he sold his idea to the youth council. Council set a date. Only one person signed up to perform. Do you cancel?

Case No. 4: A leadership/care group has planned a late night worship experience. The three who planned it are there. Only three other young people show. Do you cancel?

We strongly recommend doing everything in your power to keep from canceling an activity. In the first case, the leader should have taken the three to the rally. The three young people would have experienced a youth rally and might have come back with enough en-thusiasm to get others to go next time. With each rally, more and more youth would attend, and attending rallies would become a main event of youth ministry.

In the second case, go ahead and go roller skating, unless the two youth don't want to. But you make a stronger statement about the health of youth ministry by going ahead and having the activity. Next time more are likely to show. If you cancel, you are back where you started from. It will be harder the next time you try to get a group to go roller skating.

In the third case, the young people did not own the idea of the talent show. Obviously, the enthusiastic adult thought he had suggested a sure thing. However, what works in one church won't necessarily work in another. This one is better canceled.

In the fourth case, go ahead and worship! Those who are in leadership may be disappointed, but everyone needs to assure each other that God is pleased and desires the gathering to worship. It will be good experience for the leadership, and it may turn out to be a very special worship experience for those who are there. It could be a highlight of the year. You never know. Be open to letting God surprise you.

Two Ways to Avoid Canceling

1. In the planning stage make sure the young people have ownership. Is the activity something they really want to do? Is it something to which they are willing to make a commitment? In the area of service and mission, take care to educate everyone about a particular service or mission project. You don't want to agree to serve at a soup kitchen and have no youth sign up.

2. Make phone calls. When a deadline is approaching and only a few young people have signed up for an activity, the leadership/care group needs to get on the phone. Phone calls make all the difference in the world. In the first case cited above, instead of calling the three young people to tell them the youth rally trip was canceled, that leader should have called three other prospects who might have been delighted to be asked to go or who might have forgotten the deadline. Better still, the young people should be calling other youth.

Canceling gets you in a rut, especially when you're in the "building a youth ministry" stage. Let's say a retreat is scheduled. Only four sign up by the deadline. Don't be quick to cancel. Start calling. The leadership/care group that is responsible for the retreat should make the calls. If they don't want to, ask them why. Ask, What's not working? They will tell you.

When a youth ministry is in the building stage, everyone needs to work especially hard. Extra effort is needed to make activities happen, but this situation should change. Once more young people feel ownership, they will be more eager to attend events.

"Success" and Numbers:
Two Pitfalls to Avoid

An adult leader once said that the day she got over the canceling dilemma was the day she got over making numbers the criterion for the success of her youth ministry. She said that before that day, she could have six young people eager to go on a camping trip and be completely oblivious to their enthusiasm because of her disappointment that *only* six youth were going camping. She knew there could have been fifteen. She couldn't shake her feelings of failure.

If you're reading this and thinking, "What about those six youth?" then you are on the right track. Many readers would give anything to have six young people to take camping. Many don't even have six on the roles. Let's stop counting heads in our efforts to be successful.

> Numbers should not be the criterion for success.

What might help is to get away from the term "successful." It's much healthier to strive for a faithful youth ministry than a successful one. God has called us to a ministry with people, not numbers. God has called us to minister to each one. When we cancel, we say to the two who signed up, "you don't count."

I remember with embarrassment the time I was telling our young people about our trip to the soup kitchen. Only two young people showed up. Even though we served and I enjoyed being with the two youth, one of them later heard me telling the group that "Nobody came." She looked so hurt as she said, "I was there." Those words, "nobody came," ring in my ears. The worst thing you can do is call a young person a nobody. And I had done it.

There was a youth minister of a large church, who, at weekly staff meetings, would be asked by the senior minister to report the number of young people involved in each of the week's activities. That was all he was expected to report, numbers. I challenged him to skip the numbers at the next staff meeting and tell a story about a young person's involvement in youth ministry, and tell it with passion.

I don't think he ever did. But if he could have, it could have marked the beginning of a transformation in youth ministry in that church.

How do you measure success? By the responses of individual young people and adult leaders. When you see eyes light up with enthusiasm . . . When you see a glimmer of understanding on a young person's face . . . When you see young people caring . . . When you see adults who love young people . . . When you see young people and adults share a passion for Jesus Christ, for the church, and for others . . . then you know what success is and you know what faithful youth ministry is.

Communication—
A Key to the Delivering Stage

It doesn't matter how many mailings, fliers, and notices the young people receive about upcoming events, you still will hear, "I didn't know about the retreat," or "No one told me about the leadership/care group meeting," or "We're having a lock-in? Cool." People don't read their mail. Or fliers get thrown away by other family members.

In order to deliver the great dreams and plans the young people and adult leaders have, phone calls and personal contacts are a must. Without exception, the activities for which we phoned and contacted young people personally were the ones that were well-attended. Enthusiasm and commitment levels were up when the youth were given that extra reminder. Both youth and adults did the calling and personal contacting.

Remember the maxim from chapter 3, on the essentials of youth ministry: "So what if your program is great, if no one knows?" Often we work so hard getting together programs and retreats and working on relationships with the young people that we don't leave time for getting the word out. We fail to set up a system for regular communication and publicity. We don't engage young people in taking responsibility for promotion. The youth should be involved in spreading the word about all that happens in youth ministry. The more ownership they have, the more likely young people are to take the initiative in communication.

Promotion may be the missing link in making your youth ministry happen. As we suggest for most dilemmas in youth ministry, ask the young people how to promote. Ask them how to communicate with one another, with inactives, with new youth, with parents, and with the congregation.

Some suggestions:

• Someone needs to take notes and record ideas and decisions at all meetings where dreaming and developing takes place.
• Make sure plans get on a calendar.
• Make sure calendars get out to all young people, friends and visitors, parents, adult leaders, teachers, and anyone connected with youth. The staff of the church needs to know what's going on in youth ministry as well.
• Keep a calendar of publicity dates. These date indicate when fliers, letters, and cards should go out and when posters and phone calls should be made.
• Work out a system for working on bulletin boards and newsletters. Keep bulletin boards current.
• Young people should make announcements and report on mission trips, service projects, and special events at congregational gatherings and at worship services.
• Young people can contact friends, invite new young people, remind leadership/care group members at school of responsibilities, and make phone calls.
• Find photographers among your young people and adult leaders. Cameras should be at every event. Youth and adults can make displays of youth activities, events, retreats, service projects, and so on.
• Identify adult leaders who have organizational, promotional, and public relations skills. They, in partnership with young people with similar skills, should be responsible for communication issues.
• Look ahead. Know what's coming up. January is the month most likely to sneak up on you. As a result of Christmas busyness and vacations, January activities may not get adequate planning or communication.

Communicate youth ministry to the minister/pastors.

There is power in the pulpit. Whatever causes or programs the minister champions often are the ones that get well promoted. Youth ministry runs so much more smoothly with a pastor's support. Work to find the best ways to communicate the enthusiasm of young people and adult leaders to the pastor. Involve pastors whenever possible. Share the dream with them.

Putting Relationships before Program

When all is said and done, and adult leaders sit back and look at their youth ministry program, the one thing that seems to make the difference in whether or not the young people are catching the dream is relationships. When relationships between adults and young people are good, then it's working. It doesn't matter if a program goes sour. It doesn't matter if numbers are not consistently up. When young people know that they are surrounded by adults who truly love and care for them, then a solid, faithful youth ministry is being delivered.

As your young people and your adult leaders develop strong relationships, you will find that young people are much more forgiving than you ever expect. You can make mistakes, and it's all right. There is a sense that you all are in this together. Therefore, taking risks is possible. Young people and adults can try on new roles, can try out leadership, and can risk caring for one another.

Conclusion

It would be impossible to deliver without a commitment to the Lord Jesus Christ by those who are involved in dreaming and developing. To deliver youth ministry means to seek God's guidance at every level and to trust God's promises that God will be with us in all we do. That is such good news. We are not the ones, ultimately, who do the delivering. We help set the stage. But it is God who acts.

> Be open to what God is doing in your midst.

Therefore, remember to be open to what God is doing in your midst. Young people and adults too need to learn how to listen for God, how to look for God's Word for them in new and in common places. Be open to ways God will surprise you and to ways God will smile on you.

TEN

Adult Leaders: Roles and Responsibilities

With all this talk about youth being leaders and youth ownership, what is the role of the adult leader? What do adult leaders do? What are their responsibilities? What qualities do they have?

If you, the reader, are the only adult leader, you must know by now that it is not healthy to be doing youth ministry alone. It's not healthy for you, because going it alone invites burnout. And realistically, it can't be done alone. It's not healthy for the young people, because they need opportunities to develop relationships with other adults in the church. And it's not healthy for the church, because if you leave, so may the youth program.

So if you are the leader, please read this chapter for the purpose of recruiting and inviting other adults to join you in this exciting ministry. This chapter describes the roles and responsibilities of adult leaders. It suggests qualities that, when modeled by adult leaders, have an impact on young people.

We have found that adults are willing to be leaders if (1) they know clearly what it is they are supposed to do; (2) they are shown how to be leaders; (3) they can feel a sense of accomplishment and joy in what they are doing; and (4) they see being a leader as a good way to use their gifts as part of their Christian commitment.

Why Adults Volunteer

In a study on volunteerism, volunteers were asked what motivates them to give of their time and energy. The most common response was: knowing that they were making a difference. Too often when we recruit leaders, we say, "It won't take too much of your time" or "It's really not that hard." We try to make it easy for people to say yes by giving them the impression that they won't have to do much.

That is the exact opposite of what people want to hear. If they don't have to do much, then it's not worth their time volunteering. They'd rather give their time where they are really needed.

Adult leaders have quit youth ministry teams be-cause they didn't feel that they were doing anything. They came and helped with a few programs but were never given responsibility. The head leader did it all. The head leader wanted to make the job easy for the volunteers, didn't want to demand too much of their time, and didn't expect much. Most likely, the head leader didn't trust them to do it right.

People take volunteering seriously. Common advice is, if you're stuck in a job you're not crazy about but can't afford to leave, then find meaning and satisfaction in a voluntary "vocation." Do what you really like to do for free.

Recruiting Volunteers

Take a critical look at the way you approach volunteers. Sometimes our recruiting efforts lead us to fill slots rather than be instruments through which God calls people to ministry. The word "recruiting" has a military flavor, whereas "calling" gives a sense of seeking to respond to what God would have us do.

In seeking volunteers, spend time matching people's gifts, talents, and interests to the volunteer position that will give them a sense of joy and the fulfillment of a calling. Spend time in prayer and in discussion in order to find those special adults God is calling to do youth ministry.

Once you find those special adults, help them see the important role they will play in the life of the church and in the lives of the teenagers. If they see their role as a calling, then they are likely to respond enthusiastically to the opportunities and challenges of youth ministry.

> Volunteering is responding to God's call to a particular ministry.

People want to be needed, to be challenged to grow, to try on new roles, and to give themselves in service. Believing this should give you confidence to look for outstanding adult leaders for your young people. Expect commitment. Expect energy and enthusiasm. If you expect it, you usually will get it.

The Roles of the Adult Leader

Perhaps the best way to explain the role of the adult leader in this expanded team approach is to talk about the various roles adults play in relation to young people.

Significant Adult Friend

Adult leaders in the church are in a unique position to establish significant relationships with the young people. Young people are looking for adults who will accept them as they are. Most teenagers have shaky self-esteem. They don't like the way they look. They think they can't do anything right. They feel adults are always down on them. They feel they are never good enough for, nor can they meet the expectations of, the adults in their lives.

Young people are struggling with independence, wanting to get away from adults and make their own decisions. Yet at the same time, they want positive support and guidance from someone who has a little more experience. Often a parent is not the one they want to go to.

Here is where significant adult friends at the church can make a difference. Since their role is not parent, teacher, or coach, adult leaders of youth are free from having to be authority figures. They can have a more relaxed relationship with the young people. Their role is to accept each young person as he or she is.

We adults want so much for our young people. We want them to know, love, and serve God. We want them to care about other people. And we want them to be more responsive, less shy, better behaved, polite, courteous, respectful—all qualities that we know will help them in their adult life. It is good for adults to want to see transformation in the lives of young people. That's part of responding to God as Christians; we all need to be transformed at some level.

But young people get the idea that they are not acceptable as they are. They get the idea that adults are always trying to change them. How can adults unconditionally accept young people as they are and at the same time hope for the transformation that is a part of growing in faith? Can't adults be instruments that God uses in bringing about transformation? Of course, they can.

The answer lies with adults first accepting young people as they are, and then, in partnership, adults and young people together can experience the transformation that only God can accomplish. But first, the young people need a significant adult friend who will see them as children of God, totally acceptable.

The church can be the place where young people can go and not be criticized, nagged, lectured, or quizzed. Rather, they can find someone there who will listen caringly. A major aim of the church is to be a safe place where young people can be themselves, without fear of being put down. At church young people can find someone who will accept them, support and encourage them, and love and respect them. That is the role of the significant adult friend.

When adults are called to be on our youth ministry team, we tell them, "You've got to love the youth." That's the requirement for being an adult leader. That's the first responsibility. That's what a significant adult friend does.

In leadership training we ask our adult leaders to think back to when they were teenagers and to identify a significant adult friend in their lives. Sadly, not everyone can name one. One of our adults remarked that he wished that when he was young, he could have had relationships with adults like the relationships teenagers have today. That's a fine affirmation of the expanded team approach.

Think back to when you were a teenager. If you were a part of a church, what programs do you remember? What adult friends do you remember? More often than not it is a relationship that people remember when they recall their experiences as young people in the church. It's a relationship, not a program, that made a difference in their lives.

This special relationship is possible because the adults and young people see themselves as equals in the sight of God. When adults and youth work in partnership on planning events and leading activities, there is a mutual friendship. They are working together toward common goals in an atmosphere of Christian values—grace, kindness, joy, faithfulness, peace, love.

One group of young people put it this way:

Significant adult friends
- are interested in what youth are doing
- keep in touch with the lives of the youth away from the church
- are willing to share their own lives with the youth
- listen without feeling that they have to fix everything
- give advice from an older perspective when the youth ask for it

Guarantor

A guarantor is one who guarantees, who puts a stamp of approval on you; one who says, it's OK to be you, it's OK to have feelings, it's OK to make mistakes.

Can you remember a time when you were down on yourself, kicking yourself for mistakes you had made? Feeling like an idiot? Perhaps never wanting to face a certain person again? Then along came someone who told you it was OK to feel the way you did. Can you remember what they said? Even if you can't, can you remember the relief you felt, like a whole new world of hope opened before you? Your muscles relaxed; you could breathe again. Guarantors do that for people.

Our youth need guarantors. Young people are always kicking themselves. They see themselves in terms of "I always." They say: I always blow it; I always say the wrong thing; I always make my parents mad; I always get yelled at; I always screw up.

Guarantors help young people put things in perspective. When Felicia came to youth group one Sunday night, she was quiet. Something was wrong. Two junior girls tried to talk with her, but Felicia just didn't want to talk. After the meeting, Grace, one of the adult leaders, approached Felicia, saying, "What's going on? You look down." It didn't take long for Felicia to tell Grace the whole story, for in the past Grace had helped Felicia find hope when Felicia felt hopeless.

Grace not only listened to Felicia, she let her know it was OK to mess up. She helped Felicia identify her strengths and draw on them. Because of Grace, Felicia understood that God did not make a mistake when God created her. God loved her just as she was. Grace was a confidence builder. Grace was a guarantor.

Guarantors help young people see that they don't always blow it; they don't always say the wrong thing. Guarantors help a young person see light when all that person could see is darkness.

Partner

Of the five roles, this is the one in which the adult and the young person truly are on an equal level. All the other roles describe a relationship between an older, experienced adult and a young, unseasoned teenager. In a partnership, power is shared. The young people are not on the receiving end of being told what to do. Partners work together as equals.

Partnership is the term that best describes the adult-youth relationship in reference to the ongoing program of youth ministry. In the expanded team approach, adults and youth are partners in leadership. They are partners in the leadership/care groups. The partners have different skills and different gifts; therefore, both adults and youth can learn from each other what they need to know to accomplish the task.

Picture a team of young people and adults together pulling a rope on one side of a tug-of-war. Youth and adults are alongside one another. The young people bring to the team strength, energy, fresh legs. They come up with new ways to grip the rope. The adults bring technique, experience. They know how to pace themselves. Together in partnership youth and adults use each other's strengths to pull the rope effectively. They share tips. An adult suggests, from experience, that bending the knees may help. A young person suggests trying something new, like pulling the rope a certain way.

Partnership takes patience on the adult's part. Adults need to know that in adult-youth partnership, meetings will take longer. Young people are not as skilled in committee work or in expressing themselves. Give young people time to practice their leadership skills. Resist the urge to take over; that's not being a partner. It's easy to fall into old patterns of adults leading everything themselves.

Many adults and young people are discovering the joys of being partners on a quest for faith. Partnership, in this case, requires that adult leaders stop feeling inadequate because of their lack of biblical knowledge and open themselves to exploring the faith with young people. When adults approach Bible study with a willingness to partner with young people in seeking God, they will find youth more responsive to exploring God's word. The attitude of growing in faith together keeps adults from becoming preachy; it keeps discussions lively. When both young people and adults ask questions and express doubts, they are more likely to listen for what God is teaching them.

The concept of adults and youth sharing power is relatively new in youth ministry. In a true partnership, power is shared. One of the best ways to share power is to share information. Those who have knowledge have power. This was brought home to me when I found myself ill on the day of the first youth ministry committee day retreat. I couldn't call anyone to take my place. The retreat had never been done before; it was an experiment. And even though I had shared with another leader the agenda for the day, I had not given her enough information. She would not be able to lead the retreat.

I was the only one with the knowledge. Everyone else, youth and adults, merely needed to show up. Like puppets, they would do as I told them for the whole day. They had no power, no say, no choices.

It had not occurred to me until that morning what a big mistake I had made. I assumed that I could do it all by myself. I didn't even get anyone's feedback, which, right from the start, could have improved the entire design of the retreat.

What a wake-up call! I was not practicing what I preach. I preach that we, youth and adults, are to dream, create, and design together. That way everyone has power and ownership. I learned the hard way. It was painful, since I had to drag my sick body through the whole retreat.

Role Model

As an adult leader, you are a role model. Don't let that scare you. It doesn't mean you have to be a perfect Christian. No one can do that. Rather, it means that, as the young people get to know you, they may want to be like you, to adopt some of your qualities, or your values, or your opinions on issues. They'll watch the way you treat people and how you handle situations.

For example, Marla is a rather shy eleventh-grader. Until this year, Marla would never pray out loud. Now Marla volunteers to pray. One of the other eleventh-grade girls asked her what happened to make it easier for her to pray. She said that over the years she had watched how Donna, one of the adult leaders, had handled prayer. Donna was also shy, but would talk to God as if God were sitting across the table from her. Donna's prayers were never formal. And if she messed up in the way she wanted to word something, it didn't seem to matter. She'd say that God hears the prayer before you start praying and knows exactly what you're trying to say.

Young people are attracted to people who don't have it all together, who are still learning and still struggling with issues of faith. That should be good news to adults who fear being put in a position of leadership because they feel inadequate.

Qualities Adult Leaders Can Model

Adult leaders can model the following qualities that are particularly valuable for young people in today's world:

Caring. We can talk and talk about caring and about getting young people to stop being mean to one another. But what makes a difference is when leaders model caring.

On the way to a retreat, eighteen young people descended on a fast-food restaurant. The restaurant was short-staffed, and the worker behind the counter was irritated. He had trouble getting orders straight. Several of the young people were disgusted and mumbled about hiring more competent people. Bryan, an adult leader, edged his way up to the counter and commented to the worker on how hard it must be to have so many customers at once. Bryan then offered to help by writing down the remaining orders. The worker was visibly relieved.

What Bryan did wasn't a big deal and could have gone unnoticed, but Bryan was always doing things like that. He always looked out for people who seem less valued by our society. He spoke to bus drivers, and he thanked clean-up people in fast-food restaurants. He would remember when particular young people had tests or swim meets and would ask about them. He would ask how things were going at home. He cared.

Generosity. In a time when everyone seems to be acquiring, hoarding, getting the best deal, and seeing how much they can earn, generosity may seem old-fashioned. The following story is an example of generosity being modeled by an adult leader. A group of young people were going to a professional baseball game. They had ordered twenty tickets. By game day, only ten youth could go. The adult leader was not too excited about trying to sell tickets at the game. It occurred to her to give the tickets away. They were good seats, so it was bound to make ten people happy.

She picked out a family of four who were thrilled to be given tickets worth $36. The next recipients were three teenagers, who acted like they'd won the lottery. The last three tickets went to three students who were starting law school the next day and were grateful to be treated to a ball game the night before.

When the leader arrived at her seat, she enthusiastically introduced to the young people their guests for the game. Some of the youth looked puzzled, one a little perturbed that their leader didn't get any money for the tickets. But what the young people saw in her whole being was a delight in hospitality and generosity. She could have spent the whole game being miserable, thinking about being out $90. But the joy of giving took over. That's role modeling.

Respect. Respect is a quality that gets misconstrued when referring to teenagers and their relationship with adults. The common cry is the following: The problem with teenagers is that they don't have any respect for adults. As a workshop leader for parents and adult leaders, I have heard this cry repeatedly for years.

What I am about to say may sound backward, but I firmly believe it. The answer to the respect issue is the following: If you want respect from teenagers, respect them first. You're the adult. You're the one with knowledge and experience. You know what respect is. So model it, by respecting the teenagers first. You don't withhold your respect, or your love for that matter, while you wait for young people to earn your respect. It doesn't work that way. You can't demand respect. You model it.

Respect often has to be modeled over and over again before you receive respect from a teenager. For example, two years ago, Phil, a freshman, had a reputation as a disrespectful young person. He had a sarcastic edge. He had a chip on his shoulder and was easily angered. The real problem with Phil was he didn't believe anybody liked him. He was sure adults didn't like him. Adult leaders never called to invite him to youth activities. They probably were grateful he didn't come much, so they wouldn't have to decide how to handle his behavior.

Marc was a relatively new adult leader. He was fascinated by the "respect youth first" concept and was determined to figure out how to apply that concept to Phil. He liked Phil. In fact, he said he had been a lot like Phil when he was in youth group. He decided the first step was to call Phil and invite him to a youth meeting. While on the phone, he resisted the temptation to lay down the law on behavior. In fact, he didn't even mention behavior. He took the clean-slate approach and treated Phil as if Phil had never been a behavior problem.

At the meeting, Marc had left a notebook downstairs in the church office. He asked Phil to get the notebook. Heretofore, if Phil were to leave a room, you wouldn't see him again. But Marc decided to treat Phil like any other young person. He didn't give him a lecture about coming straight back. Phil returned with the notebook.

By the fourth meeting Marc and Phil had developed a good relationship. Marc spent time in conversation with Phil, finding out about his interests, likes and dislikes, and problems with his older brother. Marc was always glad to see Phil.

Phil did not become an angel because of Marc's attention. Phil still acted out, but it was less frequent. Whenever Phil did misbehave, Marc was the adult leader who handled the situation. Discipline works best when there is an established relationship.

Two years later Phil is very active in youth ministry. Now a junior, he has matured and gained experience in leadership. He cares about youth group; he has ownership. He acts differently because he is treated differently. The adult leaders and the young people now respect Phil.

A Gentle Spirit. We are so accustomed to violence that we have become anesthetized to it. Young people seem to enjoy portrayals of dismemberments. They laugh at gore. It's no longer just in the movies. It's on the news and it's in our lives.

On one of our trips, I hit and killed a dog with the church van. It was a horrible, gory sight. I did not know it, but some of the young people laughed. At least they cared enough not to let me see them laugh, for I was shaken. All I could think of was killing some child's pet. The youth tried to be comforting—putting an arm around me, telling me it was probably a stray.

As I thought about it later, I was glad the young people saw that I was upset. Whenever we see violence—and we see it graphically on the news—we need to let the young people see that we are affected. We need to react with compassion. Weep with those who weep. Our modeling can help young people develop their sensitivity.

Taking a Stand. Let the young people know that you are offended by mean-spirited comments, by remarks berating or belittling homosexuals, by racial or cultural prejudices. In a time when people wonder if anybody cares about anything, it is good modeling for the young people to see adults who care about issues, who have strong convictions, and who are willing to speak out and take a stand.

One of our adult leaders is easygoing and laid-back until someone makes a racial or bigoted comment. That pushes his button. Needless to say, the young people know where he stands.

It may seem that taking a stand doesn't always work. One leader may be admired for the consistency with which she supports environmental causes and reminds young people about recycling. Another leader touting the same cause will be seen as a nag. The reason for the difference is usually found in relationships. The relationship between the young people and the leader needs to be strong first, in order for the leader to be admired rather than seen as a nag.

Seeing Christ in People. A young person once shared that her role model was an adult leader who believed that you could see Christ in everyone. Five years after graduating from high school, this young person had visited this particular adult leader. She had a pressing question. She wanted to know why that leader had been so nice to her in youth group when she had been such a major pain in the neck. She said she will never forget what that leader said: "I knew there was so much more to you than your behavior. In some wonderful way I saw Christ in you, and that made it easy to be nice to you."

These examples of adult leaders modeling Christian qualities are not earth-shaking, superhuman, or idealistic. They are simple, real-life, everyday illustrations of people living out the Christian faith.

> Role models are not superhuman, super-Christian, or super-anything.

Think of other qualities that can be modeled, such as encouragement, honesty, and openness to different cultures. The idea of being a role model shouldn't scare you. Remember that young people don't expect you to be perfect. They need to know when you are struggling with issues. In fact, struggling with issues and questioning your faith are examples of good role modeling.

Talk with other adult leaders and with the young people about the kinds of values that can be modeled. Ask them what kind of role models they want to be.

Advocate

An advocate is one who speaks in favor of, or on behalf of, someone or something. Our young people need people who will say good things about them. One adult leader is forever telling parents how crazy she is about their sons or daughters. It's shocking how regularly the parents' response is a puzzled surprise.

Advocates know what's going on with the young people. They keep up with the issues the youth care about. They stand by them, advocating their concerns. They side with the young people on many issues. They let people know they care about the youth.

For instance, we have an adult leader who does a youth ministry report to the church board every month. Instead of a statistical report—how many youth attended this week—the leader tells a story about a young person's involvement in service, or about a young person's reaction to being welcomed and included, or about a need the young people have. Not only is this kind of report a good way to promote youth ministry, it's also a forum for the adult to be an advocate for youth. Granted, young people should and do report at such meetings, but to have an adult who champions youth causes, who shares passion for the young people and their concerns, is powerful.

Be an advocate for youth ministry. Tell people about youth ministry. Show your enthusiasm. If you are a member of a governing body in your church, you are in an excellent position to promote youth ministry. Speak frequently about the young people. Make youth ministry a personal priority.

Be an advocate with the church staff. Tell the staff how wonderful the youth are and how much you enjoy being with them.

What Does It Take to Be an Adult Leader?

These roles of adult leaders may sound intimidating, like something you're not sure you can do. It really is easier than you think. The main question to be concerned about is, Do you really love young people? If you truly love and care about your young people, then you will be more concerned about them than about yourself. When people are concerned about others, they tend to be less anxious about the roles they themselves play.

guard up, in a sense. As a result, they build a wall of superficiality between them and the young people. It is better to be a real person, one who makes mistakes and says the wrong thing, and thus is someone to whom young people can relate. Young people look to adults to see how they handle mistakes.

Adults are often anxious about their ability to convey the Christian faith to young people. They are concerned that they don't know enough. *Young people don't care what you know until they know that you care.* Once young people see that you genuinely care about them, then they will want to know you and know about your faith, your values, and your experiences. Stories will be shared. Adults and young people alike need to learn how to tell their stories, stories of faith, stories of experiencing God. It's your experiences that will touch the lives of your teenagers, not how much knowledge you have.

> What does it take to be a significant adult friend,
> a role model, a partner, a guarantor, and an advocate?

Be Yourself

What does it take to be all these leadership roles? First of all, simply be yourself. If you are comfortable with who you are, you'll be fine.

Being yourself means doing things you would normally do. For example, if you are a person who wears blue jeans, then wear jeans at youth activities. If you don't ever wear jeans, then don't wear them just because you think that's what youth leaders do. You're not being you; you're trying to be somebody different. That never works; the young people see through it. They much prefer that you be who you really are.

Let the young people know you as a real person, someone who experiences joy, frustration, love, loneliness, and despair; someone who feels pain and has passion. The youth need to know what you care about, what excites you, what troubles you. In that way you become a real person. That's the only way you can become a true significant adult friend.

Sometimes adults get overly anxious about their role as adult leaders. They are so concerned about being a Christian role model that they keep their

Letting the young people know you as a real person, with real emotions, is part of fulfilling your responsibility to build relationships with the young people. The relationship would be one-sided if only you got to know them. The young people want to know you.

A word of caution is in order. Being open does not mean revealing personal information that would not be appropriate. Adult leaders need to take great care in discerning what is appropriate to share with young people. For instance, a young person may ask you about personal and intimate experiences. The adult should tell them that the information is private. A disturbing development in recent years is the increase in incidences of sexual misconduct and abuse. Adult actions and conversation, though intended to be quite innocent, can be misinterpreted by young people.

Getting in Touch with the Youth in You

This does not mean act like a teenager. It means think back to when you were a teenager. Recall the insecurities, the painful experiences that may seem insignificant now but hurt deeply back then. The point is to remember how you felt back then. Then you can understand why waiting for the phone to ring is such a big deal for teenagers or breaking up seems like the end of the world.

Remember the joys. Remember the excitement of a new experience, or going to a new place for the first time. Did you have a crush on someone? Remember how it felt when that person merely smiled at you.

When seeking adults to be leaders, look for those who are secure being themselves. Young people can love a fifty-year-old leader who is comfortable being fifty. He doesn't have to apologize for not being young or for having some idiosyncrasies. If he is secure, the young people will love him, and when an idiosyncrasy comes out, the youth say affirmingly, "Oh, that's just Fred." No problem.

Getting in touch with the youth in you means relax and enjoy. Be playful. Don't feel like you need to be a watchdog. Be open to seeing things from a young person's perspective. Be open to young people's silliness and immature behavior, because it goes with the territory. Your whole being should communicate that being a Christian and a church member is a joyful experience.

Getting in touch with the youth in you does not, however, mean acting like a child. Sometimes adults are not secure about who they are and it shows up in their relationships with the young people. If you have the responsibility of recruiting, be aware of adults who might want to do youth ministry in order to relive their high school days. Perhaps high school was great and life now suffers in comparison. These adults might not have a healthy approach to the task. Or, conversely, there is the adult who had a terrible adolescence and is hoping to make up for it by "being a kid" again.

What about Discipline?

The role of disciplinarian was not included in the roles discussed so far. The word doesn't seem to fit with the kind of adult-youth relationships we've been discussing. Yet discipline is the most frequently raised issue at youth ministry workshops. What's a leader to do about disruptive behavior? Instead of being a disciplinarian, how about being a nudger, a negotiator, a reminder. Sometimes, though, adult leaders do have to play "the heavy." But disciplinarian shouldn't be a primary role. Too often that's what adults feel they are supposed to be. Help adult leaders work on the other roles, on relationship building, so that disciplinarian can remain at the bottom of the list of roles.

Instead of being a disciplinarian, think of being a boundary keeper. A need of adolescence is to know where the boundaries are. Young people are secure if they know the parameters of the playing field. Even when young people share in the setting of the boundaries, adult leaders can effectively play the role of the reminder, the one who says in a sense, "Kelly, you're crossing the line; come back."

Using the image of a yearbook staff, the adult advisor does not decide what picture will go on which page. But the advisor is the one to say "no, a picture of the principal in her bathing suit is not appropriate for the cover page."

When asked whether adult leaders should be disciplinarians, one youth responded, "They should discipline, but it's hard to explain. It has to do with interest, love, and respect."

If adults work on the roles listed above, they will build positive relationships with the young people. Once the young people know that the adults love them, like them, and respect them, then the young people are willing to respond with appropriate behavior. When behavior problems do occur, the adults and youth together—in partnership—should be able to find the solutions.

Guidelines for Minimizing Behavior Problems

Here are some hints for minimizing behavior problems:

1. *Talk with the young people about guidelines for behavior.* Talk about what is expected. People often behave inappropriately because they don't know

what is expected of them. For example, boys are willing to take off their caps during prayer, if they know that it's expected behavior. Talk about it. Don't wait until someone jumps on one of your youth for not removing his hat.

Discuss other expectations, such as asking young people to show respect for persons who are speaking by not talking while they are talking. How about, no put-downs? Do you have special needs to address—youth who disappear from the group, cleaning up after meals, throwing food, youth hanging out in the parking lot, fights, smoking?

What will you do about serious problems—someone who is continually disrupting, fighting, or bringing in drugs and alcohol? These issues need to be discussed. Everyone needs to know the consequences of negative behavior.

As a group, young people and adults together, decide on guidelines and expectations. Youth are more likely to abide by guidelines if they have a hand in creating them. That's ownership. Once young people have ownership, they are less tolerant of misbehavior that messes up what they own.

2. *Covenants are helpful and have a rich biblical tradition.* After deciding on the guidelines, the young people and adults can write a series of statements describing what both the young people and the adult leaders agree to do. The covenant can be written on poster board, and the youth can sign it as part of a worship experience.

The signing can be a ritual at the beginning of the year or at the beginning of each retreat or event. Use covenants with small groups, Bible studies, and Sunday school classes. Have a young person, rather than an adult, present the covenant to the whole group. It has a greater impact when presented by a peer.

3. *Be firm yet be grace-filled.* There may be times when a young person must be removed from a group or parents called. If that happens, make sure an adult maintains contact with that person. Even better, both an adult and a young person could maintain contact with the offender. Young people who have behavior problems, even criminal behavior problems, need significant adult friends. They need love and attention. They need the church as a guarantor.

Keep grace in mind when dealing with behavior problems and when drawing up the covenant. So many times we have seen young people surprised by grace. They were expecting adults to come down hard on them. Instead, they were wonderfully surprised by understanding and mercy. It's a prodigal son kind of thing. Consider grace issues as you create your covenant.

Alan never came to youth group. His parents made him go to Sunday school. In his sophomore and junior years he went on the ski trip, but that was the only thing he did. At one of our meetings, a young person mentioned that it didn't seem fair that someone who didn't attend youth activities could go on the ski trip. I was delighted that several young people defended our policy—anyone could come to any activity and go on any trip. Our youth were catching on to what grace means.

Sometimes you hear adults say, "You can't let the offender off, because it's not fair to the other young people." True, it may not be fair, but it is a gesture of grace. Young people are very familiar with the value of fairness. The value of grace may be new to them. Fairness tends to teach people to "look out for number one." Grace is a selfless gesture; it puts others first. Grace is love and mercy given to someone with no regard for the person's worthiness.

Adult leaders can model grace, and they can invite young people to be grace-filled by discussing the concept of grace. Talk with your young people about the message the church sends to a troubled teenager by always sticking by the rules. Talk about the message the church sends when grace replaces the rules.

We're not saying do away with rules, expectations, and covenants. We're suggesting that everyone keep in mind the spirit of a covenant. Review your goals and mission statement when you draw up your covenant.

4. *Handle behavior problems quietly.* Avoid embarrassing teenagers in front of everyone. There's no need. One of the beauties of team leadership is that there is always someone in the group who can nudge or speak to the person who is causing a distraction. It doesn't have to be an adult who does the nudging. We have found that with the expanded team, young people are willing to take on disciplinary roles; they are good at hushing one another.

Persons who are doing up-front leadership should not handle a disruptive youth. Besides embarrassing the young person, the leaders end up interrupting themselves. Then everyone is focused on the behavior problem and not on what the leaders are doing.

One simple method a leader can employ is to stop talking until everyone is listening. It gets the point across without drawing attention to one person. Another method is to ask everyone to look at you. In order to look at you, they have to stop talking to one another.

Even if the problem is serious, handle it quietly, privately. Young people who act out usually have a reason, some inner struggle or turmoil in their lives. They need to know you care. Spend time with them, not in reprimanding but in listening.

5. *Think before reacting.* Try to stop and think about how you'll react to behavior before actually reacting. It will save you from jumping to the wrong conclusion. Think why the person may be acting in a particular way. Think of the overall effect your reaction may have. Keep your overall program goals in mind. That's often hard to do, but it is a technique worth practicing.

For example, consider this situation, which happened on a retreat. The young people had been given secret partners for the weekend. On the last day they were to write an affirming note to their partners and give it to them during the worship service. When worship time came, several young people had not written their notes, so time was given during the service to write the notes. One boy, very frustrated, came up to one of the adult leaders during the service and said he couldn't do it and it was a stupid idea anyway.

The leader was about to say, "You've had the whole day to write that note," when another adult leader who overheard the conversation came along and suggested, "Let's together think of something positive you could say about your secret partner." The leader helped the boy, the note was written, the secret partner affirmed. Everybody was helped.

The first leader was ready to admonish the boy for not getting the assignment done. The second leader gave the boy the benefit of the doubt. Maybe the boy was embarrassed because he couldn't think of anything to write and knew his secret partner would be disappointed not to receive an affirmation. Maybe getting angry and attacking the activity was his way of expressing his hurt and embarrassment. Scolding him would not have helped.

Neither leader knew what the boy was thinking. All they saw was a frustrated, angry youth. One leader was ready to react in kind, to meet anger with admonishment; the other, attempted to look beyond the anger and tried to guess what might be bothering the boy.

The point of this story is the following: look at your goal. The goal in this example is not to teach the boy a lesson; the goal is to affirm the secret partner. Sizing up situations takes practice. Deciding how to react to behavior takes practice. Therefore, try to think before reacting.

6. *Address the issue when appropriate.* There are times when the whole group needs to know that certain comments and behaviors are not acceptable. If a young person makes a degrading or bigoted statement, instead of letting it go and speaking with the young person later you should say something right then. You might say, "that's not acceptable," or, if the time is right, the group can discuss the issue. When young people cut each other down, remind them of the covenant: "We agreed not to do that."

7. *Evaluate your programming.* This could be the best advice of all for preventing behavior problems. Negative behavior may be an indication that your program is not meeting the needs of the young people. Senior highs vote with their feet. If they don't like it, they won't come. Junior highs may not have an option; parents bring them. So they vote by misbehaving.

If you have a lot of dead time between activities, you lose people, and that's when behavior deteriorates. When you plan, envision the transitions between the activities. Visualize what everyone will be doing.

Look at the length of an activity. Don't expect young people to sit and listen attentively to an hour-long lecture. Fourteen minutes—sometimes less—is considered a normal attention span for listening. Vary your activities and use age-appropriate methods. Lecture is not a good method for this age group. Granted, young people do listen to lectures at school, but church should be different from school.

8. *Remember that these are teenagers.* It is normal for them to talk to one another. Some talk constantly. Part of our purpose in youth ministry is to give young people opportunities to get together and talk with one another—to build relationships.

If you find yourself constantly telling a young person to wait until after the program to talk to a friend, you may need to reconsider your program methods. Try building into the program "talk time." Give them a chance to talk about concerns they have—about school, about their families or friends, about faith, about controversial issues.

Work on raising your tolerance level. You'll be a happier adult leader. Once you accept the fact that young people don't have to be pin-drop quiet, you'll be able to relax and enjoy them.

Some people are not temperamentally equipped to work with youth. It's important to recognize that this is not a defect in their character. They simply aren't suited to working with this age group. One elementary school teacher who worked with young people finally had to stop. She was used to an orderly classroom. Being with teenagers was very different. She couldn't adjust, and that was okay. She recognized that her gifts were not with teenagers and moved on.

9. *Adult leaders need to assess their styles of relating to young people.* Some adults can play "the heavy" effectively. They can do it without embarrassing teenagers. They are comfortable going after the boy and girl who just took off for the woods after curfew. They don't mind talking with a young person about behavior.

One adult leader managed to reach a young person we thought was unreachable. The boy was disruptive. He'd run around and throw stuff while everyone else was sitting in groups, or he'd join a group and drive the leader crazy. One night, in the middle of one of the boy's disruptive episodes, Mike, an adult leader, quietly asked the boy to come with him to an adjacent room. After about five minutes, they both came back. We feared Mike had chewed the boy out.

But the boy joined his group and willingly participated. We couldn't wait to ask Mike what had happened. Mike said he simply told the boy how much Natalie, the adult group leader, liked him. Mike told him how she was always putting in a good word for him and how she had told his parents she was crazy about him.

Mike also told the boy that he was a natural leader, that the youth liked him and would follow him. Mike encouraged him to use his natural leadership qualities to influence the kids positively, instead of using his energies to draw negative attention.

We marveled at the gift Mike had for affirming that boy. He sensed that the boy needed to hear that adults liked him. A lot of young people act out because they have already decided that no adults like them or ever will like them. It took only five minutes

for that boy to hear the affirmation—Mike and Natalie were two adults who indeed liked him.

Most young people act out because they want attention. Psychologists will tell you that attention is exactly what they need. Adult leaders can help young people move away from negative attention-getting behavior and toward positive behavior.

Be careful that none of your adult leaders plays the heavy too much. On a trip to a weekend youth conference, a group of young people were accompanied by two adult leaders. The younger leader had instant rapport with the youth. He sat in the back of the van and interacted with the young people the whole trip. The older leader drove. She was burdened by the feeling that she was the only responsible adult. Her conversations with the young people seemed to center on curfews and reminders. When problems arose, she was the one to step in.

> No adult should be the heavy all the time.

At the conference she shared her concern over being perceived as the disciplinarian. She loved the youth and didn't like that role. After talking with both leaders, I suggested that they switch roles. He was to handle the reminders, the details, curfew, and any problems. She was to do nothing but enjoy the young people. On the way home he would drive the van and she would sit in the back with the youth.

In this case, the concerned adult leader needed the freedom to let go of details and concentrate on building relationships with the young people. Switching roles is a good exercise, especially for those adults who may be preoccupied with how young people behave.

Responsibilities of Adult Leaders

We've talked about the roles of an adult leader; now what does the adult leader do? What is his or her task?

Buy into the Vision

We have been talking about young people owning their program. It is equally important that adult leaders have ownership in the whole program. The adult leaders need to buy into the vision, the goals,

the adult-youth partnership, the structure, and the activities of youth ministry at your church.

Adult leaders need to spend time in the beginning learning about the particular church's youth ministry. Share with them where the program has been and where you hope it will go. Help them understand that the vision is partnership. The goal is to have youth and adults dreaming together.

It may take some adults longer than others to buy into the vision. For example, building relationships is a part of the vision. If, at every youth gathering, some adults are off to one side enjoying one another's company, then those adults have not yet bought into the vision. Or, if plans were made for each activity at a retreat to be led by a youth and an adult, and at the retreat the adult takes over, then that adult is not yet on board.

You know your adult leaders are on board when they begin taking the initiative, when they phone the young people and get them together to plan. Or, when someone comes up with an idea, if your adult leaders are the ones to say, "let's ask the youth." Then you know the adult leaders have bought into the vision of youth ownership.

Be a Team Player

Adult leaders have their own desires and hopes for the young people, which is good. However, their agenda needs to mesh with the agenda of the young people and other adult leaders. Problems occur when one adult decides that he or she knows what is best for the youth and is going to make sure that something is done a certain way.

Everyone needs to be a team player. As team players, adult leaders recognize their own skills and gifts and acknowledge those of the other team members. The "Leadership Skills" sheet on page 151 is a good tool for teams to use in order to find out what each team member is comfortable doing.

One of the best ways to get people to be team players is to share knowledge and power with them. Everyone on the team should have all the information needed: who the young people are, the goals and purposes of the activities and of youth ministry, access to resources, updated information on plans. Remember, knowledge is power. Those with the knowledge and information will be empowered to play their role on the team.

Build Relationships

It can't be overstated: Relationships with young people are more important than programs. Work at building relationships. One of the greatest joys in youth ministry is getting to know the young people. They will enrich your life and strengthen your faith. You will see Christ in them. You will see God work through them. They have so much to give.

How do you build relationships? Be available. Be a good listener. Learn about their world, their interests—school, friends, extracurricular activities, music, sports, dance, parents. Where do they go? What do they do on Saturdays? What are their families like? What influences them? (See pp. 126–127, "Who They Are.")

If the program is beginning to drag around the middle of the year, evaluate. How well do adult leaders know the young people? Have they reached out to those who have not been around for weeks? Are they spending time in conversations with the youth? Did they start the year that way but now are slacking off?

Develop and Support Young People in Leadership

In direct and indirect ways you'll be supporting, encouraging, and teaching the young people leadership. Give them many opportunities to try various roles of leadership. Give them plenty of affirmation as they go.

1. Create an atmosphere that shows confidence in the young people's abilities. Adult leaders create one of two scenarios. In the first, the adult leaders listen well and affirm the young people and their ideas. They offer the young people responsibilities and arrange to check with them to see how they're doing with their responsibilities. The young people then feel that the adults take them seriously.

In the second scenario, the adults listen to the young people, but there is the feeling that the adults will do all the work. Since the young people sense this, they don't feel the need to develop responsibility or leadership.

2. Provide a leadership lock-in or some other training in leadership for the young people.

3. Help young people see that leadership is more than standing up in front of a group.

Carry Out Programming Responsibilities in Partnership with Young People

1. Know when you have responsibilities, when you and your group of youth are planning and leading. Keep up with the calendar.

2. Contact the youth and other adults to plan.

3. Work in partnership.

4. Use an action plan (see p. 159). List all the steps needed for an activity.

5. Use resources.

Care for Young People

Sometimes in large churches it's hard for adult leaders to build a relationship with every young person on the church rolls. With the leadership/care group model, each adult leader is assigned a specific group of young people to care for—to get to know, to call, and to keep up with.

Devise some way to track the young people, that is, to keep up with who attends which activities. Taking roll is not a popular thing to do on a Sunday night; it's too much like school. However, each care group could keep a care list in place of a roll. A young person could mark who's there and who's not. Notes are made on the care list about each young person: prayer concerns, activities, trips, illness. A file could be kept with notes on each youth. List areas in the life of the church in which each young person is involved.

Contact youth who haven't attended for a couple of weeks. A phone call means a lot. Sometimes young people don't have much to say to an adult on the phone. Don't let that keep you from phoning. Relationships improve over time.

Be a Contact Person for Parents

Most of the time, parents appreciate what you do for their teenagers. At the beginning of the year, write to parents and explain the leadership/care group system. Arrange a visit with each family of your care group members. Share with them the dreams and development of youth ministry. Share your enthusiasm about their young person. Listen to their concerns. What do they need from the church to help them nurture their teenager? Take their ideas and concerns to the appropriate people—youth council, the pastor, coordinator of youth ministry.

Support groups for parents, classes in raising teenagers, and ideas for parent-youth activities may come out of these visits. Also, connect with parents concerning ways parents can support youth ministry—as cooks, hosts, drivers, or resource people, or with prayer support.

Attend Activities

An adult leader should attend youth activities even when your leadership/care group is not responsible for the activity. Being there when you don't have program responsibilities is very freeing. You can relax and spend time talking with the young people. Building relationships requires your being there as much as possible.

Attend Retreats

There is no substitute for the retreat experience for building relationships and seeing youth and adults grow in faith. Make every effort to attend the retreats—at least one. Adults who miss fall retreats report it takes them much longer to feel a part of the team, to get to know the young people, and to feel that they know what they're doing.

Attend Leadership Training and Team Meetings

Adult leaders should attend training and team meetings because this is the best way for leaders to keep one another on track. Adults need one another's support and encouragement as they seek to work in expanded teams of adults and youth together.

Communicate

All the adult leaders should let other leaders know what they need in their ministry with youth. Communicate problems. Remind one another of what's coming up. Let your coordinator know when you have to miss a leadership meeting, a planning meeting with your leadership/care group, or an activity.

Job Description, Goals, and Mission Statements

Many churches find it helpful to write a job description for leaders in youth ministry. It can be developed by the youth council, by staff, or by a Christian education committee. The young people should have input.

When putting together a job description, consider the roles and responsibilities listed in this chapter. A sample job description and mission statement are on pages 118–119. This particular sample may be helpful because it lists not only "what the church expects of you" but also "what you can expect from the church." Leaders need assurance that the church will support them. We recommend spelling out exactly how your church will support and nurture its leaders.

Job descriptions are helpful for prospective leaders as they consider joining the youth ministry team. They can see exactly what is expected of them.

Burnout

Adult leaders are less likely to get burned out if a team approach is used. Having a team of adults to share the responsibility makes it easier for adult leaders to commit to a longer period of service. Recognizing that the first year is the toughest helps. Leaders look forward to the second and third year, for they know that time allows for the building of relationships.

There is less burnout in team ministry, for adult leaders who work with young people seem to have such fun together. That's the nature of youth ministry; it is fun. Adults on a youth ministry leadership team often become a fellowship group. Serving on a leadership team is a great way for new members of a congregation to make friends who have common interests.

In the expanded team approach adults and young people together should be learning how to work as a team and how to pace themselves, so that they can avoid burnout. They should also be teaching each other to recognize when a break from leadership is needed or when God might be calling them into a form of service other than youth ministry.

Burnout can and does occur, however, even in the best of situations. When a leader starts missing a lot of activities or begs off from leadership meetings, it's time to check in. Stay in honest, open communication. Check with the person to see if it's burnout or just a busy time of the year.

Open communication is needed when an adult member of the team may need to move on to another area of ministry. Perhaps he has lost patience with the young people, or maybe her vision of youth ministry is completely different from the team's and the church's vision. Whatever the reason, talking with a leader about leaving the leadership team can be awkward. But there are times when the health of the youth ministry is at stake. In as kind and caring a way as possible, people need to be given a chance to move on from youth ministry. In the process, these people need to be affirmed for their gifts and their commitment. Finding another way for them to serve is helpful, for they need to know that they are valued.

Sample Job Description for Adult Leaders

What the Church Expects from You

1. Get to know the youth individually. Start with the young people in your leadership/care group. Speak with them whenever you see them in church. Attend at least one of their school or extracurricular activities (plays, sports, concerts, recitals). Attending just one will make a big impression. Make phone calls. Write notes: appreciation, birthdays, injuries, and so on.
2. Be responsible for the activities assigned to your leadership/care group.
3. Set up meetings with your leadership/care group to plan activities.
4. Keep up with the calendar, so you'll know when activities are coming up. Make plans early. Use an action plan.
5. Help the young people develop their leadership skills. Engage them in leadership to the extent that they are willing to lead. Support and encourage them as they try on responsible roles of leadership.
6. Participate in any leadership training offered. Attend regular leadership meetings.
7. Try to participate in all the "beginning of the year" activities—group building, cookout, fall retreat, Parent Night.
8. Participate in activities for which your group is not responsible. The more you are available, the better you will be able to build relationships with the young people. It's great to attend when you're not responsible. You're free to enjoy being with the youth.
9. Call your coordinator when you cannot make a leadership meeting, planning meeting, or activity for which you are responsible.
10. Let your coordinator know when you need help or have questions. Don't let the church let you down!

What You Can Expect from the Church

1. Not to be left alone in your ministry with youth. This is a team effort. You have a support group. Your coordinator will remind you of upcoming activities and responsibilities.
2. Resources and helps for carrying out your activities.
3. Finances for materials for your activities.
4. Registration fees and travel expenses to be paid by the church for all retreats and youth trips, as well as any leadership workshops you attend (exception: ski rentals and lift tickets).
5. Babysitting expenses incurred while attending youth ministry activities, including leadership training.
6. Publicity and communication regarding youth activities.
7. Support and encouragement from the church staff, the minister, the educator, and the youth ministry committee.

Responsibilities

1. To build relationships with the young people. Your relationship with the youth is more important than "program." Become a "significant adult friend" to these young people.
2. To share yourself and your faith with the youth. Let the young people get to know you. Share your story. Be open.

3. To support the goals of youth ministry, which can be found in the mission statement of your youth ministry, in the goals of the five areas (see appendix 3), and in the statements that emerge from the youth ministry committee and the ongoing ministry to and with young people.

4. To develop youth in leadership and to support them in their efforts. Often it is tempting and easier for adults to do everything themselves. Work to overcome this inclination. Work as partners with the youth as they try on leadership roles. Go over responsibilities and instructions with them, step by step. Make phone-call reminders.

5. To participate in leadership training. Even though you may have been a leader in previous years, each year is different. The young people are different; the program is different; the adult leadership team is different. We all need to get to know one another and each person's unique leadership styles and gifts. Attending the leadership meetings and training is essential for building a solid team.

Sample Goal and Mission Statements

Goal Statement: To give all young people opportunities to be involved in the total life of the church, in its worship, explorations, ministry within the congregation, service, and fellowship.

Mission Statement: In all that we do in youth ministry we seek to be faithful to Jesus Christ. We seek to provide a safe place where youth can love and be loved, a place to belong. We seek to nurture the faith of young people through providing opportunities for fellowship, to worship, to serve, to learn, and to lead.

Goal Statement: To enable young people to become more mature Christians, more churched people, better leaders of Presbyterian Youth Connection and the church in the future, the people God created them to be.

Mission Statement: As youth and adults, we respond to God's call through the Holy Spirit to be connected to each other, the church, and the world so that our lives proclaim with joy that Jesus Christ is Lord! (Mission Statement of Presbyterian Youth Connection)

Recruiting Adult Leaders

Qualifications

Many people assume that to be a youth leader you have to be young, energetic, outgoing, and play guitar. Not necessarily. The nice thing about having a team of leaders is you can look for a variety of ages, personality types, and talents. Young people come in varieties of personalities, and so should leaders.

The key characteristics to look for are the following:

love for young people
love for God
openness to new ideas, new methods, and various
    personalities among the young people
flexibility, tolerance of change

Some people assume that shy people can't be leaders. Not so. I remember being doubtful about asking a shy, recently divorced father of two to join the youth ministry team. He was surprised to be asked, for he thought the church wouldn't want a divorced person working with young people. My concern was not that he had been divorced, but that he might not be outgoing enough for youth ministry. Was I wrong! As it turned out, he found his niche. He was the most gentle, caring person, and had a great sense of humor. The key was that he truly loved the youth, which was evident to the young people right from the start.

He's still on the youth ministry team, some ten years later. He was a great promoter of youth ministry; he told everyone how working with youth changed his life. It deepened his faith and strengthened his relationship to the church—he became an ordained deacon. He grew in confidence; he recognized that he had gifts to offer the youth and the other adult leaders.

Every leadership team in youth ministry needs a variety of personalities and a variety of styles. You need detail people and big-picture people. You need people who will keep you on task, and you need those who can sense when a diversion is needed. How can opposites work together? That's the exciting part of team ministry. It's give and take. It's caring about one another's needs. It works because you share a common vision and calling.

People to Avoid

Avoid recruiting people who won't work out, such as people in the following categories:

- People who can't be team players—people who have their own agenda for the young people and who won't buy into the overall vision.
- People who agree to be leaders for the wrong reasons—those who feel obligated, who feel guilty about saying no, or who say yes because nobody else will do it.
- People who can't tolerate the behavior of teenagers—this will prevent them from getting to know the young people.
- People who have been abusive, either physically or sexually. It is possible to do background checks on prospective leaders. Day-care facilities and schools do so when they hire teachers. The church has become an easy target for pedophiles, since churches have not been as diligent as schools in checking out leaders.

What about Schoolteachers?

Because teachers work with children or young people all week, they may not be your best choice for prospective adult leaders. We have, however, seen excellent leaders who are schoolteachers. In these cases, it was clear that they understood what was expected of them as leaders and that they could develop good relationships with the young people. Often teachers of young children are used to a disciplined classroom and have a hard time making the transition to less-structured youth activities. Again, there are exceptions, excellent exceptions. We mention it here only as a consideration.

What about Parents?

As a general rule, we have found it is better not to recruit parents whose sons or daughters are in the youth group. Again, there are exceptions.

Parents are often the main source of volunteers for the activities in which their children are involved. For instance, parents will help out with junior choir when their child is in junior choir or Scouts when their child is in Scouts. This works well until the children become junior-high age. Then parents should give their young people a chance to develop relationships with other adults who can become significant adult friends. Parents can support youth ministry in other ways. Often, when parents are the youth leaders, the young people are not as free to enjoy becoming a part of their church through youth ministry.

Yet there are exceptions. There are parents who can be leaders and it's perfectly fine with their teenagers. We recommend always asking the sons or daughters before recruiting their parents. Usually the young person will give an honest answer.

An advantage of the team approach is that you can have a parent as a member of the adult leadership team without the young people feeling dominated by parents. One member out of a team of two, three, seven, or ten members is quite workable.

If there are parents who want to do youth ministry, suggest that they work with the other group. For example, if their son or daughter is a senior high, they could work with junior highs.

Best Prospects

Some of the best prospects for adult leaders are parents of fourth-, fifth-, and sixth-graders. These are parents who fear the day their children become teenagers. Tell them that getting involved in youth ministry at this time will give them a couple of years to get to know teenagers. Then, by the time their own children become teenagers, they will know what to expect. They will be less fearful. And their own children will benefit. In fact, after working with the young people, they will wonder what it was they dreaded.

Guidelines for Approaching Prospective Leaders

Recruiting leaders is rarely one of those things that people look forward to with undiluted pleasure. It seems like such a big job. People envision lists and lists of names that are methodically checked off as the same answer is heard: no.

It doesn't have to be a negative experience. It can be a good experience when recruiting is approached as sharing the good news about youth ministry and inviting people to join in the fun, or when recruiting is perceived as helping people to discern what God is calling them to do. It also helps if recruiting is done by more than one person.

The following guidelines may help:

1. Talk with people in person and not by telephone. You can call to set up an appointment, but you can't convey the vision of youth ministry over the phone.

2. Write a letter to those whom you and the pastor or other leaders have selected. In the letter, explain what the church is looking for in youth ministry. Introduce your team concept, mention the benefits, describe the responsibilities. Don't go into great detail, for you can explain the details during a visit. Put all recipients' names at the bottom of the letter, so everyone knows who is receiving the letter. Do not send the letter to the whole congregation asking if anyone is interested in youth ministry.

The invited adults like seeing the list of names at the bottom. They like knowing who is being contacted. They can call some of the other prospects and talk it over.

In the letter tell them you will call them in two weeks to set up a time to talk about the possibilities. Make sure to follow up in two weeks. On pages 123–124 is a sample of such a letter.

3. When you visit, be honest about the commitment of time, energy, enthusiasm, and caring that will be required. Share your enthusiasm. Share the vision. Talk about youth ownership and youth leadership. Share the job description, so they have a clear idea of what's involved. Explain the support they will have.

4. Work to convey the feeling that we are on this journey together. Your invitees need to know that every leader is valued in making youth ministry work.

5. Listen. Don't do all the talking. Let them share their experiences with youth and with the church.

6. Don't push for an immediate answer. Give them plenty of opportunities to ask questions. Give them time to think and pray about it. Let them know that you are not pressuring them. Trust that you'll find the right people with the right skills and gifts for youth ministry.

Conclusion

There is nothing like the camaraderie of a youth ministry team of adult leaders who are committed to the vision of being in partnership with young people. It may take time to get everyone on board, but once you do, it's a tremendously exciting ministry. Team ministry is a great way to get new members involved in the life of the church. They'll get to know other adults. They'll be doing a task with support.

We usually recruit leaders for a year, but we say up front that we hope they fall in love with the young people and find that this is indeed their calling. The first year is usually the hardest. It takes a while to get to know the youth. If adults hang in there for a second year and a third, it gets easier. And the benefits increase. You don't get burned out, since you're part of a team. You see kids grow in faith, change in attitudes, and become more caring and outreaching. And it's fun!

April 20

Dear Wes,

I am writing this letter to introduce you to the youth ministry team concept that we will be using at First Presbyterian this fall. As you may know, I am coordinating the Senior High Youth Ministry Team, and Tim Hodgin is coordinating the Junior High Team.

We are recruiting eight adults for Senior Highs and eight for Junior Highs. That's sixteen adults who will be involved in youth ministry. Although this may sound like a tremendous undertaking, it is a structured, effective way of giving our young people:

1. Opportunities to be involved in the total life of the church.
2. A variety of adults to whom they can relate.
3. A structured way to be involved in the planning and leading of their own program.

I am writing to you and to those listed at the bottom of this letter because you are the ones with whom we would like to talk about the possibilities of participating on the youth ministry team. This letter is not going to the whole congregation.

Let me explain how it works. The entire youth group is divided into four leadership/care groups (two adult leaders per group). The groups plan and lead four or five activities for the coming year. The youth choose activities in five areas:

Worship

Explorations: Studies, topics, issues

Ministry within the congregation: Activities involving youth with other members (young and old) of our congregation

Service: To the community (beyond the church)

Fellowship: Games, trips, retreats, and so on

Our goal is to have a balanced program of activities. We strive in our youth ministry to have an adult-youth partnership in leadership. So one of our main objectives is the training of youth in leadership.

Your responsibilities would be as follows:

1. to build relationships with the youth
2. with your group of youth, to plan and lead activities
3. to attend Sunday night activities—both those for which you are responsible and those for which you can just "be there" to build relationships. There will be retreats and activities that will occur on other days. We hope that you can participate in those as much as possible. Since you are part of a team, when you have a conflict, we can handle it.

There is a fall retreat at Camp Saddlerock in Mentone, Alabama, on September 28–29. We encourage all leaders and youth to make every effort to be there. It gets everyone on board more quickly. Other important dates are the following:

September 3 and 5—Leadership training, 7:00–8:30 P.M.
September 8—Youth Kickoff Cookout, 6:00–8:00 P.M.
September 10 and 12—Leadership training, 7:00–8:30 P.M.

There is so much more to say in describing this exciting ministry. I will follow this letter with a phone call within the next two weeks. I will not be a high-pressure salesperson. That's not my style. I am interested in exploring the possibilities with you.

We have found that team ministry with youth is a great way for new/newer members to get involved. We do become a fine fellowship group of adults.

Even though husbands and wives are listed, we are not recruiting couples. One of you may be more interested than the other.

I'm looking forward to talking with you,

(List of names of people receiving this letter.)

ELEVEN

....

Leadership Training Sessions for Adults

You might think that since we're pushing youth ownership and youth leadership, adult leadership training would not be necessary. Quite the contrary. Adults need to work on their own leadership skills, for they are the ones guiding and supporting the young people as they try on leadership roles. Sharing leadership with the youth is a challenge that requires all the adults to work together toward the common goal of partnership with the young people.

This chapter offers four sessions of leadership activities, which, if we lived in an ideal world, where people had lots of time, would be a solid leader development program. After completing the program, your adult leaders would feel confident that they are ready to build a youth ministry in partnership with the young people. They would have had time for team building, time for exploring, time to discover things about their personalities, their gifts, and their attitudes.

Since time is a problem for so many people, you'll need to consider the needs of your leadership team as you look at the twenty activities that make up these sessions. There is no one right way to do leadership training. If you choose to have four sessions, having them close together is good for team building. One church found that it was helpful to have the sessions on Tuesday and Thursday of one week and Monday and Wednesday of the next. In another church adult leaders go on a retreat the last weekend in August.

Vary leadership training each year. The first year you could have four sessions, the next year a retreat. The third year, you may have only three sessions. You could choose to use different activities each year. Just make sure that you have more than one quick leadership training meeting. Just as one leadership lock-in is not enough to develop the leadership skills of young people, so one session of leadership training is not enough to equip adult leaders for their role in leadership. You could do one session at the beginning of the year and the other three throughout the year.

It is essential that your adult leadership team attends leadership training each year, even though some of the team members have been leaders in previous years. The team is likely to change each year. The makeup of the youth group is different each year. So the adult leadership team needs to spend time team building and regrouping each year to prepare for the new configuration of young people.

Part of this leadership training should take place before the adults meet with the young people the first time. This is especially helpful when leaders are new.

Adult leaders should also meet regularly throughout the year to (1) support each other; (2) keep up with plans; (3) check on concerns relating to the young people; and (4) do additional leadership training.

These activities are designed to be user-friendly. You shouldn't need to hire an "expert" to lead them. The coordinator of the youth ministry team would be the logical one to lead these sessions. An adult leader could do it. The leader should be familiar with this book, since it serves as a foundation for these leadership activities.

Please approach these activities with the term "adapt" in mind. There is nothing magical about this format. The sessions are written with small and large churches in mind. The length of time needed for each activity varies with the number of participants. You may see that an activity will not work in your situation. Your job, as it is with most youth resources, is to adapt. Please do.

Session 1

For this and all sessions, write the agenda on newsprint and display it.

Agenda

Team Builder
Jesus as Our Model for Relating to Young People
Who They Are—Our Young People
What Do Our Youth Need?
Who We Are—Adult Leaders

Team Builder—"I am"
(15 minutes)

Preparation: Cut pieces of colored construction paper in half. Provide the construction paper, markers, and a roll of masking tape on a table.

Directions: Participants are to choose a piece of construction paper and write their first and last name at the top of the paper. Under their name they are to write the following: I am . . . They are to think of ten or twelve things they could say about themselves that complete the statement "I am . . ." They can use adjectives, nouns, whatever. They are to be creative: Instead of saying, "I am . . . a mom," they might say "a perplexed mom," or "a patient mom." They should reveal unknown facts about themselves: I am . . . an inept cook, a good speller, a stressed auto parts salesperson. They write these ten or twelve things on the name tag. (See illustration, below.)

```
┌─────────────────────────────┐
│      Morgan Morse           │
│  ─────────────────────────  │
│                             │
│  I am  ──────────────────   │
│        ──────────────────   │
│        ──────────────────   │
│        ──────────────────   │
│        ──────────────────   │
│        ──────────────────   │
│        ──────────────────   │
│        ──────────────────   │
└─────────────────────────────┘
```

Allow ten minutes for creating the name tag. Then they are to put on their name tags with a piece of tape, and walk around reading one another's statements.

Gather everyone together and show them the agenda, the list of activities for this session. People like to know where they are going.

Jesus as Our Model for Relating to Young People
(20 minutes)

The story of the Samaritan woman at the well provides an illustration of how adult leaders should approach young people. This Bible study is intended to help leaders see Jesus Christ as a model for relating to young people. Instead of avoiding the Samaritan woman, as a good Jew should, Jesus accepted the woman just as she was. Jesus knew all about her and treated her with compassion.

Preparation: Each participant will need a Bible. Leader will need newsprint and a marker.

Directions: Everyone is to turn to John 4:3–26. Ask for three volunteers to read and play the roles of narrator, Jesus, and the Samaritan woman at the well. Give them time to read the passage to identify their parts. Then have the three read and act out the passage for the group.

Point out that this is just one form of role-playing scripture, a good method to use with young people. Role-playing brings the scripture to life, and it involves the young people.

Questions (list answers on newsprint):
- What happened in this story?
- What do you know about the Samaritan woman?
- How did Jesus treat her? What did he do?
- How did she react to him?
- What is the living water?
- Reflecting on Jesus as role model, how should we relate to young people?

Who They Are: Our Young People
(20–25 minutes)

Adult leaders need to learn as much as possible about the young people. In this exercise leaders will share knowledge and observations about the world of today's young people.

Preparation: On two sheets of newsprint turned sideways, make four columns on each as shown, below:

school life	places they go	relationship to parents	friends

relationship to church	interests	influences	characteristics of this age group

Directions: Participants are to discuss what they know about the young people. Describe the world of teenagers in your area: What do they do? What influences affect them? What is school like for them? What do you know about their relationships—to parents, church, friends? List answers under the appropriate headings.

This exercise gives adults a chance to share learning and observations. If they have questions, they can ask the young people the next time they see them. They can take their adult observations to a meeting of the young people. They'll receive some helpful information.

What Do Our Youth Need?
(15 minutes)

In the woman-at-the-well passage, Jesus knows exactly what the woman needs. In this exercise participants will discuss the needs of young people in general and those of the youth in their own church.

Preparation: For each participant, make a photocopy of the "Needs of Youth" handout (see p. 129).

You'll need ten sheets of 8½ × 11 cardstock paper, five sheets each of two different colors. Cut the sheets in half lengthwise, so you have twenty sheets, ten of each color. Write the following words, one word on each card of the same color. Then prepare a second set, using paper of the second color. Cards will look like this:

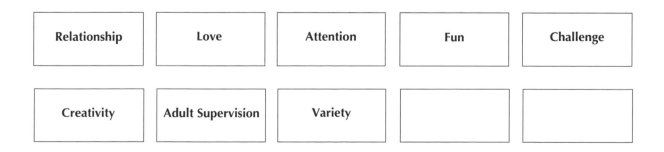

You'll have two blank cards in each set; include them in the set. (If you have more than eleven people, you'll need five more sheets of a third color of card-stock to make a third set. If you have three or four participants, you'll need only one set.)

Directions: Distribute the handout, "Needs of Youth," and allow ten minutes for everyone to look over it. Invite comments.

Then divide the group in two, giving one set of cards to each group. (If there are more than eleven people, divide into three groups. If fewer than five participants, they stay in one group.) Explain the cards as follows:

"Relationship" refers to the young people's need to develop relationships with the adult leaders.

"Love" refers to their need to know they are lovable, because God loves them first.

"Attention" refers to their need to be listened to, for adults to be interested in the youth and their world.

"Fun" refers to their need to play, to get out of the "study" or "serious" mode at times.

"Challenge" refers to their need to grow, to try new things, or to look at things differently.

"Creativity" refers to their need to let the creative juices flow, to experience new methods and media that enable them to express themselves in new ways. Youth ministry needs to be different from school.

"Adult Supervision" refers to their need to be reminded of the limits of behavior.

"Variety" refers to the need for youth ministry not to be the same every time.

If someone thinks of a need that is not in the cards, that need can be written on the extra blank cards.

The groups are to rank the cards according to what they feel are the needs of the young people in their church and community this particular year. For example, if you have a rowdy group of junior highs, you may decide that adult supervision or attention is a greater need this year. Or if you feel that your young people are ready for a challenge, you would rank challenge higher than other needs.

The groups have ten minutes to arrange their cards. Then they are to compare their ordering of the cards. Each group explains its rankings and answers this question: What are the implications for the way we do youth ministry this year?

Who We Are: Adult Leaders
(10–15 minutes)

This exercise could be used as a team builder at the beginning of the session. Or it works well here because the participants have been looking at the world of today's young people; now they will have a chance to reflect on their own adolescence.

Preparation: Choose three or four of the following sentence stems for this activity. Write them on newsprint and display them.

As a teenager, the worst thing I could have done was . . .

I would have been embarrassed if . . .

My parents could make me angry by . . .

My parents could embarrass me by . . .

I was on top of the world when . . .

What was painful for me as a teenager was . . .

When I was a teenager, a significant adult friend was . . .

Directions: In groups of three or four, each person in turn is to complete the first sentence aloud. When everyone in the group has completed the first sentence, then move on to the remaining sentences, responding to them one by one.

Alternative: Make copies of each sentence stem on slips of paper, one for each participant. Put the slips in a hat. Stay together as one group and have each person, in turn, pull out a slip and answer the question. If you have six or fewer participants, everyone could respond to the same sentence stem.

For the Next Session: Tell the participants that in the next session they will focus on team building, expectations for the young people, personality type, and leader responsibilities (job description).

Needs of Youth*

1. To be loved.

2. To be accepted.

3. To belong.

4. To be listened to.

5. To be taken seriously.

6. To have an impact.

7. Support from others.

8. Practice making decisions.

9. Practice taking responsibility.

10. Leadership skills.

11. Respect.

12. Role models.

Youth Also Need

1. To know God loves them.

2. To respond to God in love and service.

3. To explore the Bible and the Christian faith and discover how it relates to their lives.

*This page may be reproduced as needed.

Session 2

Agenda

Where Would You Be?
Team Builder
Expectations for the Young People
Personality Type
Take Me to Your Leader!
Leadership Responsibilities

Where Would You Be?
(10 minutes)

In this session the participants examine their personality type. In this exercise they explore roles they might play in youth ministry by looking at where they would choose to be during free time on a retreat with the youth.

Preparation: Make signs, using the categories, shown below on 8½ ×11 paper. Tape the signs to the wall of the room, a few feet apart from each other.

Directions: Participants are to think about where they would be and what they would be doing at 3:30 P.M. on the Saturday of a two-night retreat with the young people, during a free time scheduled from 2:30

to 5:00 P.M. They should review the choices posted around the room and move to the one that indicates what they would be doing.

Questions:
- Why are you there?
- Is there a "place" you'd rather be? Example: Someone may be in the kitchen fixing supper, but would rather be on the field with the youth.

Team Builder—Machines
(15–20 minutes)

This exercise demonstrates teamwork and the roles people play on a team. If there are more than nine participants, divide into smaller groups of five to nine each. This first exercise is from the realm of drama and pantomime.

Directions: Each group is to create a machine that has movable parts. The parts of the machine are the members of the group. Everyone should be included. The machine can be real, such as a pinball machine or a cuckoo clock. Or it could be a conglomeration of gears, levers, pumps, and so on that work together—an invention. Each group has fifteen

Taking a walk	In the kitchen helping with supper	On the field playing games with the youth
Sitting on a step talking with a youth	Sitting on the porch talking with other adult leaders	Gone to find a boy and girl who have gone off into the woods (off limits area)
Taking a nap	Working with three youth on a skit for later that night	Writing on newsprint; rearranging chairs for the next session

minutes to decide what to do and do it. Each group will then demonstrate its machine.

Questions:
- What did you discover about working together as a team?
- How did you arrive at the idea? How did you make decisions?
- What roles did each of you play, such as initiator, observer, detail person, big-picture person?
- Was everyone included?
- What about energy level—did it change as you got into the exercise?
- How is this exercise like working together as a team in youth ministry?

Go over the agenda for this session.

Expectations
(10–15 minutes)

This exercise will help everyone focus on goals, mission, purpose—the why of doing youth ministry.

Preparation: The leader will need newsprint and a marker.

Directions: Ask the participants to recall learnings from the previous session about the youth, their world, and their needs, and to refer to the story of the woman at the well (John 4:3–26).

Questions:
- How does the story of the woman at the well relate to young people and their needs?
- Jesus offered the woman living water. What do we have to offer our youth?
- What would you like to see happen with the young people in your church? What do you want for the youth?

Example: The following expectations for their youth have been suggested by various adult leaders and church school teachers. They are included merely to give you an idea of the kinds of answers you may get.

- to accept Jesus Christ as Lord and Savior
- to be challenged to grow (in faith, in relationships)
- to care for others, to love, to have a kind spirit
- to learn more about God, Jesus, the Bible
- to have Christian friends

- to be proud to be Christians
- to have significant adult friends
- to know the joy of salvation (grace)
- to be committed to the church
- to claim their calling by God to do youth ministry and to participate in the life of their congregation
- to reach out and want to reach out beyond their group to bring other young people in
- to be able to doubt, question
- to be responsible
- to be leaders in youth ministry and in the church
- to be able to express their faith, to tell their story
- to feel accepted
- to connect with people from cultures and backgrounds other than their own
- to struggle with social issues, personal issues, and faith issues
- to make decisions

Personality Type
(15–20 minutes)

Many people have taken the Myers-Briggs Type Indicator, which is a preference test for discovering how you work, what motivates and energizes you. The test results give you a four-letter type, like ENFP or ISTJ (*E*, extroversion; *N*, intuition; *F*, feeling; *P*, perceiving; *I*, introversion; *S*, sensing; *T*, thinking; *J*, judging). There are sixteen types. You also receive a description of your type that should enable you to say, "that's me." Typing helps teams function better when all members have taken the test and discussed their types. For example, some team members like everything well organized, while others are relaxed about getting things done. Such information can help everyone know which team members need extra phone call reminders, and so on.

Since the Myers-Briggs test is long, many people take the Keirsey–Bates test, a short form of the Myers-Briggs. We mention these personality tests because we believe the testing is a good idea. The Personality Style exercise that follows is a simple way of discovering personality traits.

Preparation: Make copies of "Four Personality Styles," page 152, and give one to each participant.

Directions: Participants read over the four personality styles and choose the one that is most like them. Persons may have traits from other styles, but usually one style is dominant.

Questions:
• What insights about yourself and others do you have from these personality styles?
• Do you see why you might not like doing particular jobs? Which jobs?

Take Me to Your Leader!
(15 minutes)

In this exercise participants will look at the role of the adult leader by reacting to two descriptions of leaders.

Preparation: The leader will need newsprint, a marker, and the two descriptions given below.

Directions: Before reading aloud the description of the first leader, ask participants to listen for what they like about this leader, and what they don't like. What qualities of good leadership does he or she have? What qualities need improving?

1. I am a youth leader. I have been working with the youth for ten years. I get frustrated because the children don't know the Bible. I do a lot of teaching at youth group, because it may be their only chance to hear about God. I feel like I am responsible for their learning about the Christian faith. After all, no one else is teaching them.

Youth today need direction. There are too many bad influences on youth, like peer pressure. They should be spending more time at church. There is a lot they can do to help, like picking up bulletins after church and sweeping the walkway.

I have a helper. She is kind of immature, so I don't let her have much of the program time. All she wants to do is recreation. She acts like one of the kids. I'm a parent. I ought to know what kids need. Kids today are spoiled. They don't have any respect for adults. They need to get down to business and quit waiting to be entertained.

Questions:
• How do you react to this leader?
• What are some good qualities this leader has?
• What are some not-so-good qualities? List answers to the last two questions on newsprint, divided into two columns headed "Good" and "Not so good."

Repeat this procedure for the next description.

2. I am a youth leader. I really love teenagers, especially junior highs. They're so lively. They don't have all the answers. They're not at all apa-

thetic. They're still open and willing to do almost anything. They'll talk about their faith. I love to listen. They ask such good questions. I enjoy sharing both my beliefs and my questions with them.

I am finding that the young people are willing to take responsibility but need lots of support and reminding. Lately, they have been doing their own planning. We are working toward involving them in some leadership stuff. Several of them are ready now. They lead small groups and can teach games. Two of them started a prayer chain. They organized it. They call people every week. Sometimes some of the youth are mean to each other. We talk about that a lot. When I really think they need a push, I try to challenge them . . . like to participate in Sunday school and worship, and to commit time to our service project. We have begun a Wednesday night Bible study. Three of them help me plan it.

Questions:
• How do you react to this leader?
• What are some good qualities?
• What are some not-so-good qualities? Again, list answers on newsprint, divided into two columns, "Good" and "Not so good."

Ask participants to suggest and discuss other qualities of a good leader, and add them to the list.

Leadership Responsibilities
(15–20 minutes)

Each church should have a job description for its adult leaders. Job descriptions can be designed by staff, a youth ministry committee, youth council, or adult leaders. If your church doesn't have one, the sample on pages 118–119 may be helpful. You could use the same three-part format: (1) What the church expects from you; (2) What you can expect from the church; and (3) Responsibilities of adult leaders.

Preparation: Photocopy for each participant your church's job description for adult leaders.

Directions: Hand out copies of the job description and discuss it. Ask for questions. Participants may have suggestions for the job description. Add what's needed.

For the Next Session: Tell the participants that in the next session they will focus on leadership skills, leadership styles, parents, and scripture related to God's call. They are to read each of the following passages and choose one that speaks to them about what God is calling them to do in youth ministry: John 1:35–42 (the call of Andrew and Simon Peter); Luke 15:11–24 and 15:3–7 (the parables of the prodigal son and the lost sheep); John 15:1–5 (Jesus, the true vine); Mark 4:35–41 (Jesus calms a storm); and 1 Corinthians 12:12–26 (the body of Christ).

Session 3

Agenda

Team Builder
Called by God to Do Youth Ministry
Leadership Skills
Leadership Styles
Parent Ministry

Team Builder—Operant Conditioning
(15 minutes)

The object of the game is to make a volunteer do a task without telling that person a word about what he or she is supposed to do. When the volunteer makes a move in the right direction, he or she receives positive reinforcement from the group—in the form of clapping.

Preparation: The leader will need newsprint and a marker.

Directions: Explain the rules of the game and ask for a volunteer. Have the volunteer leave the room. The group decides a task for the person to do. For example, the volunteer is to walk in the door, go over to a book, pick it up, and hand it to a designated person. The task can be simple or complicated. Everyone in the group needs to know exactly what the volunteer is supposed to do, so they can reinforce the person correctly.

Have the volunteer return. The volunteer must figure out what he or she is supposed to do. If the volunteer walks in one direction, and there is no clapping, then he or she needs to try something else.

The group only claps—no speaking, moaning, or shaking heads. This exercise is funny, sometimes frustrating, but very exciting when the volunteer finally gets it.

Allow two or three volunteers to try this and then discuss the following.

Questions:
• How did it feel being the volunteer?
• How is this game like adolescence? Write answers on newsprint.

Go over the agenda for this session.

Called by God to Do Youth Ministry
(15–20 minutes)

Several biblical passages can serve as a foundation for doing youth ministry. It is important for all involved in youth ministry to connect with God through Jesus Christ and his ministry.

Preparation: Everyone will need a Bible.

Directions: In the previous session the participants were assigned five scripture passages to read:

• John 1:35–42 (the call of Andrew and Simon Peter)
• Luke 15:11–24 and 15:3–7 (the parables of the prodigal son and the lost sheep)
• John 15:1–5 (Jesus, the true vine)
• Mark 4:35–41 (Jesus calms a storm)
• 1 Corinthians 12:12–26 (the body of Christ)

They were to choose one that speaks to them about what God is calling them to do in youth ministry.

Participants share the passages and tell how the passages speak to them about what God is calling them to do in youth ministry. If the group is larger than seven, break into smaller groups for discussion.

Leadership Skills
(15 minutes)

Not all people are comfortable doing every aspect of youth ministry leadership. To function as a team it is helpful for adult leaders to discover the skills of each of the team members.

Preparation: Photocopy the "Leadership Skills" sheet, page 151, for each participant. Prepare seven sheets with numbers from 1 to 7 (one number on each sheet). While participants are filling out the leadership skills sheets, place the numbered sheets in order on the floor in a line, with 1 at the left end and 7 at the right.

Directions: Participants are to fill out the leadership skills sheet, rating themselves from 1 (weak) to 7 (strong) on each of the skills. When everyone has finished, read the first skill and have participants move to the numbered sheets and stand on the number they wrote for the first skill. They will enjoy noticing where everyone is standing. Do the same thing for the other skills.

This exercise helps team members identify who is willing to do specific tasks. If, for example, someone is standing on 1 for making phone calls, that would not be the person to give a long list of people to call.

The coordinator of the youth ministry team should collect and file these skills sheets for reference.

Leadership Styles
(20–25 minutes)

This exercise is designed to give leaders an opportunity to consider what they would do as leaders in various challenging situations. It encourages them to identify their responses to these situations and their particular leadership styles. The styles range from highly authoritarian to the absence of leadership.

Identifying their style of leadership can help leaders understand how they relate to young people. What usually emerges from this exercise is the recognition that leaders cannot pigeonhole themselves into one particular style. They all have elements of many styles and respond differently to different situations. This is normal.

The five leadership styles that follow are not perfect depictions of five distinct styles. Encourage participants not to get bogged down debating the definition of a style, to work with the five described here. There could be variations on each.

The ultimate authority: Makes the decision. Gets the information needed and makes the decision. This is a "take charge" kind of style. Tells the group what it needs to do.

Chief: Works out a decision or solution to a problem. Presents it to the group. Invites questions and comments. Entertains alternate solutions, but has control over which solution will be carried out.

Consultor: Consults the group before making the decision. Defines options the group has, or limits within which the group can function. Still is the decision maker. Has veto power.

Democratizer: Encourages the group to make the decision. The leader and the group are equals.

This leader guides the group in examining the alternatives, helping them to see consequences, but does not sway them to a particular solution.

Hands offist: Gives the group complete autonomy. Waits to see what happens. The group makes all its own decisions, solves its own problems.

Preparation: Copy the descriptions of the five styles on five sheets of newsprint, one on each sheet. Tape the sheets to the wall in five different parts of the room. (See illustration on p. 68.)

Directions: Explain that descriptions of five styles of leadership are posted around the room. Read each aloud. Tell the participants that you are going to give them a situation. They are to decide, individually, what they would actually do in that situation. Once they have decided, they are to determine under which leadership style that decision would fall.

Below are listed seven situations. You will probably have time for only three. Consider using the others at a later date, perhaps with young people and adults together.

1. You look at the calendar and see that your leadership/care group has the program this Sunday night on "planning for college and career." It's Tuesday and your group has not done anything about it. What would you do?

2. You are on a senior high beach trip. This is the first time you have been to this particular beach. Three of the boys ask if curfew can be changed from 11:30 P.M. to 1:00 A.M. What would you do?

3. Several girls in your youth group having been spreading rumors about a girl who has just moved to town. What would you do?

4. There is one boy in the group who won't cooperate. Everytime you have a group meeting, he's either goofing off, disrupting the group, or he's sitting off by himself refusing to take part. What would you do?

5. At 1:00 A.M. on the third night of the mission trip, you get a report that somebody has brought alcohol on the trip. Everybody is in their rooms, supposedly going to sleep. What would you do?

6. A boy you've been trying to get to come to church shows up for a trip to a professional baseball game. He did not sign up. All your group tickets have been taken. He begs to go and says he'll buy a ticket when you get to the stadium. What would you do?

7. Your leadership/care group has planned a night of

games and group builders. One of the youth says to you at supper, "That's all we ever do—play games. Nobody wants to play those silly games." What would you do?

Begin by reading aloud the first situation. Participants are to decide what they individually would do and then pick the style that best matches the decision they made. Tell them to go to the part of the room where that style is posted. If someone else is there, they are to discuss solutions.

Have a person from each style speak to the whole group about what to do in the situation and how the decision reflects the particular style. If there is no representative for a style, the group should identify what that person would probably do.

After the discussion, go on to the next situation.

We have found that both adult leaders and young people enjoy this exercise—it is also included as an activity in the leadership lock-in. Not only do participants discover something about styles, but they also have a chance to discuss real problems that arise in youth ministry.

Parent Ministry
(15–20 minutes)

There are two facets of parent ministry: one is parent involvement in and support of youth ministry; the other is ministry to parents. In this exercise participants will explore ways to support and nurture parents and will evaluate the support and potential support from parents of the young people.

Preparation: The leader will need newsprint and a marker.

Directions: On newsprint list responses to the following questions:

1. What do the parents of our teenagers need from the church? from adult leaders?
2. How could we minister to parents?
3. How could parents be involved in youth ministry? How could they support youth ministry?
4. What are some ways the church and adult leaders can communicate with parents to keep them informed?

As part of your discussion, make plans also to discuss these ideas with the young people. Youth and adults together can make plans to implement some of the suggestions.

And, make plans to share concerns about family situations of your young people at a future adult leaders' meeting. It's easier for adult leaders to relate to the youth when they know something about their background. It enables them to be sensitive to particular needs of the young people.

For the Next Session: Tell the participants that in the next session they will look at specifics—planning with the young people, youth as leaders, and the fall schedule. They will also look at resources.

Session 4

Agenda

Team Builder
Planning with the Young People
Youth as Leaders
Fall Schedule
Resources
Jesus as Servant Leader

Team Builder—Knots
(15 minutes)

This is an exercise in problem solving. If there are more than thirteen participants, divide them into two groups.

Directions: Participants stand in a circle and extend their hands into the center of the circle. They grab each other's hands. Two rules: You cannot hold the hand of a person standing next to you; and you cannot hold both hands of the same person. The object of the game is to untangle the knot, without letting go of any hands. You can twist and adjust hands as you climb over and under each other's arms; just don't let go. The group should end up holding hands in a circle. It's not always possible to untangle the knot; but more times than not, it is.

Questions:
• This was an exercise in problem solving. How did you do?
• What did you discover about working together as a team?

• How can you apply this to youth ministry?

Go over the agenda for this session.

Planning with the Young People
(25 minutes)

The next three discussions deal with the details of carrying out youth ministry. Participants should have an opportunity to get their questions answered.

In this part of the session, participants will explore how to plan with the young people. They will examine the planning that has already taken place in youth ministry.

Preparation: Provide a copy of "Action Plan" (p. 159) for each participant. The leader should bring notes and information about current plans made by the youth council and leadership/care groups.

Directions: Review for this group your system, your structure for doing youth ministry. Share with participants how planning is done and how the young people are involved in the planning. If the youth are not involved, then discuss ways to get them involved. To what degree do your youth have ownership? How are you doing on adult-youth partnership in planning?

Review plans that have been made so far. Distribute and review the "Action Plan" handout. What planning still needs to be done? When do the young people and adults plan to do it? What's the next step?

As you discuss these things, remember these questions: Can a youth be doing it? How can we do it more creatively?

Write down whatever plans you make, clearly noting people assigned to responsibilities.

Youth as Leaders
(15 minutes)

In this section, participants will explore the involvement of young people in leadership.

Directions: This is a general discussion.

Questions:
• To what extent have the young people been involved in leadership?
• How can we improve in this area?
• What do we need to do to develop the young peo-

ple's leadership abilities? When and how can we do it?
• Can we do a leadership lock-in (see chapter 6)? What do the adult leaders need to do to encourage and support young people in leadership?
• Which young persons are ready to begin taking on leadership roles?
• What can the young people do in leadership? Beyond youth ministry, how can the youth be involved in leadership in the church?

Fall Schedule
(10 minutes)

Preparation: Make a copy of your program's fall schedule for each participant. It doesn't matter if the schedule is complete or in the beginning stages; just make sure everyone has a copy, so they'll know where they're heading. In light of the previous two discussions, decide what needs to be done next. When does this team of leaders meet again?

Resources
(25 minutes)

It is important to teach your adult leaders and your young people to use resources.

Preparation: Photocopy for each participant "Guidelines for Using Resources," page 158. Display youth ministry books, magazines, and curricula that have ideas, activities, and programs in the areas of worship, devotions, issues, Bible study, service, mission, recreation, and group building.

Directions: Give participants time to read the guidelines handout and to look at the resources displayed. They are to pick one resource. Using the guidelines, participants are to evaluate the resource, and then share discoveries with one another.

Jesus as Servant Leader
(3 minutes)

Preparation: Photocopy the "Jesus as Servant Leader" litany, page 165, for each participant.

Directions: Distribute the litanies. Divide the group in half. One half reads the Group #1 part, the other half reads Group #2. Everyone participates in the litany closing.

Conclusion

Adult leaders look forward to these sessions because leadership training for youth ministry is fun and also rewarding. Your adult leadership team will enjoy getting to know one another. In fact, they may have such a good time with one another, you'll need to remind them that their focus is building relationships with young people and working in adult-youth partnership in leadership. Yet, adult leaders should continue to meet regularly, perhaps monthly. They need to support and encourage one another in the process of learning to share leadership with the young people.

TWELVE

On Parents

Where do parents fit in? Do the parents support your church's ministry with youth? Are they involved? Are they over-involved? Or does it look like they don't care?

If you asked a roomful of youth leaders about parents, you would get a variety of responses: "We can't get parents involved." "We can't get them to stay out of our hair." "Ours won't bring their kids unless it's convenient." "Ours are the leaders." "Ours couldn't care less."

Since their primary responsibility is with the young people, adult leaders don't always know what to do with parents. Leaders work hard to build trusting relationships with the youth. Because they know young people need adult advocates, leaders often seem to side with the youth on a given issue. It's not that they disagree with parents; it's just that they try to understand what the young person is feeling. Their challenge is to maintain the trusting relationship with the young person without appearing to be anti-parent.

It's common to find some conflict between parental expectations and what actually goes on in youth ministry. Parents may expect leaders to keep their kids in line, when the church's goal may be to offer youth a safe place to let their hair down. Parents may expect lecture-type teaching—"Tell them what they need to know"—when leaders know that lecturing is not the best method for youth. Some parents don't understand the need for play. Some don't think that young people should be allowed to stay up late at a lock-in. Some don't believe the church should be dealing with sexuality issues.

When faced with parent opinions like these, it's not surprising that adult leaders may shut parents out and focus only on the youth. But problems with parents won't go away by ignoring them. Smart leaders realize that parents are an asset. But first, leaders must take the time to share with parents what the church is trying to do with their sons and daughters.

Communicate with Parents

We should share with parents the vision of youth and adults being called to worship, serve, explore, play, and minister to one another. For example, explain to parents why you have an "into the night" schedule at a lock-in. They need to know that you're creating a setting for group building and group caring. Tell parents that it's during those late-night, small-group conversations that you see young people becoming more responsive to what God is doing in their lives. It seems that when young people and adults are sitting or lying on sleeping bags late at night, they are more will-

ing to talk about important faith and life questions, and they are more willing to listen to one another. And when young people share personal stories, they receive affirmation and consolation from others in the group.

Parents need to know what's going on. They need to know that the church is trying to provide significant adult friends for their teenagers. Once parents understand the role adult leaders play, they are likely to support the youth ministry program. Parents will become allies of adult leaders, and not enemies. But it's up to the adult leaders to make that connection.

Suggestions for Communicating

1. **Mail information to parents.** Send a parent update, a regular mailing (perhaps monthly) that lets parents know what activities are coming up and dates of retreats and special events. Make the update promotional as well as informational. Talk about highlights of recent activities. Share your enthusiasm.

2. **Use the church newsletter.** Include information of importance to parents in your church newsletter and in youth fliers. This can be something like a "You can help" section. This encourages parents to read the newsletter and encourages the young people to share with parents information from their flier.

3. **Hold information sessions.** Gather parents together once or twice a year to share information and to hear parents' concerns. In this chapter is a description of Parent Night, a yearly gathering of parents, adult leaders, and young people. This event, which is held in the fall and led by youth and adults in partnership, both informs parents and promotes the youth ministry program.

4. **Recruit parents to serve on youth council.** Ask parents to serve on the youth council or youth ministry committee. One of the things parents bring to the council is information on school and community activities—dance recitals, arts festivals, recreation and parks activities, and so on.

5. **Start a parent advisory group.** Recruit several parents to serve in an advisory capacity to youth ministry. This group would inform those working in youth ministry of parental concerns. This group would meet periodically with the youth leaders, with a committee from the youth council, or with the youth council itself. The group would keep adult leaders informed about issues concerning home, school, and community.

Involve Parents in Youth Ministry

Adult leaders and young people should brainstorm ways parents can be involved in youth ministry. The list of ways might include some of the following:

- Serve as hosts—of an activity, of a meal in their homes.
- Prepare suppers for regular youth activities at the church.

It is helpful to recruit someone to serve as a meals coordinator. That person calls parents to enlist them as meal providers.

- Provide refreshments.
- Purchase supplies.
- Drive (cars, vans, buses).
- Use individual talents for particular tasks in the areas of drama, puppet ministry, clown ministry, liturgical dance, service projects.
- Coach or referee volleyball, softball, basketball.
- Promote youth ministry.
- Pray for young people, adult leaders, and youth ministry.
- Mentor teenagers in areas of career and college.
- Take photographs and make videos.

Should Parents Be Leaders?

There is no one right answer to the question, Should parents be leaders? Some churches have traditionally recruited parents as the advisors of their youth groups. The reason most often given is that no one else will do it. Another reason is that parents tend to volunteer in programs in which their children are involved and only for the duration of their child's involvement. For instance, parents are not likely to chaperone a fifth-grade pool party if their child is not a fifth-grader.

On the subject of recruiting parents, the question that needs to be asked is, What is best for the young people? We believe that teenagers need to develop relationships with adults other than parents who can become their significant adult friends. Indeed, there are parents who play this role in youth ministry by being significant adult friends to young people other than their own youth in the group.

A benefit of the team approach is that there are several adults in leadership. If a church has, for example, six adult leaders, having one or two parents of young people in the group on the team can work well. Some parents are excellent leaders.

When considering asking a parent to be a leader, always first ask that person's son or daughter if that is acceptable. If the young person does not want the parent as a leader, then that person's wishes should be respected. Some don't mind having their parents as leaders. Ask the young people; they will tell you.

When considering recruiting a parent, keep in mind all the issues discussed in chapter 10. The parent should be committed to adult-youth partnership and youth ownership. The intention of the expanded team approach is to get away from adult-driven youth ministry. Whenever a youth ministry becomes parent-driven, it is even harder to achieve youth ownership.

If you are in a church with a strong tradition of parent leadership and would like to see leadership expanded to include other adults, talk with the parents. Express your concerns. Talk with other adults. There are people out there who should be given the opportunity to hear the call to youth ministry. Be persistent in finding them.

One way to involve parents who wish to serve on the youth ministry team is to ask them to work with a group other than their child's. For instance, if their son or daughter is a senior high, they could work with junior highs.

Parent Night

Parent Night has become, in many churches, a traditional part of the team approach. It offers a time for parents, adult leaders, and young people to get together at the beginning of the year. Parent Night is informational, relational, and just plain fun. It offers parents an opportunity to meet the adult leaders, see adult-youth partnership and youth leadership in action, and hear all about the plans for the coming year.

As with everything else we've talked about in this book, the youth should be involved in designing Parent Night. With them, list the kinds of things to do. For example:

- Give parents an introduction to youth ministry; show them just how many opportunities there are for young people to be involved in the church.
- Share your theme, your goals, your vision for the year.
- Inform parents of activities and plans for the year.
- Let parents see youth in leadership.
- Introduce adult leaders, youth council, and the youth.
- Engage parents in ice breakers, group builders, games.
- Eat.
- Enlist parents' support by inviting them to sign up for the following:

    1. Preparing meals

    2. Hosting a gathering in their home

    3. Driving for specific outings or trips

    4. Sharing a skill (parents should list the skill)

- Address parents' questions and concerns.

The meal for Parent Night can be prepared by the young people, or it can be a covered dish supper, with parents and/or young people providing the dishes.

Preparation

Youth plan the event. They decorate the room, put up posters with photographs of youth involved in activities, posters publicizing upcoming events, posters with sign-up sheets for parents to support youth ministry in various ways, a poster with questions to discover parents' needs in areas of parenting. The youth could have baby pictures on the wall for parents to identify as they arrive. They set up the tables and the space for activities. They figure out a way to have each table include parents and young people, such as by using place cards or a mixer game. They prepare beverages. Some youth greet; some serve. Some may cook.

Schedule

Parent Night: A Sample Schedule

6:00 P.M. — Parents arrive; welcome; baby pictures

6:15 P.M. — Blessing; eat

6:45 P.M. — Icebreaker game

7:00 P.M. — Introductions; talk about youth ministry

7:20 P.M. — Games

7:55 P.M. — Thank parents; closing prayer

6:00 P.M.—Parents arrive. Youth servers arrange the food, making sure utensils are available. Youth welcome parents and guide them to an activity (like guessing baby pictures of the young people).

6:15 P.M.—Youth do the blessing, perhaps in a creative way. Parents are invited to go through the line first, if a buffet table is used. If people are being served at their tables, the young people and adult leaders can serve as waiters.

6:45 P.M.—Youth emcee the event. They lead an icebreaker or table game. Choose one of the following games:

1. What's Your Sign?

This is a name game. Everyone sits or stands in a circle. Everyone thinks of a motion for her or his first name. It can be anything, using hands, feet, body: turning around, taking a step, bending, patting head, fluffing hair. It just needs to be a motion that will help everyone remember the name. The motion could relate to the name or an interest that the person has. It should be a short motion, for everyone will repeat it. Encourage creativity.

One person starts by saying her or his name and demonstrating the motion. Everyone repeats the name and does the motion. Then the next person demonstrates name and motion. The group goes back to the first person, repeats that person's name and motion first, and then the second person's. And so on, around the circle, going back to the first person each time.

If the group is large (more than twenty), don't go all the way back to the beginning. Just go back and do the last five people each time.

2. Questions with Jelly Beans

This game is played while sitting at tables. Pass around a cup of jelly beans; each person takes out several, any number they wish. (Everyone does not need the same number of beans.) After everyone has their beans, explain the game. The leader asks a question. As each person at the table answers, he or she puts a jelly bean into the cup. As long as they have beans, people keep answering. Switch questions about every four minutes. Some suggestions for questions are the following:

Give a little-known fact about yourself.
Give an adjective that describes you.
Tell about your favorite things to do as a teenager.
Who is one of your heroes?

3. Gossip on Your Back

To be played in table groups. This game has some resemblance to the game of Gossip, where players pass on whatever is said to them. Up front is the leader, who has newsprint on an easel and a set of eight to ten drawings of objects, each drawn on a separate piece of paper. The drawings include things like: Christmas tree, jack o'lantern, cat, snowman, church, car—objects that can be drawn relatively easily. The leader is to keep the pictures from general view. Only one person from each table will see each picture.

One person from each table goes to the leader and looks at the first picture. That person goes back to his or her seat and with a finger draws the object on the back of the person to the left. That person is to draw the object on the next person's back and so forth around the table. The last person goes up to the newsprint sheet and draws what he or she perceives the object to be. Several pictures can be drawn on the same newsprint sheet. The leader then reveals the original drawing. Occasionally a table group's picture actually looks like what it is supposed to be.

The people who drew the first picture begin the second round by looking at the leader's next drawing. They go back to their seats to draw on the back of the person to the left. The game continues for about fifteen minutes or until all the pictures have been completed.

4. Three Facts/One Lie

Participants should be in groups of four or five. Pass out paper and pencils. Each person in the group is to write answers to four questions, which are displayed on newsprint. Three of the answers are to be true and one is to be a lie. Read the following four questions:

1. What is your favorite room in your house?
2. What is an embarrassing thing that happened to you?
3. What is a close call that you've had?
4. What is your favorite movie?

They can lie about whichever one they wish. They are to write down their answers.

Have someone begin by reading her or his four answers. Then the others in the group guess which one is the lie. After all have guessed, the person tells which was the lie. Then go on to the next person.

7:00 P.M.—Introductions. Begin with introductions of the adult leaders. One suggestion for introducing adult leaders is for each leader to be interviewed by a young person during supper. Interview forms, like the one on page 143, can be used. Young people then introduce the adult leaders, using information from the form.

Then introduce youth council members. A team of young people and adult leaders should explain the youth ministry vision, goals, theme, and mission statement. They could use posters as visuals. The young people from one church, for Parent Night, created posters for upcoming events. Another group created a poster for each of the five areas: worship, explorations, ministry within the congregation, and fellowship. Another time, the young people created skits for each area.

Share the calendar of activities for the coming year, or half year. If the group members have prepared posters for parents to sign up for various support functions—providing meals, hosting, driving, chaperoning, and so on—this is the time to describe what parents can do to support youth ministry. Indicate where they can sign up. Answer all questions.

7:20 P.M.—Teams of young people lead games. They begin with a group formation game to get everyone—parents, youth, and adult leaders—to form new groups. In this way, parents have a chance to meet and mingle with more people. The young people have a chance to exercise leadership. Choose one of the following games:

1. **Animals**—As a group-formation game, play Animals. Pass out slips with animal names. To find their group, participants make the sounds of their respective animals. They look for others who are making the same sound and form a group. If you play this game, have a video camera ready. It is hilarious.

2. **Machines**—In the newly formed groups, participants are to design a machine. Each group creates a machine that has movable parts. See appendix 5, page 207, for instructions.

3. **Move Left If** . . . This game is played in a large circle of chairs. See appendix 5, page 208, for instructions.

4. **I Never.** This game is also played in a large circle of chairs. See Appendix 5, page 208, for instructions.

5. Play your group's favorite games.

7:55 P.M.—Thank parents for their support. Remind them to sign up as they leave. Close with prayer. If your young people have a ritual closing, use it.

This program is designed to get parents excited about youth ministry, to energize everyone, to get them up and moving and having fun. The time flies. The tone is upbeat. The activities should reflect what goes on in your group. Parent Night should give parents a good idea of what youth ministry is all about.

Some of you may be thinking, well, we don't have an upbeat group, so how can we do an upbeat Parent Night? Review this sample schedule. Picture a group of enthusiastic young people leading this event. Picture energetic people moving from one activity to the next. That's what everyone needs to work on, and not just for Parent Night, but for all youth activities.

Introduce Leader

_____   _____
      (adjective)*   (name)

has lived in _____ for _____ years.
                   (town or area)   (number)

She/he is a graduate of _____ (Can be high school,
                            (school)
college, preschool.)

His/her family consists of _____

_____   _____.

She/he works at _____

_____ and

is a fan of _____.

He/she enjoys _____

_____   _____.

*The leader picks an adjective that begins with the same sound as the first name of the adult leader being introduced, such as Vivacious Vickie.

Family and Parent Ministry

Much is being written about expanding the focus of youth ministry to include family ministry. Some positions are becoming known as minister to families with youth rather than youth minister. The idea behind this change is to put youth ministry into the context of the family and to be more intentional about ministering to the whole family.

The concept of "family" has changed. There are fewer traditional nuclear families. Instead, many young people have several sets of families because of divorce and remarriage. For example, Will and Carrie are brother and sister, living with their divorced mother and her new husband, who has a son from his former marriage and a baby with Will and Carrie's mother. Their father is living in another part of the state with his new wife and her three daughters. Carrie and Will have a variety of roles and relationships in this family system. Carrie is close to her dad, but not her stepdad. Will and his stepdad are buddies. Will resents having to spend every other weekend with his father. And both Will and Carrie face a different set of rules in each house.

Given this situation and others like it, it is no surprise that churches are expanding their concept of family ministry as they seek to minister to young people and parents in a variety of family configurations. A teenager's life is complex enough with friends, dating, school, homework, after-school activities, jobs, and decisions! Now many must add the stress of dealing with a variety of relationships in all kinds of families—healthy, unhealthy, dysfunctional, abusive. The challenge to the church is to find ways to help families deal with these stresses and complexities. The church is in a position to connect families with agencies and counselors. The church can support families and point them to a loving God who has promised to be with them and to sustain them no matter how tough it gets.

The church can also teach parents how to be the primary Christian educators of their children. Many parents send their children to church, hoping the church will teach them about God and Jesus and faith. What churches need to do is teach parents how to nurture faith at home.

Part of the church's ministry to parents can be teaching parents how to parent teenagers. Parents often envy youth leaders' relationships with their kids. They long for that camaraderie, the relaxed, happy relationship, which parents are convinced they can't have with their teenage sons and daughters. But parents can have a good relationship with their teenagers. It's not impossible. Parents can learn the same skills that adult leaders learn: how to listen; how to affirm; how to help the young people make their own decisions.

Adult Leaders Should Encourage Ministry to Parents

Adult leaders in youth ministry are in a position to advocate parent ministry to the staff and decision makers of their churches. Adult leaders see the effects of positive and negative parenting. Leaders see the self-assurance of young people who get lots of esteem-building attention at home. All too often, though, they see the young person who is not getting affirmed at home, who is beaten down, who gets yelled at or is called "stupid" a lot. These are the young people who come to youth group looking for significant adult friends. They are hungering for affirmation.

Why is it that so many parents get in a rut of seeing only the negative things about their teenagers? When teenagers do something good, instead of affirming them, these parents ignore them and use the excuse, "Why should I say anything when they're only doing what they're supposed to do?" These parents seem to feel their only responsibility is to correct.

Church as Reward and Punishment

One of the most baffling things adult leaders see is the way church is used in raising a child. This is a typical scenario: Scott hates going to church. His parents make him go to Sunday school, church, and youth group. Even if he is grounded, he has to go to church. He lets you know with his whole body and personality that he does not want to be there. After several retreats, one of the adult leaders gets to know Scott and a significant friendship is started. Scott begins to enjoy youth group and even gets involved in planning and leading. Gradually he is included and nurtured by other youth. He begins to grow in faith and now likes to do everything connected with the church.

Scott has changed. Well, so have his parents. Now when he's being punished, he's not allowed to go to church. How ironic: They used to make him go to church; now church is off-limits.

This is one of the most frustrating parts of being in youth ministry. We want youth to be involved because they want to be, not because their parents make them. But when the young people finally get involved and enjoy it, then parents won't let them come. Either way, church is used as punishment.

How can we help parents nurture their children in the Christian faith so that there is a love of the church by both parents and teenagers? How can families, for example, avoid the battleground of Sunday mornings? We may find answers as churches develop family and parent ministry.

Suggestions for Parent Ministries

The following suggestions are descriptions of just a few programs that churches have offered to assist parents of teenagers. These ideas are not necessarily the responsibility of youth ministry, but adult leaders and young people can advocate that the church offer these programs.

A parent support group—These groups come in many varieties and can meet weekly or twice monthly. There could be groups for ninth-grade parents, junior high parents, parents of blended families, single parents. These groups often use outside resources, such as counselors who work with families of teenagers. Groups can have a spiritual focus. Or they can be topic-oriented—dating, drinking, school issues, faith, church.

A monthly parent get-together—Parents get together and talk about topics similar to those listed for parent support groups, but the ongoing support aspect is not as evident. The get-together could be a sharing session, an information session, or a time for suggestions and reactions to the youth ministry program.

A parenting class—A six- or eight-week class could be taught by a leader trained in parenting. There are videotapes that can be used as curricula. These tapes can be expensive, but they may be available from libraries or denominational or district resource centers.

A parenting Sunday school class—Many churches offer parenting classes as an elective class on Sunday mornings.

A day workshop on parenting teenagers—A workshop could be offered by the district or denominational body, or by several churches in an area.

Activity Suggestions for Parents and Teenagers

As part of ministry to parents or as part of youth ministry, there are many ways that parents and their teenagers can get together for fun, seriousness, and service. A few suggestions follow, but young people and adult leaders should think of other ideas.

Parent-youth seminar or workshop—A seminar or workshop could be created around a particular topic or study. Parents and their teenagers would attend the event together. A seminar might meet for two or three consecutive nights or once a week for six or eight weeks. A workshop might be held on a Saturday or Sunday afternoon. Topics for this kind of seminar could be: stress, music, dating, movies, television, partying, alcohol and drug use, communication, friends, making decisions, and various faith issues.

For example, the church is an excellent place to have a workshop or seminar on sexuality, especially if the curriculum for the seminar emphasizes communication between parents and their young people. One such curriculum is "God's Gift of Sexuality" (see appendix 6). It contains activities that make communicating with parents fun.

Parent-youth mission project—Many churches have mission and service projects on which parents and teenagers work side by side. Families who have had opportunities to go to a mission site either locally or away from home relate that these experiences were "the best time they'd ever had as a family." To be able to help someone else and to put faith into practice in a situation where all ages work together is a tremendous growing experience.

Parent-youth sports activities—Teenagers and their parents can play volleyball, softball, or miniature golf, or go bowling, just to name a few sports that lend themselves to parent-youth participation.

Congregational activities—Young people and adult leaders should take a look at church traditions. Look at seasonal activities. Are there areas where young people and parents or whole families might participate together?

Preparing for Parent-Youth Activities

Often when young people consider doing an activity with their parents, they react negatively. They fear that their parents will dominate, and the young people will be made to look bad or stupid or wrong. They fear it will be a case of parents making them do what they don't want to do. It doesn't have to be that way. Work with parents beforehand, preparing them to share power and ownership in the project or activity. Ask the youth to come up with the ground rules to make a parent-youth activity work. They will.

Two ground rules are a must for parent-youth activities: (1) it shouldn't be something parents force the young people to do, and (2) young people and parents should share power and ownership in planning and carrying out the activity.

Top Ten Parenting Tips

While we're on the subject of parents, in case any parents of teenagers are reading this, here is a list of parenting tips. Adult leaders and young people should feel free to share this list with parents.

1. Let your child know that you love her or him.

2. Have a sense of humor.

3. Be a good listener. Listen without trying to suggest or fix.

4. Respect your sons and daughters. That's how they learn to respect you and other adults.

5. Help your young person learn to make decisions. Don't always have a quick yes-or-no answer ready. If your daughter asks if she can go to a party, and you're not sure, tell her you're not sure, and then talk it through. Make decisions together. Don't say, "I'll have an answer for you by morning."

6. Don't be quick to judge. Be quick to affirm. Think about your youth's self-esteem. Do your words help build self-esteem or trample it? Practice talking positively about your son or daughter. Say good things. It's easy to find what's wrong with someone. Concentrate on discovering what's good and right about your son or daughter, no matter how small or seemingly insignificant. Work at it. It's a good habit to develop.

7. Be willing to admit when you're wrong. You don't always have to be right, just because you're the adult.

8. Be willing to talk when your teenager wants to talk. It may be at one o'clock in the morning.

9. Use "I" statements instead of "you." For example, say "I get frustrated when I don't know where you are," instead of "You never tell me where you're going."

10. Don't use scare tactics to teach faith. For example, "If you do that, you won't go to heaven." Or "You better be good or God won't love you."

Tips for Adult Leaders

Keep in touch with parents. Let them know that you love their young people. Let them know that the church is continually seeking ways to welcome their teenagers into the family of faith, so that the youth feel just as much a part of the church as do the adults. Let them know you are trying to nurture their sons and daughters in faith, to help them struggle with issues of faith. And let them know that "we're all in this together," that you want to assist them in any way you can. Parents, adult leaders, and young people are all on the same journey. We're all trying to live the lives God has called us to live and to care for those God has entrusted to us, whether we are parents or adult leaders or young people. We are all called to care for one another.

Appendix 1.
Leadership Lock-In Notebook[*]

A Leader

1. Leaders serve the followers.
2. Leaders are followers. They follow the will of the group.
3. Leaders are visionaries. They are dreamers.
4. Leaders motivate. They inspire the rest of the group.
5. Leaders encourage the rest of the group. They know how to build morale.
6. Leaders appreciate and affirm followers. They are aware of individuals. They treat each one with respect. Leaders believe in you.
7. Leaders lead by example. They are role models.
8. Leaders can delegate.
9. Leaders have planning and organizational skills.
10. Leaders encourage participation and involvement.
11. Leaders teach.
12. Leaders are learners. They are teachable. They are open.
13. Leaders are good listeners.
14. Leaders are good communicators.
15. Leaders care. They are empathetic. They see themselves and everyone in the group as equals. They are "we-oriented."
16. Leaders must be trustworthy.
17. Leaders hold up under pressure.
18. Leaders create change.
19. Leaders are creative.
20. Leaders are committed.
21. Leaders are enthusiastic!

Notes

Teaching Activities*

Lecture
Questions
Discussion
Small-group discussion
Fishbowl
Open-ended statements (sentence completions)
Brainstorming
Listing
Categorizing
Research
Browsing
Handouts
Silent reading
Verbal summary
Review
Reading aloud
Reading with a pencil (taking notes)
Writing
Paraphrasing
Writing a newspaper account
Rewriting in a modern-day setting
Writing a script
Writing poetry
Interviews
Surveys
Making choices
Voting: Sit down if . . .
Voting on a continuum: Standing on numbers
Role-plays
Skits
Readers' theater
Crafts
Making collages, banners, posters, murals
Drawing
Group-building exercises
Making machines, sculptures
Trust exercises
Games
Prayer
Viewing a video
Making a video
Making an audio, video, photo, or slide production
Singing
Writing songs

*Each of the activities listed above should appeal to one of four learning styles: reading, listening, observing, doing.

Discovering Your Gifts*

In each of us the Spirit is manifest in one particular way, for some useful purpose. (1 Cor. 12:7, NEB)

Check the gifts listed below that you feel you have been given by God.

_____ Intelligence	_____ Imagination	_____ Athletic ability
_____ Humor	_____ Willingness to work hard	_____ Cooking skills
_____ Musical talent	_____ Ability to teach	_____ Practicality
_____ Acting talent	_____ Ability to lead	_____ Ability to plan
_____ Sensitivity	_____ Peacemaking skills	_____ Realistic outlook on life
_____ Compassion	_____ Artistic ability	_____ Friendliness
_____ Integrity	_____ Loyalty	_____ Gentleness
_____ Honesty	_____ Ability to support friends	_____ Strength
_____ Problem solving ability	_____ Approachability	_____ Patience
_____ Enthusiasm	_____ Willingness to take risks	_____ Kindness
_____ Listening skills	_____ Efficiency	_____ Generosity
_____ Easygoingness	_____ Ability to encourage	_____ Courage
_____ Organizing skills	_____ Ability to delegate	_____ Sense of caution
_____ Mechanical skills	_____ Detail-oriented nature	_____ Affection
_____ Creativity	_____ Works-with-hands skills	_____ Dependability
_____ Spontaneity	_____ Good skills for interacting with children	_____ Empathy
_____ Commitment	_____ Good skills for interacting with older people	_____ Vision
_____ Willingness to do thankless jobs		_____ Motivation
_____ Ability to express self in words		
_____ Other _____		
_____ Other _____		
_____ Other _____		
_____ Other _____		

*Adapted from *The Giving Book: A Creative Resource for Senior High Ministry,* by Paul M. Thompson and Joani Lillevold Schultz (Atlanta: John Knox Press, 1985), 83.

Leadership Skills

Decide how well you do (or how comfortable you are when doing) the following things. Rate yourself by writing a number between 1 and 7 after each of these statements (1 = weak; 7 = strong).

1. Getting up in front of and leading a large group _____
2. Leading a small-group discussion _____
3. Giving instructions _____
4. Leading in prayer _____
5. Leading a Bible study _____
6. Leading singing _____
7. Motivating people (getting 'em going) _____
8. Delegating responsibility _____
9. Trying new things _____
10. Talking one on one
11. Listening _____
12. Making phone calls _____
13. Writing thank-you notes _____
14. Making plans, organizing _____
15. Carrying out plans (following through) _____
16. Thinking of details
17. Being on time _____
18. Doing publicity _____
19. Handling conflict _____
20. Working as a team player _____

NAME: _____

Four Personality Styles

1. Party Person
   - Prefers to be with people. Does not like to be alone.
   - Works best on group projects.
   - Wants to be liked.
   - Likes to keep people happy.
   - Likes to be perceived as a good person.
   - May have a difficult time with problems.
   - Is more people-oriented than task-oriented.
   - May need reminding of responsibilities.

2. Go-Getter
   - Prefers specific goals and objectives.
   - Is future-oriented.
   - Works well alone.
   - Likes to be given responsibility.
   - Enjoys problem solving.
   - Sticks with a job until it's done.
   - Sees problems as challenges.
   - Is more task-oriented than people-oriented.

3. Boss
   - Likes to have important jobs.
   - Wants recognition.
   - Wants to influence others.
   - Enjoys teaching and leading.
   - Can work alone or with a group.
   - Likes having authority and responsibility.
   - Likes seeing the overall picture.
   - Is persuasive.
   - Is a self-starter.
   - Can be task-oriented or people-oriented, depending on what's needed.

4. Loyal Supporter
   - Prefers to be behind-the-scene.
   - Likes to observe and then offer suggestions.
   - Does not want to stand up in front of the group and "lead."
   - Is glad to help out. Will take assignments.
   - Is a good team player.
   - Likes to make a contribution that is seen as important.
   - Can work alone or with a group.
   - Often can sense how others are doing or feeling.
   - Is dependable.

This simple assessment of personality types can be helpful in matching people with leadership roles. Many people have traits from all the types, but usually one type is dominant.

Read the four styles and choose the one that is most like you. Share your discoveries with others in your group. Turn to the "Leadership Skills" sheet. Which style would be best suited for each skill? Do you see why you might not like doing particular jobs?

Leadership Styles

The Ultimate Authority—Gets the information needed and makes the decision. This is a "take charge" person. Tells the group what they need to do.

Chief—Works out a decision or solution to a problem. Presents it to the group. Invites questions and comments. Entertains alternate solutions, but has control over which solution will be carried out.

Consultor—Consults the group before making the decision. Defines options the group has, or limits within which the group can function. Still is the decision maker. Has veto power.

Democratizer—Encourages the group to make the decision. The leader and the group are equals. This leader guides the group in examining the alternatives, helping them to see consequences, but does not sway them to a particular solution.

Hands Offist—Gives the group complete autonomy. Waits and sees what happens. The group makes all its own decisions, solves its own problems.

Sample Situations

1. You look at the calendar and see that your leadership/care group has the program on "planning for college and career" Sunday night. It's Tuesday and your group has not done anything about it. What would you do?

2. You are on a senior high beach trip. This is the first time you have been to this particular beach. Three of the boys ask if curfew can be changed from 11:30 P.M. to 1:00 A.M. What would you do?

3. A group of girls in your youth group seems always to be mean to one freshman girl. What would you do?

4. There is one boy in the group who won't cooperate. During every group meeting, he's either goofing off, disrupting the group, or sitting off by himself refusing to take part. What would you do?

5. At 1:00 A.M. on the third night of the mission trip, you get a report that somebody has brought alcohol on the trip. All the other adults and youth are in their rooms, supposedly going to sleep. What would you do?

6. A boy you've been trying to get to come to church shows up for the trip to a professional baseball game. He did not sign up. All your group tickets have been taken. He begs to go and says he'll buy a ticket when you get to the stadium. What would you do?

7. Your leadership/care group has planned a night of games and group builders. A young person says to you at supper, "That's all we ever do . . . play games. Nobody wants to play those silly games." What would you do?

Tips for Leading a Game

1. Make sure you have everything you need to play the game (pencils, ball, rope, blindfolds, whatever).

2. Let the group know the object of the game—what you are trying to do.

3. Also let the group know why you are playing the game (to demonstrate teamwork, to learn to trust each other, to get to know each other better, and so on).

4. Get the attention of the group before giving the instructions for the game.

5. Give clear, concise instructions. This takes practice. Try explaining the directions to a friend before facing the group.

6. Be enthusiastic. You'll have a reluctant group if your attitude is "this is the worst game, but we'll play it anyway." Enthusiasm is contagious.

7. Demonstrate how to play the game before actually playing it.

8. Leaders should play too.

9. Affirm people. Don't make fun of participants who make mistakes or who are slower than others. Make this policy clear to all who play: We do not tolerate put-downs.

10. If a game isn't working, suggest playing it a different way, or ask the group how the group could make this game more fun. It's always good to encourage creativity.

11. Know when to stop. It's always better to stop a game with the participants wanting more, than to wear them out. You may want to ask someone else to let you know when it's time to quit.

12. Choose games that are appropriate for the size of the group. Divide into smaller groups when you need to. Use creative ways to divide. Do not let two people choose teams. It's awful being the last one chosen.

13. Keep competition to a minimum. Choose games where the object is not to win but to have fun playing. People get tired of being losers, of being on the losing team. If you choose team games, look for those where the makeup of the teams changes as the game progresses, like "Giants, Elves, and Wizards," which is described below.

14. Choose games in which everyone can participate.

15. Choose games that are inclusive. Know your group. Are there physically challenged people in the group? Don't play games that are beyond participants' abilities.

16. Choose games that are safe both physically and emotionally.

Giants, Elves, and Wizards

Playing this game is similar to playing Rock/Paper/Scissors. It was developed by the New Games Foundation. It is an outdoor game, best played in a large field. It is a great game for large groups, but can be played with as few as eight. Give the instructions as follows:

"We play this game in a kingdom inhabited by three very different types of beings: the giants, who stand on their toes, stretch their bodies as tall as possible, spread their arms, look very, very fierce, and shout, 'Giants!' as loudly as they can; the elves, who squat down and pull in their shoulders and generally look very, very tiny as they barely peep their name; and the wizards, who stand hunched over with their hands thrust forward in the best spell-casting fashion intoning their name, 'Wizzzzzards,' in as weird and magical a manner as you can imagine."*

Explain that the pecking order, in the manner of Rock/Paper/Scissors, is: giants overcome elves, elves get wizards, and wizards zap giants. Two teams are formed, each having a goal line marked at either end of a field. The goal is about fifteen yards away from the imaginary center line. Each team huddles at its goal line and decides which of the three characters its members will be.

The teams go to the center imaginary line and line up facing each other. On the count of three the teams assume the position of their chosen character—giants, elves, or wizards, and shout, peep, or "wizzzzzard" their respective names.

The team members with the character that is higher on the pecking order chase the other team members toward their goal line. Anyone who is caught before reaching the goal line joins the chasing team for the next round. The newly formed teams huddle and choose their next character.

If both teams choose the same character, there is a groan as everyone goes back to the huddle.

The game continues for fifteen or twenty minutes, or until just before the group tires of the game.

*From *More New Games!* by Andrew Fluegelman (Garden City, N.Y.: Dolphin Books/Doubleday & Co., 1981), 167–69.

Leading a Discussion

1. Ask open-ended questions. Stay away from yes and no questions. If you ask a yes-or-no question, ask why the answer is yes or no.

2. Ask the "w" questions—who, what, when, where, why, and what do you think?

3. Relate questions to the participants' life situations. Relate the subject matter to real issues.

4. Start with easier questions. Proceed to deeper questions.

5. Wait! After you ask a question, wait for participants to think about it. That silence may seem deadly, but don't let it bother you.

6. If they look puzzled, ask the question another way. Rephrase it.

7. If they really take forever answering, start humming the "Jeopardy" tune (just kidding).

8. Always affirm a person's answer immediately after it has been shared. If an answer gets a less-than-affirmative response, the person may not respond again.

9. Invite more than one answer. This encourages greater participation. Say things like: "Good answer; does anyone have another possibility?" "Yes, that's helpful; what else?" or simply, "Thank you; what else?"

10. Repeat what you heard someone say. This will not only help those who may not have heard the answer, but it will give the person a chance to say whether or not that's what he or she really meant.

11. Don't put down an answer, or say "no, you're wrong." If the answer is not quite on target, affirm the person: "That's good thinking," or even just "okay." Then ask for more answers: "Who else wants to take a stab at this?"

12. Be a good listener. This will enable you to ask the next question based on what the person just said.

13. Encourage participants to talk to one another: "Does anyone have a response to Andy's comment?" A discussion is much more fun when people talk among themselves and not just to you.

14. You often can set the tone for the discussion. If you are asking personal questions, be the first to share. Participants will feel more comfortable sharing stuff about their lives and their feelings if they see you do it first.

15. Be enthusiastic! Your enthusiasm will make all the difference as to how the participants respond.

16. If certain people are dominating the discussion, try one of the following methods to enable others to speak:

    • Use a talking stick, which is simply an object that is held by the person who is speaking. The rule is, you cannot speak unless you are holding the stick.

    • Distribute a specific number of beans or marbles to each person in the group. When a person speaks, he or she puts a marble into a cup in the center of the circle. When the marbles are gone, that person must remain quiet for the remainder of the discussion. This method helps talkers control their talking. They have to discern which of their comments they *really* want to make. It gives others a chance to get a word in.

A Good Team

1. Everyone on the team knows the purpose and mission of the team.

2. Everyone on the team buys into the mission of the team. All have ownership.

3. Every person on the team is an equal.

4. A good team works at mission and morale. In addition to working together on the mission, a good team works on keeping up enthusiasm.

5. A good team dreams, develops, and delivers. Three aspects of the work of a good team are the following: (a) it dreams, thinks big, thinks creatively; (b) it develops a plan to carry out its dreams; and (c) it carries out its plans.

6. A good team welcomes diversity in team members—different styles of leadership; different talents and gifts; different abilities.

7. Team members share the workload.

8. Team members share responsibility.

9. Team members share in the decision making.

10. Team members care about one another.

11. Team members help and encourage one another.

12. Team spirit is evident: We're in this together.

13. The level of commitment is high.

Guidelines for Using Resources

1. Get into the habit of browsing through resources.

2. Resources are primarily used *after* you choose a topic or activity. Then you go to resources to find ideas on how to approach the topic or carry out the activity.

3. Evaluate the resource. Is it compatible with your goals and purposes? Is it compatible with the biblical understanding and theology of your church? Sometimes you encounter a resource that you are not comfortable with. Check with ministers and other church staff.

4. Are the activities, games, and so on inclusive and affirming? Stay away from those that single out people in order to make fun of them.

5. Is the resource responsible in relation to use of materials? For example, games that abuse or waste food or activities that are extremely expensive are not responsible.

6. Is the activity, study, or worship experience practical—that is, could we actually do it in our situation?

7. Share the resource with others and get their opinions. Don't grab a resource and say, "Well, this looks like fun." Make sure it fits well with your plans.

8. Remember that people are resources. So are videos, TV clips, audio recordings.

Action Plan

Start using this plan far in advance of your activity or event. Spend a half hour doing the first step.

1. On a sheet of paper, list all the steps that need to be taken. Leave space between each step. You may think of more.

2. Arrange the steps in the order they need to be done.

3. Decide who will do each step.

4. Determine by what date each step needs to be done.

5. List dates on a calendar. Use a calendar for each activity.

6. Checkpoints: Identify dates for checking on progress of the steps. *Note:* This is the key to making the plan work. Calling people to ask how they're doing with their task is often the gentle reminder that they need to perform it.

7. Publicity and promotion: Use a separate action plan for planning publicity for the activity. Again, make sure to list who will do what and when.

8. Put the action plan in the front of a file on the activity. It should help everyone keep on track with planning. It should be referred to often, so people won't get behind or forget details.

9. Evaluate and make notes after the activity is over. Keep the evaluation for the next time the same kind of activity is planned.

Steps for Planning

1. Decide what your goal is, what it is you're trying to do.

2. Write objectives, that is, statements of what you intend for the participants to do. Use action verbs like: compare, explore, discuss, demonstrate, act out, write; rather than understand, know, believe, think, care about. Objectives should be clear, measurable, and capable of being evaluated. It's hard to measure when understanding occurs. It's easier to evaluate how well people act out the understanding.

3. What is your setting? Where will you be?

4. Who will take part?

5. Describe what you are going to do. For each activity, list the following:
   - How much time it will take
   - Who will be responsible for it—who will lead it, who will get supplies or resources for it
   - Resources and supplies needed
   - The setting—in small groups, pairs, total group

6. How will you open and close the activity?

7. How will you evaluate? Set up how you will evaluate.

8. Make plans for publicity and communication.

Tips for Planning

1. Use an action plan (see "Action Plan" on preceding page).

2. Use checkpoints (see "Action Plan") to keep up with the progress of your plans.

3. Be a good listener.

4. Encourage other members of the group to participate. Encourage more than one idea.

5. Persevere. The biggest challenge in planning is to carry through the plans. When problems arise, work to overcome them. Make sure someone is responsible for overseeing the project. That person checks on those who are responsible for the various parts.

6. When evaluating, attach notes from the evaluation to your action plan, or put the evaluation in the folder for the activity, or write on the folder what needs to happen the next time you do this.

7. Be aware of significant pieces to include in your plans, such as devotions, prayer concerns, announcements, how you will make people welcome and a part of the group, a photographer.

Tips for Leading a Meeting

1. Get into the habit of starting on time.

2. Use an agenda. Tell the group what is going to happen at the meeting, so that everyone knows what to expect. If the agenda has more than two or three items, it's good to write and display it.

3. End on time.

4. Share leadership with others.

5. Be aware of those who are on the fringe and not participating. Someone should be ready to reach out to them.

6. Be enthusiastic.

7. Think through how to start the meeting. For most meetings, plan an upbeat opener.

8. Wherever possible, refer to your goal or mission statement, what you're about as a group and as part of the church. As a leader, you are a cheerleader for your group.

9. Get everyone's attention before speaking.

10. Vary your activities.

11. Plan transitions, that is, how to move from one activity to another. Avoid dead time. You'll avoid behavior problems.

12. Plan a good closing. If the group will meet repeatedly, the group should decide if they want a closing that could become a tradition, like forming a circle for a song or prayer.

13. Think creatively.

14. Think of creative ways to make announcements.

Other Areas of Leadership

Leadership role:	What is needed to prepare for this leadership role?
1.	1.
2.	2.
3.	3.
4.	4.
5.	5.
6.	6.
7.	7.

Suggestions for Evaluating

1. Leaders, leadership teams, and participants should evaluate often. In some way, every activity should be evaluated.

2. Evaluations can be oral or written. If oral, make sure someone writes down the information for future reference.

3. Written evaluations usually involve writing answers to questions or using some form of rating response, such as writing a number from one to ten indicating how well you liked a particular part of the program, or, rating items as poor, fair, good, excellent. Written answers will give you more feedback, but sometimes young people won't do the writing. Using a combination of rating and written answers is best.

4. The following questions can be used for written or oral evaluations:

   What parts did you like best?

   What did you like least?

   If we did it again, what would you change?

   What was one new thing you learned? (For example: about God; about my faith.)

   Looking at our objectives, in what ways did we accomplish them? In what ways did we not meet our objectives?

   How well did everyone participate? How could we have enabled more participation?

5. Rating suggestions:

   List each activity of the program being evaluated. Participants are to circle a number, from 1 to 5, indicating how well they liked each activity (1=not at all; 5=very much).

   List each activity, as above. Participants choose from "terrific," "great," "good," "fair," or "poor" to rate each activity.

6. Questions for the leadership teams:

   How well did our activities fit our objectives and the mission of the group? What could we have done differently?

   How did the participants respond? How well did they participate?

   How well did we meet the needs of the young people? Which individuals need attention?

   Are we growing as a group—in caring? in faith? in service?

   How can we improve? How can we be more faithful? How can we be more creative?

   What did we do well and how can we continue in that direction?

Leadership Lock-In Evaluation

After each of the following names of activities for the leadership lock-in, write a number between 1 and 5 to indicate how you rate the activity. *Note:* 1=poor; 5=excellent.

Name Tags _____
Discussion about Leadership _____
Machines _____
A What? _____
Supper _____
Communication Exercise: Gumdrops _____
How People Learn _____
Learning Styles and Sunday School _____
Discovering Your Gifts _____
Discovering Your Leadership Skills _____
Finding Out about Your Personality Style _____
What Would You Do? Leadership Styles _____
"Sister Act" Clip _____
Leading a Game _____
Leading a Group Discussion _____
Working as a Team _____
Using Resources _____
Delegating _____
Leading a Meeting _____
Worship _____

Answer the following questions:

1. Which parts did you like best?

2. Which did you like least?

3. What is something new that you learned at this event?

4. What is something you learned about yourself?

5. What do you wish we had had more time to do?

6. What suggestions do you have for changing or improving this event?

7. Would you do it as a lock-in? Why or why not?

8. What other format would you suggest? (For example: retreat; Saturday-Sunday with no overnight; five-week once-a-week class.)

9. Is there anything else you want us to know? Please put it on the back of this sheet.

Jesus as Servant Leader

Group #1: He cared about people's individual needs.

Group #2: He cared about all people, even those who were "unacceptable."

Group #1: He asked critical questions.

Group #2: He used stories and parables to teach.

Group #1: He taught people in the context of their own life experience.

Group #2: He defined himself in terms of his relationship to God and to God's will.

Group #1: He was a visionary.

Group #2: He shared his mission with his followers.

Group #1: He was committed to his mission.

Group #2: He didn't let the culture or the powerful deter his mission.

Group #1: He had patience. He never gave up on people, like the disciples.

Group #2: He delegated. He trained the disciples and sent them out.

All: He was a servant leader. Jesus is Lord.

Appendix 2.
Youth Council Day Retreat*

*This day retreat is a model for young people and adult leaders to use to begin planning youth ministry together.

When

This retreat could be held before or just after school starts in the fall. If your youth council for the following year has been formed by spring, consider having the retreat in the spring. It could be a Sunday or a Saturday. If you can make it an overnight retreat, so much the better, for this will give your council team-building time. Consult with the young people about the best time to have the retreat.

Where

Hold the retreat at a place that offers a relaxed atmosphere, yet provides adequate space to get work done. If you don't have a retreat facility nearby, consider having it at a church in a nearby town.

Purpose

Consider what you hope to accomplish during the retreat. Here, the purpose is defined by the following expectations:

Team building of the council

Dreaming of what youth ministry can be

Devising a system or structure for doing youth ministry

Getting started on planning the year

Preparation

1. Obtain resources:

    newsprint

    markers

    masking tape

    a model toy for every four or five people: car, jeep, motorcycle, truck, boat, horse

    paper and pencils

    "Five Areas Worksheet" (copied from p. 177)

    large newsprint sheet with calendar printed on it (for the year, that is, September through May)

    youth ministry resources

    copies of "Action Plan" for each participant (p. 159)

2. Prepare the closing worship. Before the retreat, find several young people who are willing to lead the closing worship. They may need resources

and adult support. Or have one or more adults and young people in partnership lead worship. Use or write a litany. A *litany* is a prayer consist-ing of phrases either recited by a leader alternat-ing with responses by the group or read by two groups of participants, alternating.

Schedule
(This sample schedule is for a Sunday retreat.)

2:00 P.M.—Team-Building Activity. (See appendix 5 for ideas such as Machines.)
2:40 P.M.—Schedule and Expectations
2:50 P.M.—Beginning to Dream
3:15 P.M.—Toy Exercise
4:10 P.M.—Developing a System for Doing Youth Ministry

5:00 P.M.—From Dreams to Reality: What We Can Do
6:00 P.M.—Reviewing Resources
6:30 P.M.—Supper
7:00 P.M.—Calendar and Activities—A Start
8:00 P.M.—Action Plan
9:00 P.M.—Closing Worship

Activities

Team-Building Activity: Machines
(30 minutes)

This exercise is from the realm of drama and pan-tomime. If you have more than nine council mem-bers, divide into smaller groups of five to nine each.

1. Each group is to become a machine that has movable parts. The parts of the machine are the mem-bers of the group. Everyone should be included. The machine can be a real object, like a pinball machine, an airplane, or a cuckoo clock, or it can be a con-glomerate of levers and moving parts. Creativity is your goal. Each group has twenty minutes to decide what to do and to practice doing it.

2. Each group demonstrates its machine. Every-body cheers the accomplishments of each group.

3. After the demonstrations, bring the groups to-gether and discuss the following questions:

How did your group decide what machine to create?
What role did each person play in the creation of the machine? (For example: came up with the idea, affirmed other people's ideas, made sug-gestions, clarified what someone was supposed to do.)
In what ways is this exercise like youth ministry? For example, if your group was slow getting started or had a hard time making a decision, how is that like youth ministry?
In what ways did your group work well as a team? What would have helped your group work better as a team?

Schedule and Expectations
(10 minutes)

Share with the council the schedule and the ex-pectations for the retreat—what you hope to accom-plish. Affirm that all who are on the council and all who do youth ministry in your church are called by God to be faithful disciples of Jesus Christ and to do this ministry. Talk about holding one another ac-countable for this ministry. Expand on what this means in your own words for your own situation.

Beginning to Dream
(25 minutes)

The following questions can help young people and adults begin to dream together. These questions encour-age individuals to reflect on their youth ministry—what their needs are, what they want, what direction to take.

1. On the walls, tape seven newsprint sheets, each with one of the following questions written at the top of the sheet:

- What would a stranger say about our youth or youth group if that person walked into our youth meeting on a regular Sunday night.
- What do you want for the youth in our church?
- What would a great youth ministry look like?
- What themes or emphases should we highlight (or work on) this year?
- Each of you is called by God to do youth ministry. What do you feel called to do in youth ministry?
- What do you need from our church in order to grow in faith?
- What struggles do you face on a day-to-day basis?

2. The council members take a marker and go around the room, writing answers to the questions on the newsprint sheets.

3. After twenty minutes, gather briefly to read all the sheets. Ask if anyone would like to add anything to any of the sheets. They will not be discussing the lists at this time. Discussion will take place later, in the "From Dreams to Reality" exercise.

Toy Exercise: On Ownership

(55 minutes)

This exercise can be done in groups as small as three or as large as eight. If you have more than eight participants, divide into smaller groups. Ideally there should be adults and youth in each group. Give each group a toy car, jeep, motorcycle, truck, boat, or horse, and paper and pencils. Begin by giving the following directions, without explaining the reason for doing this exercise.

1. Owning the Toy: Tell the groups that the toy is a model of something they could actually own. (Their small group is the owner of the object.) They have twenty minutes to respond to the following questions:

- If the group really owned the car, boat, horse, or whatever, what are five things you would do with it? List these.
- Since you own it, what are five things you need to do to take care of it? List these.
- What system can you devise for taking care of it and for doing the five things you want to do with it? (This is the hardest question, and they will struggle with it.)

Bring everyone together to briefly share their lists.

2. Owning Youth Ministry: At this point they are to relate the toy exercise on ownership to youth ministry. Invite someone to record answers on newsprint. Explain to the whole group that one of the goals of youth ministry is that it be owned by all the young people. The council is to answer the following questions:

- What are five things we can do with our youth ministry?
- What are five things we need to do to take care of our youth ministry? (This question should draw out insightful and helpful responses. The young people may never have thought about taking care of their youth ministry. They may never have thought about what it means to have ownership.)

It's fine if the council members come up with more than five answers for each question.

Developing a System

1. Explain that a system is the way an organization is structured to carry out its mission. A system might be a set of committees, planning teams, care groups, officers, "responsible persons," or adult-youth leadership teams. These groups would be responsible for the planning and carrying out of youth ministry. Then ask the following question: What kind of a system could we develop for doing both—doing what we want to do in youth ministry and taking care of it?

2. If you already have a system in place for planning and carrying out your youth ministry, this is the time for the council to evaluate the system. Does the system enable young people to have ownership? What would need to be changed in order for young people to have ownership? How do the adults function in the system? Are there adult-youth teams that do the planning and leading?

The system we suggest is leadership/care groups. The entire youth membership is divided into leadership/care groups, which see that the plans are carried out. Each group plans and leads several activities during the year. Each group is responsible for caring for the group members. (We discuss leadership/care groups in greater detail in chapter 8.)

3. After examining several system options, the youth council chooses a system that it will recommend to all the youth for carrying out youth ministry in the coming year.

4. Council members should discuss when leader-

ship/care groups (or whatever groups they choose) will meet to carry out the function of planning, leading, and caring for their youth ministry program. Great ideas will go unnoticed and unplanned if meeting times are not selected. The young people should choose these times, since they know when they are most likely to be available and willing to commit their time. The council may choose to wait and consult with the rest of the young people in this decision.

From Dreams to Reality: What We Can Do?

(60 minutes)

At this point the council is going to move from dreaming into reality. The participants take the ideas suggested during the Beginning to Dream exercise and the Toy Exercise and begin to make plans for their youth ministry.

1. Everyone is to gather as one group and sit where each can see the seven sheets which were taped to the walls earlier. On these sheets are the group's answers to seven questions that deal with needs of youth, themes, and characteristics of a great youth ministry. Review those questions and the lists of answers.

2. Discuss the following three questions, writing answers on three newsprint sheets:

- What are the needs of our young people?
- What themes and emphases should be considered for the year?
- What programs are ongoing and traditional in our youth ministry? (For example, Sunday night fellowship, Sunday school, Bible study, weeknight discussion groups, choirs, Scouts, youth in worship leadership, career guidance, sports teams, mission/service projects, retreats, Youth Sunday, confirmation.)

3. In order to develop a balanced youth ministry program, it may be helpful to work with the five areas identified earlier: worship, explorations, ministry within the congregation, service, and fellowship. Write the names of the five areas, each at the top of a newsprint sheet. Have the participants think of ideas for activities for each area, writing them on the appropriate newsprint sheet. They can pick activities they did in the past couple of years, as well as new ideas. See appendix 3 for ideas. Page 177 can be photocopied and used as a handout describing the five areas.

4. After reviewing the information that is on all the newsprint sheets, the council makes decisions regarding theme, special emphases, and goals for the year. They should take into consideration themes and emphases involving the whole church. Does the church have a special focus or theme with which the youth could connect? Are there congregational activities of which the young people want to be a part?

5. The council has two options for dealing with their lists of activities in the five areas:

- Prioritize the list of activities as to what they want to do in the coming year.
- Take the list of activities to the rest of the young people at the next youth meeting and ask for their opinions and ideas.

Reviewing Resources

Resources are not just for adults! Whatever youth ministry books and magazines are available to your church should be made available to the young people. The youth council day retreat is a good place to start giving young people opportunities to become familiar with educational resources.

1. Have several resources on a table. Don't overload the group. Too many books can be overwhelming. Invite the young people to spend twenty minutes reviewing several books and magazines, looking for ideas for: programs, topics, service opportunities, retreats, worship experiences, games, group builders, Bible study. Tell them to keep in mind what they've just discussed regarding themes, emphases, and goals.

2. In small groups of four, each young person reports on one idea they found in a resource.

Once young people become accustomed to planning and leading, they will be glad to have resources and learn how to use them. Continue to make resources available throughout the year. Adults and young people should get in the habit of using them.

Calendar and Activities: A Start

For the next hour the council will begin choosing activities, events, studies, and trips, and put these activities on a large newsprint calendar of the coming year (i.e., September through May). It is good for council members to begin looking at a calendar while they are still in the "dream" mode. It gives them a chance to see the possibilities of making the dreams a reality.

Even if your council chooses to plan a half year at a time, it will be helpful to look at the whole year, to look at the "big picture," and to be reminded of events and activities that are traditions, whether they be in the first or second half of the year.

There is no need to fill up the calendar at this time. This hour should give the council a taste of what's involved in planning and should help council members see the need for setting aside a designated time for planning.

1. Have copies of a calendar that includes assigned dates for activities already chosen. These activities would include traditions, things the young people look forward to every year. Special events involving the whole congregation should also be on this calendar.

2. Add those activities which the council is sure can be done on certain dates. If the council is excited about a new venture, then this is the time to give it a target date.

This exercise is just a beginning. There is not enough time to schedule a whole year's calendar. If the council is planning to go to the rest of the young people for ideas, then the calendar can't be completed at this time, anyway.

A Sample Calendar

The following sample calendar shows the first four months of one church's youth calendar. Note that: (1) Several events have already been scheduled: the Big Brothers–Big Sisters party, Rake 'n' Run,* and Children's Advent festival. These activities have become traditional youth-led events. (2) The fall retreat is scheduled for its usual time of the second weekend in October. (3) The Youth Kickoff Cookout, leadership lock-in, and Parent Night are scheduled, but the council needs to decide how each will be carried out. These activities should be reviewed each year and adapted to the present needs of the youth. (4) Each open date has a suggested area in parentheses to encourage the young people to keep in mind a balanced program.

Aug. 17—Youth Council Day Retreat (2:00–9:00 P.M.)
Aug. 24—Youth council finishes planning (6:30–8:00 P.M.)

Aug. 31—No activities (Labor Day weekend)
Sept. 3 and 4 (Wed. and Thurs.)—Adult leadership training
Sept. 7—Youth Kickoff Cookout
Sept. 9 and 11 (Tues. and Thurs.)—Adult leadership training
Sept. 14—Group building
Sept. 20–21—Leadership lock-in
Sept. 28—Leadership/care groups meet
Oct. 5—(A fellowship activity)————
Oct. 11–12—Fall retreat
Oct. 19—(An explorations activity)————
Oct. 26—Parent Night
Oct. 30 (Thurs.)—Big Brothers–Big Sisters Halloween party (service)
Nov. 2—(A fellowship activity)————
Nov. 9—(An explorations activity)————
Nov. 16—Rake 'n' Run (ministry within the congregation)
Nov. 23—(A worship activity)————
Nov. 28 (Thurs.)—Thanksgiving
Nov. 30—Children's Advent festival (ministry within the congregation)

Action Plan

Once an activity is chosen and assigned a date, it must be planned. An action plan is an excellent tool for planning. Groups often come up with great ideas but never carry them out. An action plan can help groups accomplish their goals and carry out their plans.

On an action plan, planners list the steps that need to be taken—to accomplish a goal, to plan and lead an activity, or to plan the year. It enables planners to get the details down on paper—who needs to do what and by what date. It has built-in checkpoints to keep everyone on track. These checkpoints are dates on which to call those who have agreed to certain responsibilities and ask them how they're doing.

1. Distribute copies of "Action Plan," from page 159, and review the steps listed there.

2. Council members should practice using an action plan by working on one for "Starting the Year." They should spend thirty minutes following the directions on the handout. This exercise will encourage the youth council to plan what they need to do after the day retreat.

---

*Rake 'n' Run is a fun-filled activity involving raking leaves. Instead of assigning two or three people per lawn, the entire group rakes each lawn and runs to the next. The job gets done more quickly, and the group enjoys working together.

3. After thirty minutes of working on the action plan, the council should do the following:

- Decide when it will meet again. If a regular youth council meeting time has not yet been determined, it should be decided while council members are present. This should be the young people's decision.
- List all that needs to be done before the first meeting of youth in the fall.
- Decide how the council will share the goals, dreams, plans, and hopes it has for the year with the rest of the youth.
- Decide to what extent the rest of the youth will be given an opportunity to participate in the dreaming and in the decision making regarding goals and activities.

Closing Worship

The worship need not be long. A song and a litany is an appropriate closing. Creativity and inclusivity in worship reminds the council of the need for creativity and inclusiveness in the entire youth ministry program. By closing in worship, council is reminded of the importance of worship in our lives together.

Conclusion

During this retreat the youth should be taking dreams and activities and playing with them like clay, forming and reforming, with no need to finish the product at this time. However, before they leave this retreat, make sure everyone knows what the next step will be. Unfortunately, many productive planning sessions become time wasted, because there is no follow-up. How much time do you need to finish the plans? The youth council needs to have a follow-up meeting to prepare for the first meeting with all the young people. Set a date.

Appendix 3.
Involving Youth in the Five Areas of Youth Ministry*

Worship

Goals: To praise God. To give thanks. To celebrate our faith in a variety of ways. To share our gifts. To offer ourselves. To be strengthened in our faith.

Issues to consider: Could youth take part in Sunday morning worship leadership? Could they do a whole service? How about scheduling worship at other times—after a football game? at a breakfast? Could they make banners or other special helps in worship? Could they use liturgical dance, handbells, guitars? How might they use drama in worship? What about using other media?

Explorations

Goals: To explore issues of faith, of the Bible, of our lives. To ask questions, to search together for understanding and guidance. To discover how our faith relates to our daily living, home, school, community, and world, and to other cultures.

Issues to consider: What topics, issues, studies might we explore? What methods other than discussion might we use for exploration? What about using role-play, case studies, projects, video? How and when should we do Bible study? Evaluate your Sunday school program, both the curriculum and the methods used.

Ministry within the Congregation

Goals: To take an active role in the life of the church. To minister to older and younger members of the congregation, as well as get to know them and let them know us.

Issues to consider: Could youth help with vacation Bible school? Could they help teach Sunday school in the younger grades? Could they do any kind of presentations for other age groups? Are there opportunities to do jobs for older members, such as raking leaves (Rake 'n' Run) or running errands or having parties? Could the youth serve on committees and task forces or as officers? For what traditional church occasions or events could youth take an active role—stewardship, mission, evangelism, Advent, Lent?

Service

Goals: To respond to God's call to love and serve others through hands-on serving beyond our congregation. To develop a lifestyle of caring for those in need. To develop the habit of service.

Issues to consider: What kinds of social service agencies do you have in your town? Where can youth be plugged in—individually and as a group? Hands-on service, such as Habitat for Humanity, working in day camps for children in need, and mission work trips, provides opportunities for life-changing experiences. Seek to perform this kind of service as well as, or instead of, "raising money" to be sent away, or other forms of activity we might call "service" but in which the young people don't have the opportunity to actually serve.

Fellowship

Goals: To get to know each other. To learn how to affirm others. To build community. To build trust. To build relationships and a spirit of teamwork and teamplay. To enjoy being together as Christians. To reach out and invite other youth.

Issues to consider: Group-building activities are a must! Retreats, trips, and extended times together are the best avenues for achieving these goals. Minimize competition. Youth are competitive in almost every aspect of their lives. Let church be different. Play games that are affirming, that do not embarrass or put down any person.

Note: Please use the "Five Areas Worksheet" to chart goals reached and those to accomplish in the five areas of ministry.

Five Areas Worksheet

WHAT WE HAVE DONE	WHAT WE MIGHT DO
Worship	Worship
Explorations	Explorations
Ministry within the Congregation	Ministry within the Congregation
Service in the Community	Service in the Community
Fellowship	Fellowship

Ideas for Activities in the Five Areas

Youth can be involved in the life and ministry of the church in a variety of ways. In fact, the opportunities are enormous. What follows is a lengthy sampling. You will probably be able to create additional activities.

Worship

During Sunday morning service:

• Give the call to worship
• Lead prayers
• Read or act out scripture
• Do a minidrama or role-play
• Perform vocal or instrumental music
• Perform a liturgical dance
• Use audiovisuals
• Give puppet shows
• Usher, carry banners, serve as acolyte
• Greet
• Announce youth activities, mission projects, or youth concerns
• Lead children's sermon

Lead entire worship service
Attend worship regularly
Participate in palm procession
Light Advent candle(s) in wreath during worship service
Attend Advent Sunday school services (fifteen-minute service at beginning of Sunday school for four Sundays in Advent)
Organize or participate in Christmas program/pageant
Make chrismons for chrismon tree
Lead early Christmas Eve service for children/families
Participate in live nativity scene
Sing in youth choir
Play in handbell choir
Make banners
Organize or attend an outdoor worship
Organize or attend a moonlight worship
Attend Lenten services/Ash Wednesday service
Attend Easter sunrise service
Attend Jewish Seder service
Design and lead worship service for children
Lead children's/junior church
Design and lead worship for vacation Bible school

Worship after football game
Worship at retreats or lock-ins
Worship spontaneously at a special place (e.g., on rug in sanctuary)
Design and lead early Sunday morning service
Lead worship for elderly
Lead praise/singing service
Visit other churches
Write on 3 × 5 cards thoughts or prayers for use in worship
Lead prayer service
Participate in prayer breakfast
Catacombs worship (simulating early Christian worship)
Worship at a meal
Have an agape meal/agape feast (worship experience designed around a meal, after the Moravian tradition)
Write hymns and songs (write words to familiar hymn or song tune)
Attend a worship workshop
Attend a New Year's Eve service
Create or participate in a clown ministry
Create or participate in a puppet ministry
Lead a prayer at congregational functions
Do a "Hymn of the Month" (youth research and publish information about hymns in bulletin or newsletter)
Design and lead worship at church picnic
Hold a progressive worship service (with other churches)

Explorations

Topics around which activities could be devised are as follows:
Going together, dating, rejection
Relationships: God, family, church, friends, opposite sex
Friends/friendship
Marriage
Racism
Prejudice
Peer power and parent power
Parent/teen communication
Problems in families
Divorce
Trust

Independence issues: parents, restrictions, decision making
Handling conflict
Gender issues
Dreams
Music: rock music, videos
Movies
Media and the affects of; advertising
Homosexuality
HIV-AIDS
Stress, anxiety, worry, stress management
Handling pressure: from parents, school, friends, peers
Why so much suffering?
Depression, suicide
Eating disorders
Drugs, alcohol, addiction
Death and dying
Afterlife, eternal life, heaven
Angels
Worship
Being a Christian, living the faith
Christian lifestyle at school
Religion in school
School: How would you change it?
Students' rights
Building Christian relationships
Success
Church school curriculum topics
Lifestyle: simplicity
Environmental issues
Politics and religion
Poverty, hunger
Child abuse
Violence in the United States
The occult
Evangelism
Global concerns
Mission
Stewardship
Prayer and meditation
Spirituality (relaxation/spirituality retreat)
Commitment
Forgiveness
Faith sharing
Bible study
Retreats on special topics
Everything-You-Need-to-Know-about-the-Bible-in-One-Day
Sexuality retreat
Confirmation retreat

Baptism and the Lord's Supper: The Sacraments
People who encountered Jesus
Life and teachings of Jesus
Meaning of Jesus Christ
Parables of Jesus
Beatitudes
Women of the Bible
Seasons of the church year
Symbols
The shorter catechism
Prophets
Prophecy
Paul
The Ten Commandments
Lenten studies
Passover and Holy Week
Apostles' Creed
Twenty-third psalm
Discussion of sermons
Intergenerational studies
Your denomination
Your church's life and ministry
Other denominations
Other religions
Visiting other churches/church members
Visiting another culture within your community
Your future
Making decisions
Career exploration
Counseling center testing
After high school
College trips
Workshops: on communication, leadership, the Bible, clowning
Local mission tour
Visiting denominational centers/offices/mission sites

Ministry within the Congregation

Lead Wednesday night supper program, other congregational events
Create a Fun Night for congregation
Lead recreation at church picnic
Lead recreation with senior group (elderly)
Rake 'n' Run (rake leaves: everybody on one yard, then run to next)
Sing Christmas carols to shut-ins
Make goody bags for shut-ins
Visit nursing homes

Sing in nursing homes (not just at Christmas)
Work with elderly and shut-ins:

- Bake cookies, make crafts
- Birthday cards, write letters
- Make emergency telephone numbers book
- Adopt a grandparent
- Clean yards, do odd jobs
- Run errands
- Take them shopping
- Do telephone check-in
- Organize or help with tape ministry

Be prayer partners with children or elderly
Make banners/posters
Hang greens/decorate church at Christmas
Make Christmas goodies for elderly or children
Lead Christmas party for children
Hold Halloween party for tots
Serve snacks for preschoolers
Organize or help with Easter egg hunt for children
Teach children's Sunday school
Team teach in Sunday school
Organize or help with Mother's Day lunch after Sunday worship
Create a dinner theater
Serve in nursery and extended session
Work with vacation Bible school—teaching, recreation, crafts, refreshments, music, nursery for vacation Bible school teachers
Run video equipment
Help prepare church school materials
Make visual aids for teachers
Help in office
Hold or help with dinners, barbecues, lunches: pancake breakfast, spaghetti supper, potato/salad bar lunch after church, Easter sunrise breakfast
Serve at regular church night suppers
Provide restaurant for church night supper: youth serve as waiters as well as do program
Design minicourse for children
Lead Advent workshop or festival (Advent crafts) for children
Participate in musicals, dramas
Provide Mothers Morning Out during Christmas vacation
Organize a craft fair
Visit youth (create a welcome wagon for new youth)
Provide new member assimilation (big brother/sister idea for new youth)
Act as big brother/sister for elementary school children

Work with children's choir
Serve on committees, task forces, church board
Assist with Parent Night or parent reception
Attend adult/youth seminars
Attend adult/youth sports events: softball, bowling, basketball, volleyball
Hold an ice cream social
Design and prepare bulletin boards
Have a talent show or time and talent auction
Bake and serve cookies between Sunday school and church (all youth present: emphasis on visibility)
Clean church yard
Have a Rent-a-Senior Day or time and talent auction
Have a puppet workshop for youth; they then present show for children or for congregational dinner
Create a video presentation of church or Sunday school, or on seasons of the church year
Devise a jeopardy game on history of the church (youth do research, long-time members play the game)
Interview adult classes (with audio or video recorders)
Participate in congregation's traditional activities

Service

Work in soup kitchen
Work on Habitat for Humanity house
Lead recreation at Big Brothers–Big Sisters events
Organize Souper Bowl
Go on in-country or out-of-country mission trip
Offer services to homeless shelter
Offer services to Girls Club or Boys Club
Volunteer with Meals on Wheels
Offer services to child-advocacy program
Hold a food collection for families in need
Hold a toy collection for families at Christmas
Do recycling projects
Hold hunger walks/runs
Hold a Work Day to raise money for mission project
Have a car wash, bake sale, barbecue for mission project
Make Christmas goodies for elderly or children in need (work through schools or social agencies), or for prisoners or for Advocacy center/abused children, AIDS victims, Big Brothers–Big Sisters
Decorate trees to give to the above
Have a Christmas party for Big Brothers–Big Sisters
Adopt a family at Christmas (buy clothes, toys, presents)
Clean up a neighborhood
Do a clown ministry to nursing homes

Have a party for or visit children's home, children's
   hospital
Summer program for preschoolers in low-income
   neighborhood
Volunteer at a day camp for children in need
Lead games for a day-care center
Give puppet shows for children
Do tutoring
Offer services to library, Saturday reading program
Shovel snow, rake leaves
Give disaster relief (trip to hurricane/tornado/flood
   area)
Take coffee to people in line at unemployment office
   (before school starts)
Educate community on social concerns with displays
   or presentation (connect to something youth
   have studied)
Help with city recreation program
Provide Christmas gifts for prisoners (make stockings
   and fill with toothbrushes, etc.)
Invite nonchurched friends to activities

Fellowship

Go on retreats
Hold lock-ins
Have a game night
Sing
Do group-building activities
Participate in a ropes course
Go on a camping trip
Hike; go backpacking
Invite other churches for recreation
Have a cookout
Go on a hayride
Play field games (new games)
Play volleyball
Play church-league basketball, softball, volleyball
Hold a progressive dinner
Watch movies, videos
Watch TV

Eat out
Take trips, car caravans
Go to beach
Go skiing
Go rafting
Have a talent show
Have a scavenger hunt
Go on a Polaroid (or video) scavenger hunt
Go skating; late-night skating
Go bowling; late-night bowling
Go cycling
Play miniature golf
Go horseback riding
Have a Super Bowl party
Have holiday get-togethers
Have a "Spontaneous Youth Group"—decide what to
   do when everyone arrives
Go to a baseball game
Go to an away football game
Have a swim party
Go on a college trip; meet with campus ministry stu-
   dents
Hold a senior banquet (put on by juniors)
Do line dancing
Have a picnic
Have an ice cream night
Have a carnival
Hold a mission fair
Play Ping-Pong
Meet at a pool
Meet in homes
Meet at a coffee house
Go on a museum trip
Attend community cultural events
Go to dances
Go to arts festivals
Go to plays
Cook dinner for parents
Do a "This Is Your Life"
Attend youth rallies
Attend district retreats and events for youth
Attend summer youth conferences

Appendix 4.
"Reach Out and Teach Someone": A Youth-Led Retreat or Workshop

It often happens that people from one church hear that another church has a good youth ministry program. So someone from the first church calls the second church for help. Let's suppose that you work with the church with the good youth ministry program. You may be able to help another church, especially if your youth ministry has youth ownership, adult-youth partnership, and young people involved in leadership.

Let's also suppose that you have been contacted to help a church. What could you do? This appendix contains a retreat design that offers a model for developing a team of young people and adults who can teach another church's young people and adults how to do youth ministry based on the expanded team approach and leadership/care groups.

This model for designing youth ministry can be carried out as a retreat or a workshop. It differs from the youth council day retreat in appendix 2 in that it is based on one specific system for doing youth ministry. At the youth council day retreat young people and adults have more options for designing and structuring youth ministry.

The goal of the model for youth ministry offered in this retreat is to give all youth opportunities to be involved in the total life of the church. Total life is defined in five areas: worship, explorations, ministry within the congregation, service, and fellowship. The young people choose activities in all five areas and use a leadership/care group system to carry out the activities.

This event is designed to be led by young people and adults in partnership. It was field-tested with a group of four youth and one adult as leaders. The team could be larger, but there shouldn't be more leadership-team young people than client-church young people. For this event to be effective, we recommend no more than thirty-five participants from the client church.

The leadership team should be trained before it can teach. Training can be accomplished in two three-hour sessions. The training involves practicing the activities of this four-session retreat/workshop. Any adult leader who can lead the leadership training sessions in chapter 11, the leadership lock-in in chapter 6, or the youth council day retreat in appendix 2 can lead the training for this retreat/workshop.

This retreat/workshop has eight hours of activities, divided into four sessions. A sample schedule and full descriptions of the activities follow.

Prearrangements

1. Send the client church a suggested schedule for this event (see p. 185) and the handouts (see "Preparation," p. 186, for a list of pages to be photocopied as handouts). The handouts will give the client an idea of what's included in the event.

2. Decide on the setting for the event. Will it be a one- or two-day retreat or a workshop? Where will it be held?

3. Find out how many young people and adults the client church will have at the event. The participants will be divided into five leadership/care groups. The client church should configure these groups before the event. The leadership/

care group handout will help them. Should the client church have less than ten youth participants, suggest that they create four, or even three, groups. The adult leader participants would be assigned, one to each group, although it's okay if a group does not have an adult in it.

A member of the leadership team will be in each group.

4. Recruit your own leadership team of at least four young people and at least one adult.

5. Set up two sessions of leadership training for your leadership team.

The Leadership Training for Your Leadership Team

All leadership team members should have a copy of:

- the schedule for the event (see below).
- the description of the activities in the four sessions of this Youth Ministry Retreat (pp. 187–196)
- their own copies of the handouts that will be distributed to participants during the four sessions

At the training session, the team should begin with Session 1, on group building, and then skip to Session 4, on how to have leadership. Session 1 contains icebreakers, which will help the leadership team in its own team building. Session 4 contains leadership exercises, which will help the team members to develop their leadership skills. Then they go over Sessions 2 and 3.

At the training session, team members should decide who is going to do what. As they go through each session of the event, they should:

- *do* each activity (not just read about it!)
- answer the questions they will be asking the client youth group
- assign parts: decide who will lead each activity and who will do the "Tell the group" parts

The "Tell the group" parts are the minilecture parts of the program. This is the scripted part. In addition, there are times when the young people will need to explain how something works or describe important points about youth ministry. The young people don't need to memorize these parts, but they should be familiar with the "script." They should have notes or an outline in hand.

It is important for the young people to actually practice the activities, for three reasons:

1. Experiencing the exercises makes it easier to lead them.
2. They need to become familiar with the resources—cards, handouts, and so on.
3. *Doing* the exercises—as opposed to reading and talking *about* them—involves movement, which makes a three-hour training session more fun.

At the retreat or workshop, all the leadership team members should participate along with the members of the client youth group. In this way they will model participation. It is an important principle of leadership that leaders participate along with the group. Leaders, whether adults or young people, should not stand off to the side and observe.

The team should cover as much as possible at the first training session, so that at the second, team members can review, rework, and firm up the four sessions. Everyone should know exactly what she or he is going to do on the retreat.

Saturday-Sunday Retreat: A Sample Schedule

Saturday
SESSION 1: YOU HAVE TO BUILD A GROUP!
11:00—Name Game
11:15—Zip Zap
11:25—Name Tags
11:40—Virginia Reel Conversation
11:55—Three Facts/One Lie
12:10—Machines
12:30—Lunch
  2:00—Ropes Course or Trust-Building Activities
  4:15—Free Time

SESSION 2: YOU HAVE TO KNOW YOUR YOUTH!
  5:00—Group Builder (Mingle or Operant Conditioning)
  5:20—Being a Teenager Today
          Youth Worries and Concerns
          Being a Teenager in (town/city/area)
  5:45—Needs of Youth
  6:15—Supper

SESSION 3: YOU HAVE TO HAVE A PURPOSE AND A PLAN!
  7:15— What Would a Great Youth Ministry Program Look Like?
  7:30—Five Areas
  8:00— Rotation
  8:20—Leadership/Care Groups Work on Areas
  9:00—Break
  9:20—Leadership/Care Groups Reconvene
  9:45—Presentations
10:15—Game

Sunday
SESSION 4: YOU HAVE TO HAVE LEADERSHIP!
  8:00—Breakfast and Packing up
  8:40—Clean Up; Pack
  9:00—Group Builder
  9:15—Review
  9:25—Leadership: Coordinator and Youth Council
  9:45—Take Me to Your Leader!
10:05—Leader Skills
10:20—What Can Young People Do in Your Church?
10:30—Leadership Styles
11:00—Youth Ministry Is More Than a Program: Eight Essentials
11:20—Taking It Home: Action Plan
11:40—Closing Worship

Preparation

Make the following eleven cards out of poster board. Write each numbered phrase on a separate piece of poster board. These will be used during the workshop.

1. You Have to Build a Group!
2. Give Everyone an Opportunity to Participate.
3. Have a Lot of Variety in the Activities.
4. You Have to Know Your Youth!
5. Relationships Are More Important Than Program.
6. You Have to Have a Purpose and a Plan!
7. Vision
8. Goals
9. Giving All Youth Opportunities to be Involved in the Total Life of the Church
10. The Five Areas:

Worship

Explorations

Ministry within the Congregation

Service

Fellowship

11. You Have to Have Leadership!

Prepare "worry cards," a set for each group of six or seven people (see p. 190, Activity 2, for instructions).

Prepare newsprint with Three Facts/One Lie questions (see p. 188, Activity 5, for instructions).

For Session 4, Activity 7, prepare leadership style newsprint sheets (see p. 196) by writing one leadership style description on each of five sheets.

Photocopy as a handout for each participant and each leadership team member:

"Youth Council or Youth Ministry Committee" (p. 9)

"Leadership Skills" (p. 151)

"Action Plan" (p. 159)

"Five Areas Worksheet" (p. 177)

"Ideas for Activities in the Five Areas" (pp. 178–181)

"Leadership/Care Groups" (pp. 197–198)

"Eight Essentials for Youth Ministry" (p. 199)

"Litany" (p. 200)

Make samples of the various types of name tags (see Activity 3, p. 187, and appendix 5, pp. 201–202).

Resources

colored construction paper, cut in halves, for name tags (Session 1, Activity 3); full sheets for "worry cards" (Session 2, Activity 2).

markers

crayons

tape

newsprint

paper

pencils

poster board for 11 numbered cards

sample of a poster promoting one of the five areas, if you have one (see pp. 193–194, Activity 4)

the five leadership styles (see appendix 1, p. 153)

handouts

Session 1.
You Have to Build a Group!
(90 minutes)

A leader holds up card number 1 and then tapes it to a wall.

1. Name Game
(15 minutes)

One of the leadership team members announces the first activity, which is a name game, explains how to play it, and leads the game. (Six name games are described in appendix 5, pp. 203–204. The leader for this activity has chosen one ahead of time.)

Tell the group: This was what we call an icebreaker, as well as a good way to learn names. It's fun; and it gets everybody moving. There are several other name games that you might want to use in your youth group . . . especially at the beginning of the year, or when new youth join your group—games like Zip Zap, which we'll teach next.

2. Zip Zap
(10 minutes)

As in Activity 1, the leader for this game, which is described on pages 203–204, explains the game and leads it.

Tell the group: You have to learn names. Did you ever notice that if you're not sure of a person's name, you tend to avoid that person? You just aren't comfortable around him or her. You're embarrassed to ask the person to tell you the name again. But avoiding people is the opposite of what we're trying to do in youth ministry. So we need to spend lots of time at the beginning of the year getting names straight. You'll be a lot nicer, warmer, and more welcoming to people if you can use their names. And sometimes *you* may know everyone's name, but there may be a new youth or a new adult leader who doesn't know everyone's name, so a round of name games is a good idea.

It's also a good idea to use name tags every once in a while. There are lots of creative ways to do name tags.

3. Name Tags
(15 minutes)

The leader has chosen one of the name tag activities from appendix 5, pages 201–202, and gives the directions. Participants will need construction paper and crayons or markers, and masking tape to put on the name tag. Have a display of sample tags showing the group other ways to make tags (refer to appendix 5, pages 201–202): -ing or -able Name Tag, Symbols Name Tag, Acrostic Name Tag, Four Corners Name Tag, Slogan Name Tag, Right Now I Feel . . . Name Tag.

Participants should put on their name tags with masking tape and walk around reading each other's tags and looking at the display of samples.

Tell the group: Your group may want to think of other creative ways to make name tags. Creative name tags give people something to talk about as they mingle.

Moving on—For the next three activities, you'll be in groups of two, four, and then eight. The purposes of these groupings are, first, group building and team building—you'll be gradually building a team as you join with another group for each activity. And second, variety: it's good for a group to move around and not stay in the same place. It's easier to build enthusiasm.

4. Virginia Reel Conversation
(15 minutes)

For the first group-building activity use the Virginia Reel Conversation. (Instructions are on pages 204–205.) The leader for this activity gives the directions, and then asks the first question, and so on. Use the questions listed below, or come up with your own.

1. What is a favorite Christmas tradition in your family?
2. What do you (or did you) like about school?
3. What don't you like about school?
4. If you could have dinner with two famous people, who would they be?
5. Where would you like to live, other than your present location?
6. What is something that makes you angry?
7. What was something you feared as a child?
8. What is one way parents could do a better job bringing up their kids?
9. If Jesus were here on earth today, what would he say to you?
10. What are two things you would do if you were president?
11. Why do you think people go to church?

5. Three Facts/One Lie

(15 minutes)

Have the participants form groups of four: from the Virginia Reel Conversation, the first two pairs in line form a group of four. Then, the next two pairs form a group, and so on.

Pass out paper and pencils. Each person in the group is to write answers to four questions, displayed on newsprint at the front of the group. Three of the answers should be true and one should be a lie. The four questions might be:

• What is your favorite food?
• What is an embarrassing thing that happened to you?
• What is something you did even though your parents told you not to?
• What is your favorite TV show?

You could think up your own questions instead of using those suggested above.

Someone begins by reading her or his four answers. Then the others in the group guess which answer is the lie. After all have guessed, the person tells which was the lie. Then go on to the next person in the group.

6. Machines

(20 minutes)

Form groups of eight by having two of the groups of four from the previous activity come together. The leader gives the directions (see p. 207 in appendix 5). After the participants have created and demonstrated their "machines," the leader asks participants what they discovered about working together as a team. They are to discuss within their groups questions such as:

• How did you do?
• In what ways did you work together as a team?
• Was it hard to get started? Why?
• How did you decide what machine to make?
• Who emerged as leaders?
• What role did you play?
• How did the energy level of the group change as you started putting the machine together?
• How is this like youth ministry or youth group? What would help your group work well together? In what ways can youth be leaders?

Tell the group: In the Virginia Reel Conversation, you started out in conversation groups of two. You were gently forced to participate. Only one person heard what you had to say, so you didn't have to worry about what other people might be thinking. Everybody was doing the same thing, so it should have been easier to talk to someone you didn't know very well.

Then you moved to small groups of four, and then to a bigger group of eight and did a task that required teamwork. The advantage of breaking into small groups, whether it be in twos, fours, or teams, is that more people get to participate. Did you ever notice that in a large group discussion, two or three people tend to dominate the conversation? That's not a problem with small groups.

So what have we been doing? (Hold up cards number 2 and number 3.) Two goals of youth ministry are to: (1) *give everyone an opportunity to participate,* which is helpful for building groups and teams, and to (2) *have a lot of variety in the activities.* Notice how the activities got you moving around a lot. There's no chance for boredom here. It's important to keep things lively.

Put the cards up on the wall. Tell the participants that in Session 2 they will be looking at "who the youth are" in their youth ministry program, in their church, and in their community.

Recreation and Free Time
Between Sessions One and Two

The schedule for this retreat allows free time and time for recreation in the afternoon between Sessions 1 and 2. This would be an ideal time for team-building and trust-building activities, such as the kind provided by a ropes course. If your retreat setting has such facilities, arrange for guides to take the group through a ropes course. If not, check out resources which offer trust-building activities and "new games." (See the listings under Community Builders and Games in appendix 6.)

Ropes Course

If you have access to a low ropes course, perhaps the group could have an hour or two on the course. A ropes course is an outdoor series of problem-solving tasks involving ropes, logs, and cables. Trained guides take the group through each element. Communication and trust are the essential ingredients for each element. For example, there is an element called "the web of life," which looks like a spider web. The group passes its members through the spaces in the web without touching the ropes (the web). It is a timed activity, so the group must plan how they will work together to accomplish the task. Another element involves getting the whole group up and over a 10- to 15-foot wall. The guide then leads the group in debriefing the experience.

Groups quickly learn that in order to accomplish these tasks, they must work together, communicate, make group decisions, exercise leadership, delegate, and trust each other—all the things that go into teamwork. The young people have to care about every person in the group in order to succeed.

Tell the group: Ropes courses and trust-building exercises are ways to give people a taste of Christian caring. They provide an excellent way to start the year. Many youth groups have problems with cliques. Teenagers (and many older people) stick with their own little groups. It's more comfortable that way. But it's tough on newcomers and youth who don't have a group. Therefore, groups must work on team building.

Session 2.
You Have to Know Your Youth!
(55 minutes)

Hold up card number 4; then tape it to a wall.

1. Group Builder
(15 minutes)

If there are more than eight participants, play Mingle (see p. 207 in appendix 5). Discuss how the game is like adolescence.

If there are fewer than eight participants play Operant Conditioning (see pp. 207–208 in appendix 5). Discuss how the game is like adolescence.

2. Being a Teenager Today

Youth Worries and Concerns
(15 minutes)

Preparation: Using poster board or sheets of construction paper, make a set of "worry cards" (see below) for each group of six or seven people.

Tell the group: As you start developing a youth ministry, you need to look at who the youth are. What are they like? What's their world like? What issues concern them? What do they worry about? What are

School performance	About my looks	How well other kids like me
Parents might die	Hunger and poverty	Violence in this country
Sexual abuse	Physical abuse by parent	Might lose my best friend
Drugs and drinking	Might not get a good job	That I might kill myself

their needs? You'll also need to get to know each individual in the group. This takes time, but it's crucial. Both young people and adult leaders need to work at getting to know and care about *all* the youth.

For this exercise, participants should be in groups of six or seven. The leader should use a "divide up" exercise (see appendix 5, p. 205) to form the groups.

The leader gives each group a set of worry cards and explains that the task is to work as a team to put the cards in order of importance. Arrange the twelve cards on the floor, deciding as a group the most pressing concern of youth and putting that card at the top, with the remaining cards below it in descending order of importance.

After ten minutes, everyone reviews the other groups' arrangement of cards. Participants will have fun comparing.

Gather everyone together for discussion. The leader asks the following questions:

• How were your arrangements alike?
• How were they different?
• How do you explain your arrangement?

The leader invites comments to get the young people talking about how they see their life and their world. There are no right or wrong answers. Issues vary from one group to the next.

Being a Teenager in (town/city/area)

(10 minutes)

The leader continues and broadens the discussion by asking:

• What is it like being a teenager in [use name of town/city/area]?
• How would you describe teenagers in your area—what school is like, what's in, what's not in? This information will be helpful to the adult leaders who are hearing the young people describe their world.

3. Needs of Youth
(15 minutes)

The leader writes at the top of a sheet of newsprint, "Needs of Youth," and asks the participants: What do teenagers need? Encourage them to consider psychological needs, spiritual needs, and needs particular to this age group. The leader lists on the newsprint all their answers.

If they haven't included the following, the leader should add:

to be loved
to be accepted
to belong
to be listened to
to be taken seriously
to have an impact
support
practice making decisions
practice taking responsibility
leadership skills
respect
role models

and

to know God loves them
to respond to God in love and service
to explore the Bible and the Christian faith and to discover how it relates to their lives

Tell the group: We've spent a lot of time this weekend on the subject of building a group and getting to know each and every young person, because (hold up card number 5) relationships are more important than program. This is a basic principle for youth and adult leaders. In the next session we'll be spending a lot of time working on planning a great youth ministry program. But the best program in the world is never worth as much as the relationships that can be developed between youth and adult leaders, and among the young people themselves.

Tape card number 5 to a wall.

Session 3.
You Have to Have a Purpose and a Plan!
(3 hours with break included)

Hold up card number 6; then tape it on a wall.

Preparation: This session is a work session and requires a room with tables. Set up five tables in five areas of the room, in such a manner that the participants can rotate in groups to each table. If there are fewer than five groups of participants, then one or two groups will have two area sheets at one table.

For the first discussions, the participants are together in a large group.

1. What Would a Great Youth Ministry Program Look Like?
(15 minutes)

The leader asks the participants this question and lists their answers on newsprint. This is a brainstorming session.

Tell the group: We need a *vision* of what youth ministry can be, so we know where we're heading. (Hold up card number 7; then tape it on a wall.) This helps us discover what our purpose is. Why do we have youth group, anyway, or Sunday school, or any other youth program?

The leader asks the following questions:

• Why do you have youth group? Why do you do youth ministry?
• What do you want for the youth in your church?
• What do you hope will happen spiritually, in their relationships with God, the church, friends, family, and others?
• What do you hope will happen in their lives?

(If the discussion is slow getting started, the leader might offer an answer or two, such as for the last question: To know that they are loved by God, or to see how the Christian faith relates to their lives.)

The leader lists participants' answers on newsprint. (Hold up card number 8; then tape it on a wall.)

Tell the group: Discovering what you want for the youth in your church will help you discover your goals for youth ministry.

If you want to have a solid, faithful youth ministry, one of your goals could be to provide opportunities for youth to be more involved in the life of the church. You want youth group to be an important part of *[name of church]* Church. You want young people to be taken seriously as members of your church. To expect anything less is to shortchange your youth. There's a phrase, "You get what you expect." If you don't expect much, years down the road you'll be wondering why you never had a good youth program.

At this retreat, we are going to introduce a team approach to youth ministry that is based on the following goal: *Giving all youth opportunities to be involved in the total life of the church.* (Show card number 9.) To define the life of the church, we'll use five areas: worship, explorations, ministry within the congregation, service, and fellowship. (Show card number 10, and tape both cards on walls.)

This goal can get you started on planning your year's program.

2. Five Areas
(30 minutes)

The participants divide into leadership/care groups, which the client church identified before the retreat. These groups can be as small as three persons. There should be an adult leader and at least one youth from the client church in each group, and there should be a member of your leadership team in each group. Announce that these groups will serve as leadership/care groups for planning and carrying out their youth ministry program back home.

What We Have Done

Pass out copies of the "Five Areas" handout (see p. 177) and pencils to each of the participants (youth and adults). On the "Five Areas Worksheet," "What We Have Done" is near the top of the left side and

"What We Might Do" is near the top of the right side. The groups will work on the left side first.

Participants should think of all the activities, topics, events, projects, retreats—anything that youth have done in the past year as a youth group or as individuals in the church—and list them in the appropriate space. If the group has been less active, they can include activities from the past several years.

Give the participants ten minutes to fill out the left side of the sheet (what they have done). After they have finished, ask if some areas have more activities listed than others. Which ones? Which areas have fewer items?

Tell the group: In most churches, the list is longest under Explorations and Fellowship. Youth group programs usually are topics and recreation. Some churches have a hard time finding service opportunities for youth. Youth Sunday is often the only worship area activity. Ministry within the congregation is often overlooked.

What you are striving for is a balanced youth ministry in which youth do things that are important to their church and to their community. It may take time to figure out what you actually can do in each area, but it's worth it.

What We Might Do

Assign each group one of the five areas of ministry and tell them that for the rest of the session, they are to work on this one area. They will become the "experts" and the "advocates" for this area. (If there are only four groups, one group can work on ministry within the congregation and on worship. If there are just three groups, combine service and fellowship as well.)

On the right side of the "Five Areas Worksheet," participants are to write ideas of what they might do in their assigned areas. Give them five to ten minutes. Then pass out the "Ideas for Activities in the Five Areas" handout (see pp. 178–181). This handout lists activities that other churches have done. Each group looks specifically at activities listed for its area.

Give each group a blank sheet of newsprint (two sheets if the group is working on two areas). They are to write the name of their area across the top of the sheet and list three of their ideas as suggestions of what their youth might do in the coming year.

Have them take their newsprint sheets to the tables in the room, putting one sheet on each table (or two sheets on one table, if a group is working on two areas).

3. Rotation
(15 minutes)

The participants visit the table for each area and write on each area sheet their own ideas for what they would like to do in the coming year. Everybody gets to write ideas on each newsprint sheet. They have only three minutes at each table. One of your leadership team members should be at each of the tables to answer any questions about the particular area. This part of the process is fun and gets everyone moving around.

4. Leadership/Care Groups Work on Areas
(40 minutes)

Participants go back to their groups, with one person from each group taking their respective sheet with them; that is, the service group takes the service sheet, and so on. They will now function as leadership/care groups for their area.

Distribute the "Leadership/Care Groups" handout (see pp. 197–198).

Tell the group: In order to see great ideas happen, you need a system or structure for planning and carrying out the activities. In this model of youth ministry, planning and leadership of activities is done by leadership/care groups. (Go over the description and responsibilities on the handout you just distributed.) You can take this handout back home and share it with those who are not on this retreat.

Leadership/care groups give youth a chance to own their youth ministry. Instead of programs being planned and led by adults, everything is planned and led by youth and adults in partnership. When there is youth ownership, everyone is more enthusiastic about participating. It's easier to get excited about ideas that you create, plan, and lead.

On this retreat, the leadership/care groups will accomplish the following tasks:

- Become familiar with your area. Look over your area's description on "The Five Areas" handout (see p. 177).
- Create a skit to promote the area.
- Create a poster to promote the area. The skit and poster are active, fun ways to begin to understand the five areas of ministry. And they give

you practice in promotion and publicity. A great youth program is a waste without promotion.

• Look at all the activities participants suggested for your area. Pick three favorites, the three that your group would recommend to your full youth group that they do this year.

5. Leadership/Care Groups Reconvene

(25 minutes)

Groups continue working on the four tasks listed in the previous activity.

Session 4.
You Have to Have Leadership!
(3 hours with break included)

Hold up card number 11; then tape it on a wall.

1. Group Builder

(15 minutes)

Begin the session with a group builder, such as Knots (see appendix 5, p. 208). After the game, the leader asks the following questions:

• This was an exercise in problem solving. How did you do?
• What did you discover about working together as a team?
• How can you apply this to youth ministry?

2. Review

(5 minutes)

Tell the group: You've got a goal, a purpose for youth ministry: *To involve all youth in the total life of the church.* You've got a program, based on the five areas: *Worship, Explorations, Ministry within the congregation, Service, and Fellowship.* You've got a

6. Presentations

(30 minutes)

One by one, the groups present their skits, their posters, and their recommendations.

7. Game

(15 minutes)

Close the session with a favorite game that the client group can teach the leadership team or that the leadership team can teach the group.

system for making it work: *Leadership/Care Groups.* Are there questions about what you've done so far?

3. Leadership:
Coordinator and Youth Council

(15 to 20 minutes)

Tell the group: This design, using leadership/care groups, needs coordination. It needs a *coordinator,* someone who

• oversees the entire program;
• keeps up with the calendar of activities;
• contacts the group leaders to remind them of their upcoming responsibilities and to check on individual concerns of young people in their groups.

Next, pass out the "Youth Council or Youth Ministry Committee" handout (see p. 9).
Tell the group: Having a youth council or a youth ministry committee is a good idea for several reasons:

• It's better to have a group making policy decisions than one leader.

- It gives youth opportunities for decision making and leadership.
- It connects youth ministry to the life of the church, and to other committees. In many churches, this committee comes under the Christian Education Committee.

Let's look at the handout. If you have, or choose to have, a youth council or youth ministry committee, it should look at your present youth ministry program. What are all the programs that affect youth—choirs, Scouts, sports team? Are there traditions, like Youth Sunday, or a Christmas festival with youth choirs? What are special things that the youth do every year? Traditions are important. No doubt, with the team approach, you'll find new activities that will become traditions.

The youth council would take ideas from a planning retreat like this one and:

- share the ideas with those who couldn't go on the retreat.
- put chosen activities on the calendar for the year (September through May) or half-year. If you plan for a half-year, you could have a miniplanning day in January, and plan for summer in March.

A faithful youth ministry needs everyone, young people and adult leaders. Youth and adults, together in partnership, design it, plan it, and lead it. We are going to take you through a quick leadership training program, in which you will

- identify qualities of a good leader;
- discover the skills of leadership you already have;
- learn something about your "style" when it comes to leadership and handling problems.

4. Take Me to Your Leader!

(15 to 20 minutes)

Tell the group: We're going to read descriptions of two adult leaders. Listen for what you like about each leader, and what you don't. What qualities of good leadership does he or she have? What not-so-good qualities? The descriptions are of adult leaders, but you'll see qualities of leadership that apply to both youth and adults.

Read aloud: "I am a youth leader. I have been working with the youth for ten years. I get frustrated because the children don't know the Bible. I do a lot of teaching at youth group, because it may be their only chance to hear about God. I feel like I am responsible for their learning about the Christian faith. After all, no one else is teaching them.

"Youth today need direction. There are too many bad influences on youth, like peer pressure. They should be spending more time at church. There is a lot they can do to help, like picking up bulletins after church and sweeping the walkway.

"I have a helper. She is kind of immature, so I don't let her have much of the program time. All she wants to do is recreation. She acts like one of the kids. I'm a parent. I ought to know what kids need. Kids today are spoiled. They don't have any respect for adults. They need to get down to business and quit waiting to be entertained."

Ask the following questions, and list answers to the last two on newsprint, divided into two columns headed "Good" and "Not so good:"

- How do you react to this leader?
- What are some good qualities this leader has?
- What are some not-so-good qualities?

Repeat this procedure for the following description:

"I am a youth leader. I really love teenagers, especially junior highs. They're so lively. They don't have all the answers. They're not at all apathetic. They're still open and willing to do almost anything. They'll talk about their faith. I love to listen. They ask such good questions. I enjoy sharing both my beliefs and my questions with them.

"I am finding that the young people are willing to take responsibility but need lots of support and reminding. Lately, they have been doing their own planning. We are working toward involving them in some leadership stuff. Several of them are ready now. They lead small groups and can teach games. Two of them started a prayer chain. They organized it. They call people every week. Sometimes some of the youth are mean to each other. We talk about that a lot. When I really think they need a push, I try to challenge them . . . like to participate in Sunday school and worship, and to commit time to our service project. We have begun a Wednesday night Bible study. Three of them help me plan it."

Ask the following questions:

- How do you react to this leader?
- What are some good qualities this leader has?

• What are some not-so-good qualities?

Ask the participants to suggest and discuss other qualities of a good leader, and add those to the list.

5. Leader Skills
(15 minutes)

Pass out the "Leadership Skills" handout and pencils (see p. 151). Ask the participants to read the instructions at the top of the handout and rate their leadership skills.

6. What Can Young People Do in Your Church?
(10 minutes)

Ask the participants to identify all the things that young people can do in their church and in youth ministry that would be considered leadership opportunities. As the group talks, the leader should list the answers on newsprint.

7. Leadership Styles
(20 minutes)

This is a fun exercise. Young people get into good discussions about the situations. Although it was designed for adult leaders and will benefit those adults present, youth enjoy talking about what they think the adults should do, as well as what they would do as "youth" leaders.

Newsprint sheets listing the five leadership styles (see p. 153) should be taped to the walls in five different parts of the room. Read these descriptions aloud. Then read aloud one of the "Sample Situations" on page 153. Tell the participants they have three minutes to decide individually—no discussion—what they would do in that situation. Then they are to decide which of the five leadership styles best matches their decision and go stand under the description of that style on the wall. If others have chosen that style, they are to discuss what they would do in the situation and why they chose that style.

Ask one person from each style to report on the group's discussion. Then go on to the next situation,

repeating the procedure. You should have time for three situations.

8. Youth Ministry Is More Than a Program: Eight Essentials
(20 minutes)

Tell the group: We've looked at a goal, which suggests involving youth in the church in a variety of ways, and which, as you have seen, can result in a well-planned year of activities. You could now pick several of your ideas, put them on a calendar, and you'd have a great program. But if you really want a youth ministry that's exciting, a youth group that attracts youth, you've got to think about more than program.

Distribute the "Eight Essentials for Youth Ministry" handout (see p. 199). Participants are to rate their youth ministry as directed on the handout. Invite comments and questions.

9. Taking It Home: Action Plan
(20 minutes)

Distribute the "Action Plan" handout (see p. 159).

Tell the group: We've covered a lot of ground at this retreat. Now you need to decide what to do when you get back home. How will you share your ideas with those who are not here? How will you implement the ideas and "make it happen"?

An action plan can help you. We're going to spend the next twenty minutes working on an action plan for "Planning Youth Ministry," deciding what steps need to be taken and who needs to do what.

The group then brainstorms about the action plan, arriving at a consensus and completing steps 1–4 of the plan.

10. Closing Worship
(5 minutes)

Tell the group: For worship, young people and adults can write their own litanies by taking a scripture and adding phrases or responses.

Pass out the "Litany" handout (see p. 200). To use it for this closing worship, divide everyone into two groups, Group #1 and Group #2, and read the litany aloud as indicated.

Leadership/Care Groups*

Leadership/care groups are responsible for:

1. *Planning three or four activities* for the coming year. Choosing activities can be done in two ways:

   a. Each group plans activities in one particular area. One group does worship, one explorations, one ministry within the congregation, one service, and one fellowship. Or, if you have four groups, combine worship and ministry within the congregation.

   Advantage: A group learns a lot about a particular area in the life of the church.

   b. Each group, in turn, chooses an activity from the five areas, until all the activities have been assigned. In this way a group may plan a fellowship activity, an exploration, and a service.

   Advantage: A group gets to plan a variety of activities. There's less chance that young people will wish they were in another group.

2. *Leading the activities* for which their group is responsible. Part of planning is deciding who will do what. What kind of leadership roles are the youth willing to take? These roles include leading a small group discussion, giving instructions, leading in prayer, doing the devotions, leading a game, preparing the resources and materials, making the announcements, promoting the activity, making phone calls. *Tip:* If adult leaders have a tendency to do everything themselves, remind them to ask: Can a youth be doing this?

3. *Working in partnership with the adult leader/s* in the group. The adult leader(s) assigned to the group should make a special effort to get to know the youth in their group—make phone calls, write notes, find out individual interests, give special care. This way, no youth is overlooked.

4. *Doing team-building and trust-building exercises* at the beginning of the year. This greatly increases the closeness of the group. It makes possible the fusing of a fun group out of a group of youth who don't normally hang out together. It helps nurture the Christian spirit of love, care, and openness that you are trying to encourage.

5. *Caring for each other.* Pray for each other. Reach out to those who have not been participating. This group has the opportunity to develop into a group that bonds, that shares highs and lows, joys and pains.

*This page may be photocopied as needed.

Creating Leadership/Care Groups[*]

How Leadership/Care Groups Are Structured

The following are three ways to structure leadership/care groups.

1. *Well-mixed groups.* The youth membership is arbitrarily divided into groups. Each group has relatively equal numbers of youth from each grade. Each has a balance of very active and not-so-active youth. Each has a balance of personalities—from aggressive to shy. Each has a balance of males and females.

2. *Grade groups.* The youth membership is divided by classes. Each grade group serves as a leadership/care group. Freshmen meet together to plan and lead an activity for which they are responsible. Sophomores meet together, and so on.

3. *By areas.* The youth membership is divided into as many groups as the church has areas of ministry. According to our team approach, there would be five groups, to correspond with areas of worship, explorations, ministry within the congregation, service, and fellowship. These groups are responsible for planning and leading activities in their respective areas. This option gives groups a chance to specialize and learn about a particular area of ministry.

The membership of these area groups could be either well-mixed or grade groups. If grade groups, and there are four grades, then an adjustment must be made to accommodate the five areas. One option is for each grade to take one of the first four areas and all four groups to add a fellowship activity as part of their responsibility. Other options are to combine the areas of ministry within the congregation and worship, or to combine ministry and service.

Who Leads the Leadership/Care Groups?

Whenever possible, a young person and an adult should lead the leadership/care group. Or two youth and an adult, or better yet, two youth and two adults. Youth council members are logical choices for care group leaders. Or any young person who volunteers to lead the group. Ask the young people how to structure the leadership and the groups.

Who Drafts the Membership of Each Group?

Adult leaders who know the young people should start the process of assigning youth to groups. The youth council should have input and approval.

Every young person on your membership rolls should be in a leadership/care group. Include those young people you never see. Even if they never show up for a group meeting, at least they are not forgotten; someone will be looking at their names periodically. And someone should be contacting them periodically. Don't give up on any young person. The exception is when an inactive person tells you to remove her or his name.

*This page may be photocopied as needed.

Eight Essentials for Youth Ministry*

Rate your youth ministry from 1 (weak) to 7 (strong) on each of the essentials, writing your rating after each essential.

1. *Youth ministry must be Christ-centered.* _____

We are different from other youth organizations. What makes us different is a belief in Jesus Christ as Lord. We believe that Christ calls us to love and care for one another. We believe that God loves us and, therefore, we can love and serve others.

2. *You have to love the youth.* _____

All adults who work with young people *must* love the young people, just as they are.

3. *You must build relationships. Relationships are more important than program.* _____

The first responsibility of an adult leader is to build relationships with the youth. Adults should become "significant adult friends" to the young people. Building relationships among the youth is another primary function of youth ministry. Developing each youth's relationship with God through Jesus Christ is another primary purpose. All these relationships are more important than any activity.

4. *Youth need ownership. Youth ministry should be youth-driven.* _____

Youth should play a major role in making decisions and in planning, carrying out, and leading their youth ministry activities. Adults and youth should work in partnership. If adults are doing too much, they should ask: Can a youth be doing this?

5. *Commitment is critical. Commitment of youth* _____, *of adult leaders* _____, *of parents* _____, *of the church* _____, *of the pastor/s.* _____

Getting people involved in the vision of youth ministry leads to their commitment. Listening to youth, adult leaders, parents, and pastors also encourages commitment. Recognizing that those who are involved in youth ministry are responding to God's call inspires commitment.

6. *Program: Think big. It's more than Sunday night.* _____

Youth ministry includes all that young people do in response to living as a follower of Jesus Christ. Youth ministry includes everything that youth do in the church. Recognize and affirm the various ways youth are involved in the life of the church.

7. *Program: Here's the beef.* _____

What actually happens on Sunday night, or a weeknight, is important and should reflect all the essentials. Sometimes the weekly program is a young person's only connection to the church.

8. *Promote! Promote! Promote! So what if your program is great, if no one knows.* _____

Communicate and publicize. Make phone calls! Talk it up!

*This page may be photocopied as needed.

Litany*
(Based on Eph. 4:1–6, 11–16)

Group #1: We are urged to live a life worthy of the calling we have received.

Group #2: God is calling us to do youth ministry in (name of place).

Group #1: We are called to be completely humble and gentle.

Group #2: To be patient and to bear one another in love.

Group #1: We are to make every effort to keep the unity of the Spirit through the bond of peace.

Group #2: We are one in the Spirit, we are one in the Lord.

Group #1: There is one body and one Spirit—just as you were called to one hope when you were called.

Group #2: We are called to work and play together in unity.

Group #1: To worship and serve together in community.

Group #2: One Lord, one faith, one baptism, one God and Father of all, who is over all and through all and in all.

Group #1: It was Christ who gave some to be apostles, some to be prophets, some to be evangelists,

Group #2: Some to be pastors and teachers,

Group #1: Some to be leaders of youth ministry.

Group #2: To prepare God's people for works of service,

Group #1: So that the body of Christ may be built up.

Group #2: Speaking the truth in love, we will in all things grow up into him who is the Head, that is, the Christ.

Group #1: From him the whole body, joined and held together by every supporting ligament,

Group #2: Grows and builds itself up in love, as each part does its work.

Group #1: To this we have been called.

All: We will love and serve the Lord.

*This page may be photocopied as needed.

Appendix 5.
Group Builders and Games

Group Builders

Group builders are activities that facilitate interaction in a group. It is hard for young people to walk up to someone they don't know and carry on a conversation. Group builders are games or exercises that, through a structure, help people relate to one another. You could say they gently force people to get to know one another.

These activities are also called community builders or team builders. Some are called icebreakers, because they are used at the beginning of a meeting to help people feel comfortable being in the group. Young people who are shy or feel like outsiders need something to get them involved with the group.

These activities can be used at regular meetings, at retreats, in Sunday school, wherever. They are not solely for the beginning of the year. Some, such as open-ended statements, can be used throughout the year as methods to explore studies or issues. Others are beneficial when new young people join the group. The task of building a group should be ongoing.

Introduction Activities

Name Tags

Creative name tags can be used as an "arrival" activity. As people arrive, they are guided to a table where they find colored construction paper (cut in half), markers, tape, and instructions. They spend five to ten minutes making the name tag, put it on with the tape, then move around reading one another's name tags. Below are several varieties of name tags.

1. *-ing or -able Name Tag.* Write your name on the name tag paper. Think of four or five things that you enjoy doing or characteristics about yourself. Make the words end in -ing and -able. They don't have to be real words. Example: singable, soccering, bookable, energeticable, soap opering, travelable.

2. *Symbols Name Tag.* Write your name on the name tag paper. Think of four or five things about yourself (interests, hobbies, job, likes), and draw a symbol for each. (See the illustration, below, for an example.)

3. *Acrostic Name Tag.* Write your first name down the left side of the name tag paper. For each letter of your name, write a word that tells something about you. For example:

Loving
Open-minded
Responsible
Independent
Night person
Dependable
Active

4. *Four Corners Name Tag.* Write your name in the center of the name tag horizontally.

In the upper left corner, write where you were born.
In the lower left corner, write your favorite toy when you were a child.
In the upper right corner, write your favorite restaurant.
In the lower right corner, write a favorite movie.

Or you may think of other ideas for the four corners. (See the illustration, below, for an example.)

5. *Slogan Name Tag.* Write your name on the name tag paper. Think of a slogan or bumper sticker that would tell something about you. Write that slogan on your name tag. (See the illustration, below, for an example.)

6. *Right Now I Feel . . . Name Tag.* Write your name at the top of the name tag. Draw a picture of how you feel right now. (See the illustration, below, for an example.)

NOTE: Sometimes young people get tired of making name tags. They say that everybody knows each other. Remind them that even if everyone does know each other, the name tag exercise reveals facts that not everyone knows.

One way to get around the aversion to name tags is to call them "group builders" or "team builders" instead.

7. *Team Builder: "I Am."* Write your name on the paper. Under your name, write: I am . . . Think of ten or twelve things you could say about yourself that complete the statement, I am . . . Use adjectives, nouns, whatever. Be creative. Instead of saying I am . . . a tennis player, say, I am . . . a tennis-playing fanatic. Reveal little-known facts about yourself. I am . . . a first-rate chocolate chip cookie baker, a pitiful speller, a stressed student, and so on.

Name Games

What's Your Sign?

Participants are in a circle. Have everyone think of a motion to use for their first name.

Tell them: It can be anything. Use hands, feet, body. Turn around, take a step, bend, pat head, fluff hair. It just needs to be a motion that will help everyone remember your name. The motion could relate to your name, or an interest that you have. It should be a short motion, for everyone will repeat it after you do it. Be creative.

One person starts by demonstrating her or his name and motion. Everyone repeats the name and does the motion. Then the next person does her or his name and motion. The group now goes back to the first person, repeats that person's name and motion first, and then the second person's. Go around the circle, going back to the first person, second person, and so on, each time.

If the group is large (more than fifteen), don't go all the way back to the beginning. Just go back and do the last five people each time.

Delightful Debra

This name game is similar to What's Your Sign? Have everyone think of an adjective that begins with the same letter as their name. If they can, they should pick an adjective that matches their personality. The game can be played two ways:

Version 1: The first person says the adjective and her or his name, as in Delightful Debra; the second person says the first person's adjective and name and then her or his own: Delightful Debra, Witty Whitney. The game continues around the circle with each person naming all the persons who have gone before. The last person has a lot of names to remember. Ask if anyone else wants to try to name everyone.

Version 2: The first person says adjective and name, and everyone repeats it. The second person says adjective and name. Everyone says the first person's, then second person's adjective and name. Use this second alternative when you are concerned any participant, such as one who has a learning disability, might be embarrassed to play.

Name Choo Choo

The starter is in the center. Everyone else is in a circle. The starter walks over to someone and asks, "What's your name?" The person answers, "Morgan" (for example). That starter yells "Morgan" over his or her shoulder and does a "dance"—right foot out, says "Morgan"; then left foot out, says "Morgan"; then right, left, right, saying "Morgan" three times. (This is like the Mexican hat dance.)

The starter turns around; Morgan puts her hand on the starter's waist and follows as the starter goes to someone else. "What's your name?" the starter asks. "Sam," the new person says. The starter yells "Sam" over his shoulder and Morgan yells "Sam" over her shoulder: "Sam . . . Sam . . . Sam, Sam, Sam," starter and Morgan say and dance together.

The starter and Morgan drop hands, and turn around in place. Sam puts his hands on the starter's waist. Morgan is now the head of the choo choo line. She chugs over to a new person. The game continues.

If you have more than fifteen participants, do two choo choo lines in the same circle.

John, John, John, John

Everyone is in a circle. The leader is in the center. The leader moves around the circle, pointing at different people. When the leader points, everyone says that person's name in a resounding chorus four times. When a name comes a little slowly to the group, the leader should stand over that person and keep pointing until everyone is saying, "Natalie, Natalie, Natalie, Natalie" or whatever with assurance.

Zip Zap

Arrange chairs in a circle, or have everyone sit in a circle on the ground. This could be played while standing, but not for too long.

Find out the first name of the person on your left. That person is your *Zip.* The person on your right is your *Zap.* The leader stands in the center of the circle. The leader points to a person and says: "Zip, one, two, three, four, five." That person must shout out the name of the person to the left within the count of five. If the leader points to a person and says: "Zap, one, two, three, four, five," that person must shout out the name of the person to the right. If the person pointed to fails, he or she takes the leader's place in the center of the circle and the leader takes that person's chair. (Left is your *Zip.* Right is your *Zap.*)

Introduction Interview

Pass out paper and pencils. Have each person pair up with someone he or she does not know well. Everyone should have a partner.

Everyone is to find out as much as possible about the partner in six minutes—where born; favorite food, TV show, movie, singer, hobby; pets; likes; dislikes; etc. They jot all this down on paper. Partners are to interview each other at the same time.

After six or seven minutes, call time. Have everyone gather in one group, if there are fourteen or fewer people, or in groups of seven to ten, if there are more than fourteen. Ask someone to start by introducing to the group the person he or she interviewed, using the information from the interview. Go around the circle until everyone has been introduced.

Get-to-Know-You Better Activities

Sign My Card

Create a form with an item on each line. Leave space for a signature next to the item. The following is a list of possible items; use items of your own too.

Has had tonsils taken out _____
Loves spinach _____
Has two brothers _____
Has always lived in _____ (town/city/area)
Has a coin collection _____
Has red hair _____
Watches cartoons on Saturday mornings _____
Sings in the shower _____
Wears socks to bed _____
Went to Sunday school last Sunday _____
Has at least six stuffed animals at home _____
Watches soap operas _____
Eats Cheerios for breakfast _____
Has won a trophy _____
Is taking French in school _____
Likes to ride a horse _____
Plays guitar _____
Works out _____
Likes to dance _____

Provide a copy of this form for each person. Everyone is to mingle, finding people who fit the statements. Have people sign their names after the appropriate item. Participants are to try to get as many different signatures as possible.

Virginia Reel Conversation

Directions: Have everyone line up Virginia Reel style, in two lines of equal length. Participants sit on the floor (or in chairs) with lines facing each other, a foot apart.

Ask the first question from the list below. The pairs have two or three minutes to talk with each other about that question, each giving the other an answer.

Call time. One line—not both—moves to the right one person. The end person comes around and fills the empty space at the other end. Each person has a new conversation partner. The leader reads the next question. Again, each person talks with the person opposite for two or three minutes. Time is called. The line moves to the right again, and so on.

Questions (you'll want to create more of your own):

1. What was one of the best vacations you've had?

2. What do you (or did you) like about school?

3. What don't you (or didn't you) like about school?

4. If you could have dinner with two famous people, who would they be?

5. Where would you like to live, other than your present location?

6. What is something that makes you angry?

7. What is a quality you greatly admire in your mom or dad?

8. What is one way parents could do a better job bringing up their children?

9. If Jesus were here on earth today, what would most distress him?

10. What are two things you would do if you were president?

11. Why do you think people go to church?

Ways to Divide into Groups

When getting people to move into smaller groups of three, four, eight, or whatever, instead of saying "get into groups of . . .," it's better to use some kind of creative divide-up exercise. If people choose their own groups, they will seek their friends. Someone will be left out and feel excluded. The purpose of group building is to encourage people to mix and get to know people they don't know well.

If the group has just used the Virginia Reel Conversation, it's easy to form groups of four, for example, by suggesting that the first two people in both lines form a group, then the next two, and so forth.

At other times, use one of the following divide-up exercises, or think up others.

- Line up according to your shoe size, from smallest at one end to the largest at the other end.
- Line up according to birthdays.
- Line up according to first letter of first name, last name, or middle name.
- Line up according to your lucky number.
- Give all persons who are to be in one group the same song/jingle (on slips of paper). Each group gets a different song/jingle. All sing their songs until they find their groups.
- Same as preceding, but use animal sounds.
- Give each person a name tag, each name tag with a red, blue, green, or whatever dot indicating the group.

Small Group Activities

Three Facts/One Lie

Form groups of four or five people. Pass out paper and pencils. Each person in the group is to write answers to four questions displayed on newsprint at the front of the group. Three of the answers are to be true and one is to be a lie. The four questions might be the following:

What is your favorite food?
What is an embarrassing thing that happened to you?
What is something you did even though your parents told you not to?
What is your favorite TV show?

You could think up your own questions instead of using those suggested above.

Someone begins by reading her or his four answers. Then the others in the group guess which one is the lie. After all have guessed, the person tells which was the lie. Then go on to the next person.

In Event of Fire

Pass out paper and pencils. Tell the participants to imagine that their houses are on fire and they have only four minutes to save their most valuable possessions. Ask the following question: Other than people, what four things would you try to save? They write their answers. Then each, in turn, tells the four things. Suggest they explain why they chose those particular items.

Stranded on an Island

Use the same procedure as for the "fire" exercise. Tell the participants to suppose they are stranded on an island and can have their wish for four things, anything they want. Each person lists the four things he or she would wish for, and shares the answers.

A Special Dinner

Ask the following question: If you could have a special dinner and invite four famous people, who would you invite? Tell everyone to make a list and then share it with the group, explaining why those four were chosen.

Open-Ended Statements

These are single-answer statements that can be used for a variety of group-building, value-oriented, or study-related activities. The leader makes the statement and goes around the group, letting each person complete the statement. The following are suggestions. Make up your own.

If I had half a million dollars given to me, I would . . .
My favorite thing to do on a Saturday is . . .
What makes me angry is . . .
The most important quality in a friendship is . . .
If I were an animal in a zoo, I would be . . .
If I were in a circus act, I would be . . .
Something I did when my parents told me not to was . . .
At age ten my hero was . . .
I am happiest when . . .
An adult who means a lot to me is . . .
My parents can embarrass me by . . .

If I could work for six months anywhere in the world it would be in . . .
I am proud of . . .
If I knew I wouldn't get hurt, I would . . .
A crazy thing I did as a child was . . .
The think I like best about school is . . .
The thing I like least about school is . . .
To improve my school, I would . . .
People can hurt my feelings by . . .
I wish my parents would . . .
Being a Christian means . . .
Something I worry about is . . .
If I have children, I want them to . . .
Something I am afraid of is . . .
My favorite thing to do on a vacation is . . .
If I had a T-shirt designed, it would say . . .
A quality I would like to have is . . .
A question I would like to ask God is . . .
The hardest decisions I have to make have to do with . . .
If I had a lot of power, I would . . .

A Few Games

Who Am I?

Prepare a set of stick-on name tags, each with the name of a famous person. Make enough for everybody.

Stick a name tag on each person's back and instruct participants not to tell people the name that's on their backs. All are to mingle and ask questions about who they are.

Rules: Questions must be answered by yes or no. Don't ask the same person more than one question. You must move around, asking different people questions.

When you discover who you are, call it out. See how long it takes for the first person to discover who he or she is. Play until all have guessed who they are.

Suggestions for names (you can think of your own):

The Lone Ranger
Miss Piggy
Abraham Lincoln
Marilyn Monroe
Forrest Gump
Queen Elizabeth
Superman
Napolean
Snoopy
Charlie Brown
Big Bird
Noah
John the Baptist
Simon Peter
Scrooge
Peter Pan
Frankenstein
Fred Flintstone

Pooh Bear
Sylvester Stallone
Muhammad Ali
Little Red Riding Hood
Cinderella
Tarzan
Al Capone
Henry VIII
Oprah Winfrey
Michael Jordan
Billy Crudup
Albert Einstein
Martin Luther
John F. Kennedy
Martin Luther King, Jr.
Tiger Woods
Santa Claus
Barney

Name Charade

Prepare a stack of stick-on name tags with names of characters, movie stars, celebrities, politicians, biblical characters.

Stick one name on the back of one person. Everyone looks at the name and pantomimes the character, until the person guesses the name. No talking or sounds of any kind—strictly pantomime.

A What?

This game can be played in groups of eight to fifteen. Everyone is sitting in a circle. One person is the starter. Give that person a set of salt and pepper shakers, salt shaker in the left hand and pepper shaker in the right hand. Hold up the salt shaker and say: "This is a dog." Hold up the pepper shaker and say "This is a cat." The starter shows the salt shaker to the person to the left and says, "This is a dog." The person says back to the starter: "A what?" to which the starter responds, "a dog" and gives the salt shaker to the person on the left. Then that person shows the person on the left the salt shaker and says, "This is a dog." "A what?" the person responds. Before a person can take the "dog," it must be confirmed all the way back to the starter that it is a dog. So you have, "A what?" "A what?" "A what?" "A dog," "A dog," "A dog."

At the same time, the starter says to the person on the right: "This is a cat," referring to the pepper shaker. The person on the right says back to the starter: "A what?" to which the starter responds, "A cat," and gives the person the "cat," who then passes it on to the next person on the right with the same drill.

The fun comes when the person half way around the circle receives a dog from the right, a cat from the left, and hears from both sides: "A what?" It is a fun game filled with lots of laughs and, of course, lots of confusion. Tell the participants that the object of the game is to get the dog and the cat back to the starter.

Let several different people be the starters, so that lots of folks get the challenge of getting the dog and cat to cross and get on "home."

To make the game more challenging, use a several-word item, like "a freshly baked peach pie" and "a jar of watermelon pickles."

Machines

Directions: Tell participants that they are to create a machine using their bodies. The machine must have moving parts and everyone must be included. The machine can be real, such as a pinball machine or a cuckoo clock, or it could be a conglomeration of gears, levers, pumps, and so on that work together—an invention.

Give the group fifteen minutes to think of the machine, decide how they are going to do it (who's going to do which part), and practice. If you have more than thirteen participants, divide into two or more groups.

Groups demonstrate their machines.

Discussion: Ask group members what they discovered about working together as a team.

Mingle

Directions: You'll need an area where there are no chairs or tables. Tell everyone that they are to mingle until you call out a number. They are to get in groups of that number. Those who are left over are "out" and should stand over to the side. The remaining people mingle again until you call another number. They get into groups of that number. Play for four or five minutes. Then call all the "out" people back in. Play it again.

Discussion: Ask the participants how this game is like adolescence.

Operant Conditioning

The object of the game is to cause a person to do a task without telling that person a word about what he or she is supposed to do. When the volunteer makes a move in the right direction, he or she receives positive reinforcement from the group—in the form of clapping.

Explain the object of the game to everyone. Have a volunteer leave the room while the group decides on a task for the volunteer to do. For example, the volunteer is to walk in the door, go over to a designated book, pick it up, and hand it to a designated person. The task can be simple or complicated. Everyone in the group needs to know exactly what the volunteer is supposed to do, so they can reinforce that person correctly.

Have the volunteer return. The volunteer must

figure out what he or she is supposed to do. If the volunteer walks in one direction, and there is no clapping, then he or she needs to try something else.

The group only claps. No speaking, moaning, or shaking heads. This exercise is funny, sometimes frustrating, but very exciting when the volunteer finally gets it.

Knots

Have the group stand in a circle and extend their hands into the center of the circle. They are to grab one another's hands. Tell them: There are two rules. You cannot hold the hand of a person standing next to you; and you cannot hold both hands of the same person. The object is to untangle the knot, without letting go of any hands. You can twist and adjust hands as you climb over and under each other's arms; just don't let go. The group should end up holding hands in a circle.

It's not always possible to untangle the knot, but more times than not it is.

Move Left If . . .

The group is sitting in chairs in a circle. The leader is in the center. The leader says something like, "Move left three chairs if you're wearing white socks." If you are wearing white socks you must move three chairs to the left and sit. If there is someone in that seat, sit on top of them. Then the leader says, "Move one chair to the right if you have a sister." And if you have a sister, you must move. And so forth. It gets hilarious when there are five people sitting in one chair. Sit lightly, so you don't break chairs!

I Never

The group sits in chairs in a circle. There are no empty chairs. One person stands in the center. That person identifies something he or she has never done, such as, "I've never worn pierced earrings." Everyone who *has* worn pierced earrings gets up and runs to another seat. At the same time the person in the center tries to get a seat. Whoever is left in the center says the next "I never . . ."

Appendix 6.
Youth Ministry Resources

GENERAL

Burns, Jim. *The Youth Builder.* Eugene, Ore.: Harvest House, 1988.

DeVries, Mark. *Family-Based Youth Ministry.* Downers Grove, Ill.: InterVarsity Press, 1994.

Gallup, George H. *Growing Up Scared in America.* Princeton, N.J.: The George H. Gallup International Institute, 1995.

Howe, Neil, and Bill Strauss. *Thirteenth Gen: Abort, Retry, Ignore, Fail?* New York: Vintage Books, 1993.

Keirsey, David, and Marilyn Bates. *Please Understand Me: Character and Temperament Types.* Del Mar, Calif.: Prometheus Nemesis Book Company, 1984.

Martinson, Roland D. *Effective Youth Ministry: A Congregational Approach.* Minneapolis: Augsburg Publishing House, 1988.

Saito, Rebecca N., and Dale A. Blythe. *Understanding Mentoring Relationships.* Minneapolis: Search Institute, 1992.

Schultz, Thom, and Joani Schultz. *Why Nobody Learns Much of Anything at Church: And How to Fix It.* Loveland, Colo.: Group Publishing, 1993.

BIBLE STUDY

Life-Changing Bible Studies from the New Testament. Loveland, Colo.: Group Publishing, 1992.

McNabb, Bill, and Steven Mabry. *Teaching the Bible Creatively.* Grand Rapids: Zondervan Publishing House, 1990.

Murray, Dick. *Teaching the Bible to Adults and Youth.* Nashville: Abingdon Press, 1993.

The Youth Worker's Encyclopedia of Bible-Teaching Ideas: Old Testament. Loveland, Colo.: Group Publishing, 1994.

The Youth Worker's Encyclopedia of Bible-Teaching Ideas: New Testament. Loveland, Colo.: Group Publishing, 1994.

BOOKS FOR YOUTH

Coleman, William L. *What You Should Know about Living with One Parent.* Minneapolis: Augsburg Publishing House, 1993.

Gootman, Marilyn E. *When a Friend Dies.* Minneapolis: Free Spirit, 1994.

COMMUNITY BUILDERS AND GAMES

Ball-Kilbourne, Debra. *Mudpie Olympics and Ninety-nine Other Nonedible Games.* Nashville: Abingdon Press, 1994.

Group Publishing. *Quick Crowdbreakers and Games for Youth Groups.* Loveland, Colo.: Group Publishing, 1988.

Halverson, Sam. *55 Group-Building Activities for Youth.* Nashville: Abingdon Press, 1996.

McGill, Dan. *No Supplies Required: Crowdbreakers and Games.* Loveland, Colo.: Group Publishing, 1995.

———. *One Hundred and One Affirmations for Teenagers.* Loveland, Colo.: Group Publishing, 1993.

Rice, Wayne. *Up Close and Personal.* Grand Rapids: Zondervan Publishing House, 1989.

Rice, Wayne, and Mike Yaconelli. *Play It!* Grand Rapids: Zondervan Publishing House, 1986.

———. *Play It Again!* Grand Rapids: Zondervan Publishing House, 1993.

Rice, Wayne, and Mike Yaconelli, compilers. *Creative Crowd-Breakers, Mixers, and Games.* Winona, Minn.: Saint Mary's Press, 1991.

Rohnke, Karl. *Silver Bullets.* Dubuque, Iowa: Kendall/Hunt Publishing Co., Project Adventure, 1984.

———. *Youth Group Trust Builders.* Loveland, Colo.: Group Publishing, 1993.

DRAMA

Bolte, Chuck, and Paul McCusker. *Short Skits for Youth Ministry.* Loveland, Colo.: Group Publishing, 1993.

Mitchum, Naomi. *Fun with Drama.* Nashville: Abingdon Press, 1987.

Nappa, Mike. *Super Plays for Worship and Special Occasions.* Loveland, Colo.: Group Publishing, 1994.

Sturkie, John, and Marsh Cassady. *Acting It Out.* San Jose, Calif.: Resource Publications, 1990.

Tanner, Charles M. *Acting on Faith,* vol. 1. Nashville: Abingdon Press, 1994.

Watson-Burgess, Linda. *Reader's Theater.* Nashville: Abingdon Press, 1988.

Wolfe, William D., and Sheryl J. Anderson. *A Message in a Minute.* Valley Forge, Pa.: Judson Press, 1992.

ISSUES

Ekstrom, Reynolds R. *Access Guides to Youth Ministry: Media and Culture.* New Rochelle, N.Y.: Salesian Society, 1992.

Kirby, Michael. *Street Smarts.* San Jose, Calif.: Resource Publications, 1995.

Lynn, David. *Rock Talk.* Grand Rapids: Zondervan Publishing House, 1991.

Vos Wezeman, Phyllis. *Creating Compassion: Activities for Understanding HIV//AIDS.* Cleveland: Pilgrim Press, 1994.

LEADERSHIP TRAINING

Carver, Dave. *Building Relationships with Teenagers.* Loveland, Colo.: Group Publishing, 1990.

Christie, Les. *How to Recruit and Train Volunteer Youth Workers.* Grand Rapids: Zondervan Publishing House, 1992.

Harpine, Elaine Clanton. *Youth-Led Meetings.* Loveland, Colo.: Group Publishing, 1989.

Johnston, Ray. *Developing Student Leaders.* Grand Rapids: Zondervan Publishing House, 1992.

Marcum, Walt. *Youth Ministry Essentials.* Loveland, Colo.: Group Publishing, 1990.

———. *Teenagers and Group Dynamics.* Loveland, Colo.: Group Publishing, 1991.

Noon, Scott C. *Youth Ministry Leadership Skills.* Loveland, Colo.: Group Publishing, 1990.

Schultz, Thom, and Joani Schultz. *Kids Taking Charge.* Loveland, Colo.: Group Publishing, 1991.

MINISTRY TO JUNIOR HIGH STUDENTS

Dockrey, Karen. *Junior High Retreats and Lock-Ins.* Loveland, Colo.: Group Publishing, 1990.

Gillespie, Mike. *Good News for Stressed-Out Teens.* Cincinnati: Standard Publishing, 1992.

Johnston, Ray. *Developing Spiritual Growth in Junior High Students.* Grand Rapids: Zondervan Publishing House, 1994.

Parolini, Cindy, ed. *Groups Best Junior High Meetings,* vols. 1 and 2. Loveland, Colo.: Group Publishing, 1987, 1989.

Youth Specialties. *Creative Programming Ideas for Junior High Ministry.* Grand Rapids: Zondervan Publishing House, 1992.

MISSION AND SERVICE

Benson, Peter L., and Eugene C. Roehlkepartain. *Beyond Leaf Raking.* Minneapolis: Search Institute, 1993.

Burns, Ridge. *The Complete Student Missions Handbook.* Grand Rapids: Zondervan Publishing House, 1990.

Moore, Joseph. *Learning to Serve, Serving to Learn.* Director and student books. Notre Dame, Ind.: Ave Maria Press, 1994.

Parolini, Stephen. *Videotaping Your Church Members' Faith Stories (Projects with a Purpose).* Loveland, Colo.: Group Publishing, 1994.

Reynolds, Brian. *A Chance to Serve: A Leader's Manual for Peer Ministry.* Winona, Minn.: Saint Mary's Press, 1983.

———. *A Chance to Serve: Peer Minister's Handbook.* Winona, Minn.: Saint Mary's Press, 1983.

Woods, Paul. *Serving Your Neighbors: Projects with a Purpose.* Loveland, Colo.: Group Publishing, 1994.

PARENTS

Cline, Foster, and Jim Fay. *Parenting Teens with Love and Logic.* Colorado Springs, Colo.: Pinon Press, 1992.

Elkind, David. *Parenting Your Teenager.* New York: Ballantine Books, 1993.

Gaetano, Ronald J., and Jim Grout. *Please Talk with Me.* Dubuque, Iowa: Kendall/Hunt Publishing Co., 1991.

Grimbol, William R. *Befriending Your Teenager.* Minneapolis: Augsburg Publishing House, 1993.

Kochenburger, James. *Fun Devotions for Parents and Teenagers.* Loveland, Colo.: Group Publishing, 1990.

Lynn, David. *Parent Ministry Talksheets.* Grand Rapids: Zondervan Publishing House, 1992.

One Hundred and Thirty Ways to Involve Parents in Youth Ministry. Loveland, Colo.: Group Publishing, 1994.

PROGRAMMATIC RESOURCES

Amazing Tension Getters. Grand Rapids: Zondervan Publishing House, 1988.

Bimler, Richard W. *The Youth Group Meeting Guide.* Loveland, Colo.: Group Publishing, 1984.

Cannon, Ann B. *When God Scrambles Your Plans.* Nashville: Abingdon Press, 1997.

———. *Something's Cookin'.* Nashville: Abingdon Press, 1994.

Cannon, Chris. *Great Retreats for Youth Groups.* Grand Rapids: Zondervan Publishing House, 1994.

Headline News Discussion Starters. Loveland, Colo.: Group Publishing, 1990.

Lynn, David. *Talksheets, More High School Talksheets, More Junior High Talksheets.* Grand Rapids: Zondervan Publishing House, 1992.

Parolini, Stephen. *Controversial Discussion Starters for Youth Ministry.* Loveland, Colo.: Group Publishing, 1992.

Schultz, Thom, and Joani Schultz. *Do It! Active Learning in Youth Ministry.* Loveland, Colo.: Group Publishing, 1989.

PUBLICITY

Bargmann, Dale, and Robert M. Moyer. *Classy Clip Art.* Loveland, Colo.: Group Publishing, 1991.

Christie, Les. *Great Promotion and Publicity Ideas for Youth Ministry.* Grand Rapids: Zondervan Publishing House, 1994.

Hunt, Steve, and Dave Adamson. *Youth Ministry Clip Art.* Loveland, Colo.: Group Publishing, 1987.

———. *Youth Workers' Promo Kit.* El Cajon, Calif.: Youth Specialties Products, 1993.

Kruback, Rand. *Outrageous Clip Art.* Loveland, Colo.: Group Publishing, 1988.

SENIOR GIFTS

Moore, James. *Can You Remember to Forget?* Nashville: Abingdon Press, 1991.

Neinast, Helen R., and Thomas C. Ettinger. *What About God? Now that You're Off to College: A Prayer Guide.* Nashville: Upper Room Books, 1992.

Seuss, Dr. *Oh, The Places You'll Go!* New York: Random House, 1990.

Willimon, William H. *Good-Bye High School, Hello College.* Nashville: Dimensions for Living, 1992.

SEXUALITY

Berry, Woody, et al. *God's Gift of Sexuality: Leader's Guide.* Louisville, Ky.: Presbyterian Publishing House, 1989.

———. *God's Gift of Sexuality: Older Youth Guide.* Louisville, Ky.: Presbyterian Publishing House, 1989.

———. *God's Gift of Sexuality: Parent's Guide.* Louisville, Ky.: Presbyterian Publishing House, 1989.

———. *God's Gift of Sexuality: Younger Youth Guide.* Louisville, Ky.: Presbyterian Publishing House, 1989.

SMALL CHURCH

Chromey, Rich. *Youth Ministry in Small Churches: Creative How-Tos, Plus Twenty-eight Involving Activities.* Loveland, Colo.: Group Publishing, 1990.

Rice, Wayne. *Great Ideas for Small Groups.* Grand Rapids: Zondervan Publishing House, 1986.

Rice, Wayne, and Mike Yaconelli, compilers. *Creative Activities for Small Youth Groups.* Winona, Minn.: Saint Mary's Press, 1991.

Warden, Michael. *Small Church Youth Ministry Programming Ideas.* Loveland, Colo.: Group Publishing, 1994.

SPIRITUAL GROWTH AND SMALL-GROUP MINISTRY

Edwards, Steven L. *Connections.* Philadelphia: Judson Press, 1986.

Gooch, John. *Is My Nose Growing?* Nashville: Abingdon Press, 1992.

Marcum, Walt. *Living in the Light.* Nashville: Abingdon Press, 1994.

————. *Sharing Groups in Youth Ministry.* Nashville: Abingdon Press, 1991.

Thompson, Paul M., and Joani Lillevold Schultz. *The Giving Book.* Atlanta: John Knox Press, 1985.

WORSHIP AND DEVOTIONAL

Keffer, Lois, ed. *Creative Worship Ideas.* Loveland, Colo.: Group Publishing, 1993.

Koch, Carl, ed. *Dreams Alive: Prayers by Teenagers.* Winona, Minn.: Saint Mary's Press, 1991.

Koch, Carl, ed. *More Dreams Alive.* Winona, Minn.: Saint Mary's Press, 1995.

Student Plan-It Calendar. Yearly. Loveland, Colo.: Group Publishing, 1996.

Swanson, Steve. *Faith Prints.* Minneapolis: Augsburg Publishing House, 1985.

Ten-Minute Devotions for Youth Groups, vols. 1, 2, 3. Loveland, Colo.: Group Publishing, 1993.

Weems, Ann. *Reaching for Rainbows.* Philadelphia: Westminster Press, 1980.

Index